BISON
BOOKS

HENRY HITCHCOCK
IN LATER LIFE

MARCHING WITH SHERMAN

PASSAGES FROM
THE LETTERS AND CAMPAIGN DIARIES OF

HENRY HITCHCOCK

MAJOR AND ASSISTANT ADJUTANT GENERAL OF VOLUNTEERS

NOVEMBER 1864—MAY 1865

EDITED, WITH AN INTRODUCTION, BY

M. A. DEWOLFE HOWE

INTRODUCTION TO THE BISON BOOK EDITION
BY BROOKS D. SIMPSON

University of Nebraska Press
Lincoln and London

Introduction to the Bison Book Edition © 1995 by the University
of Nebraska Press
Manufactured in the United States of America

⊛ The paper in this book meets the minimum requirements of
American National Standard for Information Sciences—Perma-
nence of Paper for Printed Library Materials, ANSI Z39.48-1984.

First Bison Book printing: 1995
Most recent printing indicated by the last digit below:
10   9   8   7   6   5   4   3   2   1

Library of Congress Cataloging-in-Publication Data
Hitchcock, Henry, 1829–1902.
Marching with Sherman: passages from the letters and cam-
paign diaries of Henry Hitchcock, major and assistant adjutant
general of volunteers, November 1864–May 1865 / edited, with
an introduction by M. A. DeWolfe Howe; introduction to the
Bison Book edition by Brooks D. Simpson.
p.   cm.
Includes index.
Originally published: New Haven: Yale University Press, 1927.
ISBN 0-8032-7276-6
1. Hitchcock, Henry, 1829–1902—Diaries. 2. Sherman's March to
the Sea. 3. Sherman's March through the Carolinas. 4. United
States—History—Civil war, 1861–1865—Personal narratives. 5.
Soldiers—United States—Diaries. I. Howe, M. A. De Wolfe
(Mark Antony De Wolfe), 1864–1960. II. Title.
E476.69.H67 1995
973.78378—dc20
95-2996 CIP

Reprinted from the original 1927 edition published by Yale
University Press.

INTRODUCTION

Brooks D. Simpson

On 12 September 1864, ten days after the fall of Atlanta to Union soldiers, Ulysses S. Grant dispatched staff officer Horace Porter to the headquarters of General William T. Sherman to discuss what to do next. Porter had never met Sherman, although he had heard more than enough from Grant about the general and the man. Eight days later, he approached Sherman's headquarters, a brick house off the courthouse square, and saw the general sitting on the porch, scanning a newspaper. "With his large frame, tall, gaunt form, restless hazel eyes, aquiline nose, bronzed face, and crisp beard," the staff officer recalled, "he looked the picture of 'grim-visaged war.'" Sherman called on Porter to take a seat and began to talk, exhibiting "a peculiar energy of manner in uttering the crisp words and epigrammatic phrases which fell from his lips as rapidly as shots from a magazine-gun. I soon realized that he was one of the most dramatic and picturesque characters of the war." He is also one of the most controversial figures in American military history, primarily because of his willingness to bring the war home to Confederate civilians—a policy most vividly demonstrated in the March to the Sea (November–December 1864) and the March through the Carolinas (February–April 1865). [1]

Henry M. Hitchcock, who joined Sherman's staff as military secretary some six weeks later, got a chance to observe the general up close during the military campaigns which would mark his chief claim to fame—and infamy. A nephew of General Ethan Allen Hitchcock, he had practiced law in St. Louis before the war. For three years he had watched the course of conflict; by 1864, he wanted to participate, and so his uncle presented him to Secretary of War Edwin M. Stanton with the words, "Here is a young fellow spoiling for a fight." He was assigned to the Judge Advocate General and sent to Sherman (who had met him in St. Louis).

Sherman deemed him of "infinite assistance" and remarked, "He is a lawyer and scholar and can draw up my rude thoughts in better array, as well as lend me a hand in the voluminous work of the office." The admiration was reciprocated and more. In later years Hitchcock would judge Sherman "a man of genius" and a great general. "To the casual observer," he remarked, Sherman's "quick and nervous manner, the flash of his eagle eye, the brusque command, might give token of hasty conclusions, of disregard of detail, of eager and impatient habits of thought. There could be no greater error. . . . The atmosphere of his mind was lucidity itself. What he saw was pictured there, once for all." [2]

The major's letters and diaries offer readers a clear picture of Sherman at the high point of his military career; in conversation with his military secretary the general shared his philosophy of war. They also trace Hitchcock's growing acceptance of the general's perspective, suggesting that he, too, was hardened by what he encountered, although a sense of discomfort never quite left him. Finally, Hitchcock's writings introduce us to the officers and men of Sherman's command and help us understand why they waged war as they did. In short, they provide wonderful and insightful testimony about two campaigns that did much to crush the Confederacy and the man who directed them. [3]

On 2 September 1864, Sherman notified the authorities at Washington, "Atlanta is ours, and fairly won." Almost lost in the celebrations and hundred-gun salutes across the North that followed was the fact that much remained to be done. John Bell Hood's Army of Tennessee remained a dangerous foe in the field; the armies under Sherman's command were dependent for supplies upon a single rail line extending back to Chattanooga. Once Atlanta was a prize dearly sought; now it could prove to be an albatross around Sherman's neck. He had to decide what to do next—and soon. As he pondered his alternatives, he thought long and hard about his next target. He settled upon the will of Confederate citizens to continue the struggle. "I propose to demonstrate the vulnerability of the South and make its inhabitants feel that war and individual ruin are synonymous terms," he declared. [4]

For some time Sherman had wanted all Confederates, civilians and soldiers alike, to feel the hard hand of war. Within
a week of the fall of Atlanta, citing military necessity, he
ordered all civilians to evacuate the city. When civil officials
protested, he replied, "War is cruelty and you cannot refine
it." Hood tried to entangle Sherman in a war of words about
the decision, declaring that it "transcends, in studious and
ingenious cruelty, all acts ever before brought to my attention in the dark history of the war." This made little impression on the Union commander. "To be sure, I have made war
vindictively," Sherman remarked to an Episcopal bishop.
"[W]ar is war, and you can make nothing else of it; but Hood
knows as well as anyone I am not brutal or inhuman." Indeed, the fabled burning of Atlanta by Sherman's departing
columns on November 15 (one of the most memorable scenes
in *Gone with the Wind*) was in fact limited to areas of military importance; within days many citizens had returned to
their residences. [5]

Contrary to the popular image of Sherman the ruthless
destroyer, the general cared little for the destruction of property for its own sake. "Sweeping around generally through
Georgia for the purpose of inflicting damage would not be
good generalship," he told Horace Porter. [6] Nor was wanton
destruction sanctioned by orders; while Sherman instructed
his men to live off the land, he also directed them not to
enter the homes of non-combatants; only officers could au-
thorize the destruction of property. However, he did not always enforce his own orders, thus contributing to some ex-
cesses. Nor would the director of destruction consent to be
the agent of revolution. True to his conservative views on
slavery, Sherman, disregarding Grant's instructions to make
use of black refugees, treated the flood of freed people as a
hindrance to his military operation. His oft-cited Special Field
Order No. 15, setting aside land for blacks along the Atlantic
coast, was a temporary measure designed to shake off the
burden of providing for the growing number of refugees following his columns.

At one point it looked as if Sherman would not have to
bring the war to white Georgians. When three Unionists,

led by Joshua Hill, visited Sherman after the fall of Atlanta, the general shared his willingness to keep his columns on the roads if Governor Joseph Brown would sue for a separate peace. Brown wavered, withdrawing the state militia from Confederate control, but went no further. The following year, after his men relished the opportunity of punishing the residents of South Carolina for their prominent role in bringing on the war, Sherman made sure that North Carolina would not be subjected to the same treatment, in large part to encourage a Tarheel peace movement. "I pledge you that my study is to accomplish peace and honor at as small a cost to life and property as possible," he told the daughter of a South Carolina unionist. But for the Palmetto State he held little back. "You need not be so careful there about private property as we have been," Sherman remarked to Army of Georgia commander Henry W. Slocum. "The more of it you destroy the better it will be. The people of South Carolina should be made to feel the war, for they brought it on and are responsible more than anybody else for our presence here. Now is the time to punish them."[7]

That Sherman's men destroyed much is true: but myth, exaggeration, and Confederate apologists have left many Americans with a misleading impression of utter and complete devastation. Some ninety years after the march through Georgia a survey of the area from Covington to Milledgeville concluded that claims of destruction were overblown; one would be at a loss to explain why some houses still stand if all were destroyed. The foraging had limited long-term effect on the primarily agricultural region along which Sherman's men marched in Georgia: those who cite the burning of Columbia, South Carolina, as evidence of Sherman's inflammatory tendencies overlook the rather peaceful occupation of Savannah seven weeks before. Crimes against civilians were exceedingly rare. John F. Marszalek notes that "a great deal of damage was done, but people were generally left alone. Rape and murder were practically nonexistent. The march to the sea saw a land ravaged by enemy and friendly forces alike and the will of its people broken. Their bodies, however, usually remained whole."[8]

Nevertheless, at times things got out of hand. Sherman did not exercise complete control over his men, and to some extent shares responsibility for what followed. Some members of his command were rather thorough in carrying out their orders; so-called "bummers"—Union soldiers who straggled and otherwise eluded their commands—proved especially enthusiastic in bringing the war home to white southerners. So did stray Confederate cavalry, deserters from both armies, escaped slaves, and outlaws—facts often overlooked by present-day critics of Sherman. Such chaos seems to have accounted for a good deal of the destruction in Georgia. Similarly, although it is true that South Carolina came in for especially harsh treatment by Sherman's men, Columbia's fate was due to several factors, including Confederate orders to burn cotton in the streets rather than let the bales fall into enemy hands. A third of the city was consumed by flames spread as much by wind as by torches: Sherman actually took steps to contain the blaze. To remark that Sherman's men *would* have burned Columbia in any case is to evade what actually *did* happen—although to this day even well-informed historians still insist that "Sherman's men burned Columbia." [9]

Those who portray Sherman as an advocate of hard war to exterminate the South will have trouble reconciling this image with the generous and lenient peace terms he offered Joseph E. Johnson at the Bennett farmhouse outside Durham Station in April 1865. As soon as Confederates were willing to give up the cause of independence, Sherman demonstrated his willingness to make reconciliation as painless as possible—to the point that some Northerners suspected him of treason. It would be Henry Hitchcock to whom Sherman entrusted the draft of the surrender terms for delivery to Washington—and it would be Hitchcock who would return with Ulysses S. Grant as the general-in-chief sought to repair the damage while soothing his comrade's feelings. [10]

In justifying his plan of operations in the fall of 1864, Sherman told Grant, "This may not be War, but rather Statesmanship." Such an attitude was evident in his willingness to consider a deal with Governor Brown. Nevertheless,

Sherman's declaration invites inquiry. What sort of statesmanship did he practice in these campaigns? How did it shape
not only the winning of the war but also the restoration of
peace? As one Union officer noted, "In what way will the
destruction of so much property aid us in restoring peace,
harmony and union to our distracted country?" Or did
Sherman's marches, embittering though they might have
been at the time, gain their present fame—or infamy—as
defenders of the Confederate past sought justification and
revenge against those who did the most to insure that there
would not be a Confederate present?[11]

To a large extent Sherman did succeed in eroding Confederate will. Mention of his very name sent chills down the
back of many a Southern white; others viewed his success as
a sign that the Confederacy was done for. As Sherman waited
outside Savannah, Mary Chesnut noted, "Desolation—mis-
management—despair . . . the country is demoralized." Two
months later, Robert E. Lee remarked that North Carolina
soldiers, "influenced very much by the representations of
their friends at home, who appear to have become very de-
spondent as to our success," were deserting to protect their
homes. Whatever actual destruction was committed by
Sherman's soldiers, it was the fear of such destruction—and
worse—that white Southerners dreaded. It was psychologi-
cal warfare as waged by a master.[12]

Yet Sherman's very success in terrorizing white Southerners led them to exaggerate the extent of the actual damage of the march. It seemed as if every building had been
put to the torch; Sherman's men were also accused of rape
and murder. "Before they came here, I thought I hated them
as much as was possible," declared Emma LeConte days after Sherman's columns left a still-smoldering Columbia,
South Carolina; "now I know there are no limits to the feeling of hatred." Whatever chance there was that these feelings would fade in the hearts of many Southern whites was
lost when Sherman defended his action in his *Memoirs,* which
appeared in 1875. In it he actually added to the myth of the
marches, describing Atlanta as "smoldering and in ruins"
and expressing no regret over the burning of Columbia. When

such comments were added to the terror of his words in letters, dispatches, and testimony—which often outstripped his
acts—one senses that the general's vivid language and exaggeration of expression were as responsible as anything else
for shaping the image of him as a half-mad avenging angel.
The memories of Sherman's marches, real and imagined alike,
embittered many Southern whites—and continue to do so to
this very day. Merely the mention of Sherman's name can
provoke a sharp response among present-day Confederate
wannabes; they cite the march as the best example of Yankee wartime atrocities. Sherman remains the best-hated
Union general in the hearts and minds of many an aficio-
nado of the Lost Cause.[13]

Sherman dismissed such complaints by white Southerners. "Those people made war upon us, defied and dared us to
come south to their country, where they boasted they would
kill us and do all manner of horrible things. We accepted
their challenge, and now for them to whine and complain of
the natural and necessary results is beneath contempt." He
never felt remorse for what he did—and grew angry with
others who did. "The war, no matter what its course or conduct, was an epoch in our national history that must be sanctified, and made to stand justified to future ages," he told
Grant. For the marches Sherman had no apologies, no regrets.[14]

The popular image of Sherman's campaigns during the
last six months of the war illustrate the malleable nature of
historical memory. It is futile to note the rather limited scope
of the devastation on Sherman's line of march, or the general's
willingness to punish those of his soldiers who committed
unprovoked acts of violence against civilians. It is pointless
to remark in reply that Sherman characterized war as an
inhumane act of hellish cruelty, or to cite in response the
Confederate massacre of black soldiers at Fort Pillow. Nor
does it matter much that one might counter that the institution of slavery itself, that "cornerstone of the Confederacy"
as Confederate vice president Alexander H. Stephens called
it, was an atrocity, one for which many Americans shared
the responsibility—a point Abraham Lincoln raised in his

second inaugural address. Such contentions miss the point even as they enliven argument. For those residents of the former Confederacy who cannot quite come to terms with the Civil War or its outcome, Sherman will always stand as the embodiment of Yankee brutality, regardless of fact. The memory of the marches and of the man who directed them are indelibly etched in the mind of many a white Southerner as a lasting nightmare. The embers still smolder; the wounds remain tender.

NOTES

1. Horace Porter, *Campaigning with Grant* (New York: Century, 1897), 289–90.
2. W. A. Croffut, ed., *Fifty Years in Camp and Field: Diary of Major-General Ethan Allen Hitchcock, U.S.A.* (New York: G. P. Putnam's Sons, 1909), 468–70; Henry M. Hitchcock, "William T. Sherman," Military Order of the Loyal Legion of the United States, Missouri, *War Papers and Personal Reminiscences, 1861–1865,* vol. 1 (St. Louis: Becktold, 1892), 421–23.
3. Several books offer great insight into Sherman's conception of his operations. They include John F. Marszalek, *Sherman: A Soldier's Passion for Order* (New York: Free Press, 1993); Lloyd Lewis, *Sherman: Fighting Prophet* (1932; reprint, Lincoln: University of Nebraska Press, 1993); Charles Royster, *The Destructive War: William Tecumseh Sherman, Stonewall Jackson, and the Americans* (New York: Knopf, 1991); and Charles Edmund Vetter, *Sherman: Merchant of Terror, Advocate of Peace* (Gretna: Pelican, LA, 1992).
4. Vetter, *Sherman: Merchant of Terror, Advocate of Peace,* 234.
5. Marszalek, *Sherman,* 285–86, 299.
6. Porter, *Campaigning with Grant,* 292.
7. Marszalek, *Sherman,* 320.
8. Marszalek, *Sherman,* 306, 551 n.27. Reid Mitchell in *The Vacant Chair: The Northern Soldier Leaves Home* (New York: Oxford University Press, 1993), 106–8, suggests that black women were much more likely to be the victims of rape.
9. On the burning of Columbia, see Marion B. Lucas, *Sherman and the Burning of Columbia* (College Station: Texas A&M University Press, 1976); Joseph T. Glatthaar, *The March to the Sea and Beyond: Sherman's Troops in the Savannah and Carolinas*

Campaign (New York: New York University Press, 1985), 143–46; Mitchell, *The Vacant Chair,* 107.

10. See Brooks D. Simpson, *Let Us Have Peace: Ulysses S. Grant and the Politics of War and Reconstruction, 1861–1868* (Chapel Hill: University of North Carolina Press, 1991), 95–101.

11. Simpson, *Let Us Have Peace,* 68; Glatthaar, *The March to the Sea and Beyond,* 146; Vetter, *Sherman: Merchant of Terror, Advocate of Peace,* 265–66; John B. Walters, *Merchant of Terror: General Sherman and Total War* (Indianapolis: Bobbs-Merrill, 1973), 204–7.

12. C. Vann Woodward, ed., *Mary Chesnut's Civil War* (New Haven, 1981), 694; Clifford Dowdey and Louis H. Manarin, eds., *The Wartime Papers of Robert E. Lee* (Boston: Little, Brown, 1961), 910.

13. Earl Schenck Miers, ed., *When the World Ended: The Diary of Emma LeConte* (1957; reprint, Lincoln: University of Nebraska Press, 1987), 60.

14. Marszalek, *Sherman,* 316; Simpson, *Let Us Have Peace,* 246.

CONTENTS

ILLUSTRATIONS

The reproduction of pictures in *Harper's Weekly* through
the first half of 1865 has a special fitness for this volume,
since Theodore R. Davis, the *Harper's* "special artist at
the front," is frequently mentioned in the text, sometimes
with direct reference to pictures here given.

This map of Sherman's Marches through Georgia and the Carolinas is
made by joining two maps from *Sherman and His Campaigns,* by Col.
S. M. Bowman and Lt. Col. R. B. Irwin (New York, 1865).

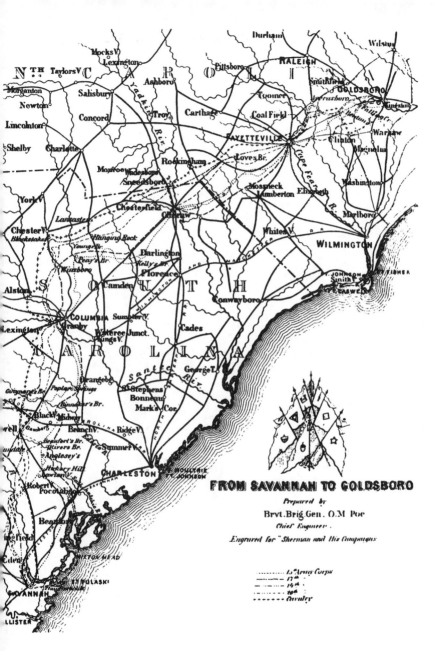

FROM SAVANNAH TO GOLDSBORO

Prepared by

Brvt. Brig. Gen. O.M. Poe
Chief Engineer.

Engraved for "Sherman and His Campaigns"

.... 15 Army Corps
————— 17th
— · — · — 14th
········· 20th
— ·· — ·· Cavalry

The officer who prepared them is frequently mentioned in Hitchcock's narrative as Col. O. M. Poe, Chief Engineer. The vertical line across the map indicates the division between the parts of which it is made.

THE CAREER AND CHARACTER
OF HENRY HITCHCOCK

THE purpose of this volume is to save from oblivion a remarkable young man's record of an experience quite extraordinary—his close association with General Sherman for the seven months in the course of which he made his historic marches across Georgia and northward through the Carolinas. At thirty-five this member of Sherman's staff was not to be counted a young man so much in comparison with his fellow officers of the Civil War as in the light of the seventy-three years he was destined to live. At thirty-five he could bring to the experience that faced him not only the enthusiasm of his younger manhood but also a well-trained mind and lofty character already disciplined. These qualities he turned to valuable account, performing his daily duties to the evident satisfaction of his chief, and including faithfully among them the writing of elaborate diaries and detailed letters to his wife—a record now first permitted to see the light after nearly sixty years.

This Civil War experience of Henry Hitchcock's stood as a detached episode in his long and fruitful life. Before discussing it in any detail, let us see what preceded and followed it. Though born (July 3, 1829) at Spring Hill, near Mobile, Alabama, neither his father, Judge Henry Hitchcock, nor Colonel Andrew Erwin, the father of his mother, Anne Erwin, were natives of the South, the one having emigrated thither from Vermont, the other from the north of Ireland. His father, soon after graduating from the University of Vermont in 1813, had moved to Alabama, where he became an eminent lawyer and finally Chief Justice of the Su-

preme Court of the state. The father of the Alabama
Judge Hitchcock was himself Judge Samuel Hitchcock
of Vermont, a native of Brimfield, Massachusetts, a
graduate of Harvard in the Class of 1777, Attorney
General of Vermont from 1790 to 1793, active in the
legislative, legal, and educational affairs of his adopted
state, and finally appointed United States Circuit
Judge by President John Adams. His wife was the
second daughter of Ethan Allen, the hero of Fort
Ticonderoga. Through this ancestry both an uncle and
a brother of the Henry Hitchcock of Sherman's staff—
Major General Ethan Allen Hitchcock, U.S.A., and the
Hon. Ethan Allen Hitchcock, first United States Am-
bassador to Russia and Secretary of the Interior—received the name they bore in common.

Back of Vermont the Hitchcock line ran through
western Massachusetts forbears to Luke Hitchcock, an
early Connecticut settler from Warwickshire in England. It is told in the annals of his family that "he was
peculiarly fortunate in cultivating the friendship of the
Indians who in testimony of their attachment to him
gave him a deed of the town of Farmington. This deed
was a clear and valid title to the land, but was so little
thought of that it was destroyed by his wife, who used
it to cover a pie in the oven." Americans who go back
far enough sometimes encounter such instances of an-
cestral error.

From the blended inheritances of New England on
his father's side and of North of Ireland Presbyterian-
ism on his mother's, Henry Hitchcock must have derived many of the qualities which, affected by the circumstances of his own life, made him so typical an
American of his generation. It was natural for such an
one to seek the best educational equipment for whatever might lie before him. After his father's death
from yellow fever, in 1839, his mother moved from Mobile to Nashville, Tennessee, and in 1846, at seventeen,
he took the degree of A.B. at the University of Nash-

ville. Thence he proceeded to Yale, where he graduated
with the Class of 1848, delivering an "oration" on Commencement Day. After a few months in a New York
lawyer's office, he became assistant classical teacher in
the high school at Worcester, Massachusetts, and held
this position for the year ending November, 1849. Then
for two years he pursued his legal studies in Nashville,
and in September of 1851 moved to St. Louis, where, in
the following month, he was admitted to the bar.
Through the year of 1852 he served as assistant editor
of a Whig newspaper, the *St. Louis Intelligencer,* but
found a continuance of this work incompatible with his
growing law practice.

Through the decade leading up to the Civil War
Henry Hitchcock established an unquestioned place for
himself among the younger St. Louis lawyers of out-
standing promise and achievement. Both then and
thereafter he declined criminal practice, and applied the
fruits of his sound studies of legal principles to questions of equity and commercial law. In 1857 he married
Mary, the eldest daughter of George Collier, a prominent merchant of St. Louis, and began a domestic life
recalled by those who knew it as marked by a rare
charm and distinction. Twelve years later, in 1869, his
younger brother, Ethan Allen Hitchcock, married Mrs.
Henry Hitchcock's younger half-sister, Margaret D.
Collier. The double family circle thus established must
be counted among the central elements of his life.

For the events immediately preceding Henry Hitchcock's active participation in the Civil War no better
summary can be found than in a paragraph from an
autobiographical sketch which he prepared, in 1898,*
for the fiftieth anniversary of his graduation from
Yale. It should be read with a consciousness of that
tendency to understatement which modest men of large

* His two sons, Henry Hitchcock, Jr., and George Collier Hitchcock,
are graduates of Yale in the classes, respectively, of 1879 and 1890.

achievement are prone to indulge when writing such
records:

Never engaged actively in politics but always interested in
public affairs. Was a Whig until the Republican party was
formed, but in 1860 advocated the election of Lincoln, and
since then have always been a Republican. In January, 1861,
was elected on the "unconditional Union" ticket a member of
the Missouri State Convention, which was called by a secession
legislature for the purpose of taking Missouri out of the
Union, but which disappointed their expectations, no ordinance of secession being then introduced; was one of the six
Republican members of that body, consisting of 99 members in
all, which in July 1861 deposed the rebel Governor and Legislature, appointed a provisional state government, being con-
vened from time to time, and adjourning *sine die* July 1, 1863.
Attended all its sessions, took an active part in its proceedings,
and remember with satisfaction having voted as one of a minority of four to ninety-one against the approval of what was
known as the Crittenden Compromise of 1861.

From the testimony of others it is manifest that the
clear thinking and cogent speaking of Henry Hitchcock
in the Missouri Convention made him as effective a
worker for the Union cause as if he had followed his
own inclination to enter the army at the outbreak of
the war. We shall see how he turned finally from a civilian's to a soldier's participation in the conflict, but for
the present—leaving the military episode of his life to
stand by itself in immediate conjunction with his own
record of it—we may best proceed to follow him,
though hastily, through the many years of his life after
the war.

Mustered out of service in June, 1865, he gave himself, before resuming his professional work at home,
the respite of four months' travel in Europe—an experience enriched by association with such men in England as John Bright, Thomas Hughes, and Jowett of
Oxford, and in France as Edouard Laboulaye. Before
the end of the year he was back at his law office in St.

Louis, employed in the professional, civic, and educational labors which—save for an interruption in 1870 and 1871 due to overwork—were to engage him steadily until he died on March 18, 1902.

It was said of him after his death that "he devoted himself to his profession, not simply as a business, but as a public duty," and also that "he was in all things and at all times a public servant." A high and exacting sense of obligation to the common good, the counterpart of a stern sense of duty in all his personal relations, carried his activities far beyond his individual practice at the bar. Even before the war he became a director of Washington University, and in 1867 took an active part in organizing its law department, the St. Louis Law School, in which, from 1867 to 1881, he served both as a professor and as dean of the faculty, a labor of love. In 1878 he was one of the fourteen signers of a call which led to the formation of the American Bar Association. In the work of this body he bore an important part, preparing the majority report of a committee that advocated a plan subsequently pursued by Congress in establishing the United States Circuit Courts of Appeal; and delivering the annual address before the Association in 1887, on "General Corporation Laws." Yale had already honored him with the degree of LL.D. in 1875, and in 1889 the American Bar Association elected him its president—a national recognition of high significance.

In other states than his own his public addresses on special occasions, relating to constitutional and legal questions, marked him as a man whose opinions were of weight with his profession throughout the country. For some years he was a member of the executive committee of the National Civil Service Reform League, and in 1896 he served as a delegate from Missouri at the American Conference on International Arbitration assembled at Washington. These instances of a far-reaching activity—to which may be added the signifi-

cant item that in the preface of the first edition of
Bryce's *American Commonwealth* he is named among
those to whom the author was "especially indebted"
for help—are enumerated for what they suggest of a
quality of citizenship which, of course, found its chief
expression in Henry Hitchcock's own community.
There he stood not only in the forefront of his profession, but representing so fully the most significant life
of his city that his house became and long remained
the scene of gracious and distinguished hospitalities
through which his fellow citizens were well content that
eminent visitors, both American and foreign, should
make their acquaintance with St. Louis. The personality and motive force behind this quality of repre-
sentative citizenship are clearly suggested in a single
sentence from the resolution adopted by the directors
of Washington University at the time of Henry Hitchcock's death:

His inimitable charm of conversation, his literary attain-
ments, his broad grasp of political information, his profound
learning and marked success in his own profession, and his
zealous support of every educational interest, all found their
origin in his undivided devotion to common welfare.

Having seen in some measure what made Henry
Hitchcock the man he was before his military experience and what he became through the years that followed it, let us now turn back to the year 1864 and consider particularly the circumstances out of which proceeded the letters and diaries which give this volume
its occasion for existence.

In staying out of the army until so late as September,
1864, Henry Hitchcock yielded his own convictions and
desires to those of his friends and advisers, who felt
that he could be of more use to the Union cause as a
member of the Missouri Convention and in other patriotic activities than as a soldier at the front. This was
especially the advice of his uncle, General Ethan Allen

Hitchcock, whose military training and long experience lent much authority to his opinions. "Neither of us realized," said Henry Hitchcock in later years, "the magnitude of the conflict, or that the Civil War must educate its own officers. I reluctantly acted on his advice, but year by year regretted it more, till in September, 1864, before the fall of Atlanta and when the issue of the war still seemed doubtful, still against his earnest protest—although he was then himself in the service as Major General of Volunteers—I applied in person to Secretary Stanton for a commission and obtained one; not in the hope, at that late day, of rendering military service of any value, but simply because I could not endure the thought of profiting in safety at home by the heroism of others, and of having no personal share in the defense of my country against her enemies in arms."

When Henry Hitchcock went to Washington in 1864 to seek an opportunity in the army his uncle proposed at first to introduce him to Seward with a view to finding a place in the State Department. The younger man would none of it, nor, when General Hitchcock introduced him to Stanton as "a young man spoiling for a fight," would he accept the post of Judge Advocate at St. Louis which the Secretary of War offered to him; service at the front, he insisted, was what he sought. Thereupon, General Sherman, a friend and admirer of General Hitchcock's, was asked by letter whether there would be a place for Henry Hitchcock on his staff in the event of his receiving a commission, and answered, "I will be most happy to have him assigned to me," adding, "and you may show this to the Secretary of War and he may construe it into an application for him." In this telegram he said, besides: "I knew Mr. Hitchcock very well at St. Louis," and "Though universally I have favored the appointment of young officers already in the service, yet I esteem this case as one that may safely be made without endangering the rule.''[*] Thus, having received on October 1, 1864, the appointment of Assistant Adjutant-General of Volunteers with the rank of Major, Henry Hitchcock presented himself, when the month was ending, at the headquarters of the Army of the Mississippi, then on the point of setting forth on its march from Atlanta to the sea.

The record of his experiences, conscientiously made in letters and diaries, and long withheld from publication, is the record to be expected of a sensitive, yet vigorous, intelligent, and educated man. Its value is at once biographical and historical. As a biographical document this record illustrates well the highest type of American volunteer officer in time of war—a figure of identic general outline in our Civil War and in the World War, educated for civil life, at an early stage of a promising career, turning from it at the call of his country to venture all in its service, returning when the work is done to the ways of peace, and devoting the remainder of his days to the enrichment of the life of his time. The World War is not yet far enough behind us for a full measurement of the contributions of its American soldiers to the civic life of the nation. Henry Hitchcock was typical of the younger men of the sixties, who, in the fullness of their years, carried over into our own century their great example of unselfish devotion to the common good. Their memory brings confidence in the corresponding contributions still to be expected from the young civilian soldiers of 1917-1918.

The historical interest and value of Henry Hitchcock's narrative will be found unquestionably great. Sherman's Georgia and Carolina campaigns, by reason both of the intensity of feeling which they incited and of their important part in bringing the four years' struggle to a conclusion, are perhaps more familiar to

---

[*] See *Fifty Years in Camp and Field: Diary of Maj. Gen. Ethan Allen Hitchcock, U.S.A.*, p. 468.

Americans of the present time than any other campaigns of the Civil War. Certainly they have left behind them such a legacy of bitterness in the South that any mitigating knowledge of their conduct should be welcome. They have indeed taken their place in history as the classic, though modern, examples of the military invasion of an enemy's country, and inevitably invite comparison with earlier and later instances of corresponding warfare. Fresh light upon them must be counted among the lasting, not merely timely, materials of history.

Sherman's own *Memoirs*, first published in 1875, are the chief source of information in this field—and Hitchcock's record is often found to supplement that of his chief. Immediately after the war, in 1865, came such books as *Sherman and His Campaigns*, by Colonel S. M. Bowman and Lieutenant Colonel R. B. Inman, and *The Story of the Great March, from the Diary of a Staff Officer*, by Brevet Major George Ward Nichols, who appears frequently in Hitchcock's letters and diaries. In the ensuing decades other books followed, but they all bear, in varying degrees, the marks of composition after the event. Henry Hitchcock's record is unique in that it is a strictly contemporaneous narrative, written obviously without reference to publication, and dealing with matters which became controversial while they lay still quite outside the field of controversy.

What particularly distinguishes this record is that it represents with perfect frankness the feelings of a high-minded, intensely patriotic man, impelled by an unwavering sense of duty, at the same time so just and essentially humane that he was in frequent distress over the severities of Sherman's soldiers toward the enemy. Time and again this led to discussions of the destructive methods of the army with his fellow officers and with Sherman himself—with some resulting modifications of his own views of the cruel necessities in the case. The immediate first-hand reports of Sherman's conversations with Major Hitchcock, with Southern whites and negroes encountered on the marches; the palpably honest account of the burning of Columbia, written as soon as possible after its occurrence, and confirming in vital particulars the conclusions of so careful an historian as Mr. Rhodes; the narrative of his observations as Sherman's messenger entrusted with conveying to Washington the terms of Johnston's first surrender, of his return with Grant, when those terms were disapproved, to Sherman's headquarters, and of the momentous scenes then ensuing—the record of all these things constitutes an historic document of unique and permanent importance. Throughout the narrative the intensity of war-time feeling inevitably expresses itself in terms of the moment. Yet in the most vigorous utterances of honest indignation the reader will note the emphasis upon larger issues, the absence of hostility to individuals except as exponents of the cause with which the writer was in conflict.

The letters and diaries of Henry Hitchcock now to be drawn upon are separated by a natural line of division. When it was possible to reach his wife promptly by letter, he wrote to her. When the lines of communication between the army and the world at home were cut—as through the weeks of Sherman's marches from Atlanta to Savannah and from that point northward through the Carolinas—Hitchcock recorded his experiences in three slender account books which he called his "campaign diaries." They were kept for the benefit of his wife and friends—as his own words about them will show—and were sent home, in lieu of letters, as opportunity offered. They were written, usually in ink, in a script incredibly minute, accurate, and legible.

More than the diaries, the letters—in the very nature of the case—contain much that is intimately personal and inappropriate for publication. More than the letters, the diaries abound in military detail and also in abbreviations. For the purposes of publication it has seemed best to treat letters and diaries alike, giving the preference to passages of relatively greater human and historic value, and, in the interest of fluent reading, generally to substitute the complete for the abbreviated word.

At no other time during Major Hitchcock's more than six months on Sherman's staff did he write so abundantly to his wife as in the period between his arrival at the front, on October 31, 1864, and the beginning of the March to the Sea, on November 12. Atlanta had been occupied by Sherman's troops on September 2. Hood, who had abandoned the city on the preceding night, had made what Mr. Rhodes calls "an adroit and audacious movement" in getting into the rear of the Union army, with consequent danger to its lines of communication. Sherman meanwhile had been planning his march across Georgia, involving the voluntary severance of all contact with the usual avenues of supplies and intelligence, and the transfer to Thomas, well reenforced at Nashville, of the responsibility for dealing with Hood.

On November 2 Sherman, having laid fully before Grant what he calls in his *Memoirs* his "long contemplated project of marching to the sea-coast," received a telegram from his commander ending with the words, "I say, then, go on as you propose." His army at the end of October was "strung from Rome to Atlanta." His plans for the march were in process of completion when Hitchcock joined his staff. From that time forth, the young officer's record speaks for itself—and much besides.

I

THROUGH GEORGIA TO SAVANNAH

LETTERS

HEADQUARTERS,
MILITARY DIVISION OF THE MISSISSIPPI*

IN THE FIELD. ROME, GA. October 31 1864

(Monday morning)

I HAVE this moment (10½ A.M.) arrived here at the General's Headquarters and finding him gone down town improve the minutes till he returns by sending a word to you. I am perfectly well, and in the best spirits —have had a very quick, pleasant and fortunate trip though with just enough "roughness" to make it spicy: met nor heard of any guerrillas on the road, save the evidences of where they had recently been along, and have had good luck and good company all the way. I was very sorry to write you so hurriedly from Nashville and Chattanooga, but it was something to do that: and you must take it for granted once for all . . . that when I write thus, and if I do not always write often, it is because one cannot always do as they would "in the field."

I met Fullerton,† as I mentioned, at Chattanooga,— a fortunate encounter and very jolly for us both. His (4th) Corps arrived there that (Sunday) morning and was passing through westward while we were there, which was only for an hour. My note thence to you was written in the open air, sitting on my valise with a pile of other baggage, on a piece of paper lent me by a friend. By the way Margie's‡ nice portfolio is locked, and I don't find the key yet—but I'll get it opened soon. Tell M. that I found time to open my valise and make a

---

* It was Maj. Hitchcock's habit to write on letter paper bearing this printed heading, here reproduced once for all.

† Bvt. Brig. Gen. Joseph S. Fullerton, Chief of Staff, Fourth Army Corps.

‡ Mrs. Hitchcock's younger sister, Margaret Collier, afterwards Mrs. Ethan Allen Hitchcock.

formal presentation of *the sword;* tell her it was done
in the presence of hundreds if not thousands of officers
and soldiers (*entre nous* they were all minding their
own business and the "presence" means a radius of a
½ mile)—that I made an eloquent and inspiring
speech, but omitted to mention the donor's name,—and
that the gallant Colonel was so overcome by his feelings
that he made no reply at all but to say that (being in a
hurry) he would postpone *that* to another occasion.

I do not yet know what my duties will be, nor will till
I see the General,—but find that they will not be those
of Judge Advocate, for there are none such to do, now
at least, on this staff. So much the better. Gen. Sherman
asked for me, and if he can't find something for me to
do I'm mistaken and it's none of my business anyhow.

Don't "you'uns" fret about Hood, not a bit. The
story is that he has crossed the Tennessee,—for which
if true we are understood to be very much obliged to
him. Lt. Col. Kittoe,* (Med. Director on Gen. S's staff)
just said to me that Hood's late movement north had
been a *faux pas,* and of more good to us than him; and
if I was a prophet I should tell you, probably, that
within the next fortnight Hood will hear news from
below that may make him wish he had staid there.
However, once for all, for obvious reasons, I do not expect to deal in predictions. Letters sometimes miscarry,
and predictions sometimes do harm where it was not
intended.

I am glad to find that my "transportation"—one
valise and one roll of bedding—is universally pronounced very moderate and entirely within bounds;
also my French cot is greatly admired for convenience
and compactness. I was indebted to it last night for a
comfortable bed at Kingston in a room 10 ft. 5 in. x 9 ft.
3 in. (by measurement), which had bare walls and floor
for furniture and which four of us were very lucky to
get control of. More than that, seventeen of us,—offi-

* Edward D. Kittoe.

cers *en route* for Headquarters—were thoroughly grateful to the Agent of the U. S. Sanitary Commission at Kingston for a most welcome supper, after all other chances had failed,—served on tin plates and tin cups, and consisting of fat bacon, boiled beef (cold) in "chunks," dried apple sauce and baked beans, with what was understood to be coffee, and being brown and warm, *was* undoubtedly such. So a meeting was duly organized, and as Chairman of a "Committee on Resolution" I submitted one the original draft of which is inclosed and which was adopted *nem. con.*

After the rest left I wanted to pay the Agent something—he wouldn't touch it. I then insisted that I had a right to subscribe to the funds of the Sanitary Commission at Kingston as well as at New York, for the benefit of the soldiers,—but he couldn't see that either, and refused positively anything whatever under any pretext. What must these men do for the soldiers when their kindness comes so welcome to officers.

. . . I cannot tell you how I rejoice to have entered the service. I understand perfectly well,—did so before, and cannot do so more truly hereafter,—what its realities are. I have no boyish impulse or nonsense about it, but the satisfaction of hoping to do a manly part and share the risks which these men take. It was a singular thing to be and travel with the men I was with, most of them, as it happened, younger than I, who have been in the service one, two and three years, and to whom the names of events and places which to us are only historic, are the mementoes of their own experience. I have been fortunate in meeting in almost every case, quiet, manly pleasant fellows who made no pretense, and had no brag about them. I have uniformly been received and treated with frank and pleasant courtesy, and though I felt like being very quiet with men who had seen and done what I have only read of, nothing in their manner or words claimed any merit. Of course this was right and all that; but it is creditable too.

I have even more reason than I knew of to be glad of an appointment on Sherman's Staff,—among others, it implies facilities in the way of sending and getting letters and packages which I might not have elsewhere.

At Nashville I was lucky to be just in time to come down with one of the General's special messengers, bringing down his mail and sundry boxes, etc., for his staff—a good fellow, quick, ready and smart, as well as knowing his place. I have made a friend of him and shall need his services.

As I wrote before, address all letters and everything for me to "Headquarters of The Military Division of the Mississippi, *Nashville,* Tenn." They will be all attended to there. And remember that when an army and its Headquarters are moving, it is no easy matter always either to send things from or to the same, even for the General himself. The Headquarters which are here today may be somewhere else tomorrow (*will* be somewhere else very soon)—and even our special messenger had to telegraph ahead from Chattanooga Sunday morning to Rome, to learn by a dispatch which met us at Kingston, whether we should come here or go on direct to Atlanta to find these same "Headquarters." So you must not think it strange if you hear from me irregularly,—and what troubles me is that I can hear from you only at intervals. But well you know . . . that while I am here hoping to serve my country it is you who are to me the visible embodiment of what hallows that name.

It is plain enough and sad enough to see that this region is and has been the seat of war. I wish I had time to describe to you the scenes I have already looked on, —I do not mean, of course, any of the active scenes of war, but its visible results. Houses in towns and by the roadside of which only charred timbers and ruins are left; buildings converted into fortifications by embankments, and their brick walls pierced for musketry; and all along the railroad from Greysville, Ga., to near

Kingston the half burnt ties, and bent and twisted rails
lying by the newly built track, as well as the new water-
tanks and new timber, etc., in bridges, telling of the destruction which only two or three weeks ago Hood
vainly thought would ''coop up'' Sherman and result
in all sorts of terrible things. But somehow it didn't
work. I do not wonder at the intense and universal admiration his soldiers feel for ''Uncle Billy.''

I find another thing everywhere,—that so far as I
can learn by inquiry, and from conversation both with
and between others, *one* in ten would be a large estimate of the McClellan men in the army. This is true
even of the *New Jersey regiments,* of which there are
three or four in this army.

I must close this to be sure of sending it back by today's messenger. I will write whenever I can,—and
how I hope and long to hear from you and all of the
dear ones at home. Give them my dear love, and kind
words to friends who may inquire for me. Pray for me
. . . that I may do my duty to God and man; . . .
trust in God, and believe me ever and always in truest
devotion

Your

H.

In the Field, Rome, Ga. Monday Night
October 31st 1864

The enclosed note on note paper was written this A.M.
expecting the mail to go today. The courier does not
leave till early tomorrow morning, and as it is very
likely the last mail we shall get through northward for
some time I cannot but add something more.

Gen. Sherman did not return to his Headquarters
till after 2 P.M., when I saw and reported to him at
once, and was received in his frank, kind, off-hand way
and put at once at my ease. He tells me that he intends
to turn over his correspondence to me for the present
to take care of, and that in good time I shall have

"more elaborate matters" to look after. As to a Judge Advocate's duty there is none of it here now at any rate.

I wish it were possible for me to write you fully about my first day on the staff, for I dare say it might be interesting; but I write late in the evening, in the Adjutant General's office, and have but little time. The house occupied as Headquarters,—a double one-story frame residence, nicely built and in grounds which were once pretty, with a large inclosure round the house and a number of handsome trees in front and on both sides—is devoted to offices. The General and staff all occupy tents pitched in the yard, one of which vacated by Lt Col. Kittoe today, is turned over to me. It is a question with the staff whether on the campaign just about to open,—and for which I am just in time, we shall have any tents at all, or anything better than a "fly." Our meals also are served in an open tent on a plain pine board table,—I being one of the General's mess, which comprises part of the staff, while Gen. Barry,* his Chief of Artillery, takes the rest in his mess.

Everything is as plain as possible, but the dinner was good enough for anybody, including the soup, though that was served in tin platters. —Dinner, by the way, was about 5 P.M. and after it we sat round the camp fires in front of the tents. Gen. S. asked me many questions about St. Louis people, and talked with the same frank, off-hand unreserved way he always had. Tell Mr. Yeatman† that the General spoke of him in the kindest and highest terms,—of his devotion to the cause, of his efficiency, his admirable good sense and management, and of the judicious, sensible and *effective* way in which he (Mr. Y.) personally did his noble work. He could hardly have spoken more warmly in his

---

* Brig. Gen. William F. Barry.

† James E. Yeatman, vice-president of the Sanitary Commission at St. Louis.

praise than he did. He also spoke of Uncle Ethan* in exalted terms,—of his purity of character, his accomplishments, and his fine intellect,—which I have written about to Uncle E. just now. Briefly, I could not desire a more frank, kindly unaffected welcome than I have received both from the General and his staff, and I am most fortunate in every respect in thus entering the service.

Hood *has* crossed the Tennessee River, last night, with his army, numbering about 30,000 men. You need not for a moment imagine, if you hear that he has cut the Nashville & Chattanooga Railroad, and even if he attacks Nashville, or gets *into Kentucky,* that this means either permanent disaster to our cause or unexpected danger to us. Gen. Sherman expects that within three or four days Hood (with Forrest's cavalry) *will* cut that railroad, very likely at or near War Trace, some 60 miles below Nashville,—possibly at or near Tullahoma or Decherd. Of course this will interrupt our communications, both by mail and telegraph, and you will probably not hear directly from me again for some time after you get this letter. Hood's movement is a bold one, but it will be a failure in its real purpose, which is to strike behind Sherman, and frighten him into bringing his whole army northward and so give up Atlanta.

When Gen. Sherman gives up Atlanta it will not be worth much to the Johnnies. Within a few days, probably three or four, *we* shall move,—*not* northward, no matter what Hood does. He told me this evening, briefly, his plans, adding—"It's a big game, but I can do it,—I *know* I can do it." And you may be sure of one thing,—that what he says he can do, he *can.*

I find I cannot write many minutes more; all the rest

---

* Maj. Gen. Ethan Allen Hitchcock, who had served with gallantry in the Mexican War, and, declining high command in the Civil War, served at Washington in an advisory capacity. His career is fully set forth in *Fifty Years in Camp and Field: Diary of Major General Ethan Allen Hitchcock, U.S.A.* Edited by W. A. Croffut, Ph.D., New York, 1909.

have gone to their tents, and the orderly in charge of the office has come in to go to bed, as it is late. . . .

I am very much afraid I shall not be able to get a letter off to Ethan* by this courier, and that for the present means not at all. Pray write to him at once and tell him that while I have no good excuse to offer for my long silence, it was not intended, and that I am grieved and troubled that I should have been guilty of it. He has good right to be hurt, and to doubt even my affection for him; but tell him, God bless him, he was never dearer to me, nor could anything have been more touching than his few lines of August 12th. How could I but love him, the dear, noble fellow, and only the more that I have treated him badly. Ask him to forgive it,— and I will surely write him when I can. . . .

You may not hear from us save through the rebel papers for a time—perhaps my next letter to you will come by *New York*. But remember, in that case, not to trouble yourself about their lying accounts, for this very place—Rome,—where I write, they published recently that Hood had taken, which was simply a lie. It has been held ever since Sherman first took it last Spring, by our own troops. By one, judge all. Believe in "Uncle Billy" as his soldiers do,—and believe in a higher than mortal protection which I should need no less were I quietly at home, and could not more surely receive there than here. But I cannot bear to write about dangers which I do not fear, nor to counsel you against anxieties which you will not allow to harass you. . . .

IN THE FIELD, ROME, GA. November 2

(Wednesday noon) 1864

I make the most of a few minutes' waiting for a special train which is to take down to Kingston the General and one or two of his staff today—the rest to march down there by tomorrow. I owe my ride on the

---

* H.'s younger brother, Ethan Allen Hitchcock. See *ante*, p. 2.

car, I presume, to my being as yet dismounted, having
found it impossible to get a horse for permanent use as
yet, though I had arranged for the use of one, kindly
loaned by a brother officer, for this trip. As it is an
ugly, chilly, rainy day, I am quite as well satisfied to
take the cars with as good company as there will be.
"Uncle Billy" is capital company, always in the same
frank off-hand flow of spirits and talk when not actually busy, and even then without the slightest affectation. As I write, in the room used as the Adjutant General's office, he is lying on a wooden settee with an Aid
writing a dispatch on one knee at his side. What would
Hood give to see that dispatch!

You may draw your own inferences from *my* going
from here. I would not have written as much as I did
on Monday as to future possibilities but for the fear
lest you might be alarmed by what Mr. Hood might do
north of the Tennessee River. As it was, I don't know
that it should have been written, in view even of the
possibility of that courier coming to grief. If this letter
goes through, Hood will have done less than is regarded as *possible*,—not probable, perhaps,—but if it
does not, he cannot do more than somebody else is waiting and ready for.

I have slept two nights in a tent, the first of them
cold and windy, the last, cold and rainy; and having
slept comfortably (you'll believe that) and not caught
any cold, I am "all serene."

During this my first visit to Rome I have obeyed the
adage and found it very pleasant to do as the (*most*
modern) Romans did: particularly as those did who
kept company with a very Roman-nosed General. I
have become entirely at home, and find my associates
on the staff an exceedingly pleasant and gentlemanly
set of men,—as I was told, before seeing them. All of
them have seen service, some of them as much as anybody. Gen. Barry, our chief of artillery, who is a finer-
looking man than his photograph in your album, is, as

you know, a West Pointer; as are most of the staff, I think; Gen. Barry held a similar position with McClellan, and is very honorably known in connection with the Army of the Potomac. He is very much of a gentleman in all respects, and a man of cultivated taste, I should judge, quite aside from his profession.

I told you what my duties were for the present, and am told by one of the Aids that it is considered something of a compliment to be placed at once in the confidential relation which this implies even on the Staff. Since then the General has foreshadowed to me other duties hereafter to be taken up, which make it somewhat clearer why he thought I might do him service,— and if I can properly fulfil them it will exactly meet my hopes and wishes. I looked over and answered for him a few letters yesterday, some private and some military. I enclose you the original of one of the former, and copy of my reply, which reminded me a little of writing letters for the Sanitary Fair.* The fun of it was the directions given me as to the sort of reply to write—so brief and comprehensive that I have endorsed them exactly as given, on the back of the enclosed copy of reply. Read this endorsement before reading the reply. The General seemed not only satisfied but very much pleased with the latter when I read it to him before mailing. He also requested me yesterday to look over his letter-books, containing copies of all letters and telegrams sent by him, including those sent in cypher; and it was a commentary on the history of his campaigns and movements, so far as I have read yet, which was interesting enough, you may guess. It was a little odd that the first one copied in the first book

---

* The letter, accompanying a gift of fruits from three ladies in Newark, Ohio, bore on its back a note of Sherman's instructions for the reply: "Somethin' sweet, you know, as the feller said—molasses and honey." This bears out what Sherman wrote to his wife, April 5, 1865 (*Home Letters of Gen. Sherman*, p. 340): "Hitchcock, nephew of the General, writes private letters not needing my personal attention, such as autographs and locks of hair."

I took up—that of latest date,—was his telegram to Kelton* in September which resulted in my appointment. I considered it no harm to take a copy of that, which I herewith also enclose to you; and you can now judge for yourself of the epithet which Kelton applied to the telegram in his letter to me.

This town of Rome is very prettily situated on a point or peninsula formed by two rivers—see map—and is set upon and among several hills and ridges which make quite a charming landscape. Our Headquarters are on one side of the town, perhaps a quarter of a mile or less from the broad principal street running through it. It was evidently a thriving and somewhat important country town, contains two or three well-built churches, and some very respectable buildings.

I must stop for the present; hope to finish this at Kingston and send it thence if an opportunity offers.

(1 P.M.)—The train is not yet ready or at least not announced, and I continue my scribbling till it is. Lunch has been announced and discussed, however, meanwhile. The domestic economy of this "military family" is not very elaborate. Our boarding-house as well as our respective lodgings, is in a tent—a wall-tent, open at both ends and consecrated to breakfast, lunch and dinner, for we don't take supper, but have tea and coffee (tea sometimes, coffee always) at dinner instead. The sumptuous board is a planed pine table without cloth or cover. The ware is good stout china, especially the tea cups which do duty for tumblers. The soup plates are of a fine variety of tin ware, no doubt originally as lustrous as silver; whether the spoons are pewter or tinned iron I am not metallurgist enough to decide, but one or the other. For lunch today

* Col. J. C. Kelton, Assistant Adjutant General. The message is printed in *Fifty Years in Camp and Field: Diary of Maj. Gen. Ethan Allen Hitchcock, U.S.A.*, p. 468, and is quoted in the Introduction to this volume (p. 7).

we had slices of ham or bacon, flanked by a dish of stewed dried apples, the other wing being composed of what our *cordon bleu,* Manuel, considers "fust rate biscuit,"—and they are good enough,—with a bottle of molasses and a smaller one of jelly thrown out as skirmishers and the rear-guard I believe was another dish of bacon;—for liquor, good water. The train is ready and the ambulance coming to the door—Good bye.

KINGSTON, GA. November 2d—7 P.M.

WE left Rome this afternoon a few minutes after the above was written, and as it turned out I was the only one of the staff who was to or did come down by rail with the General, besides his orderly. The "special train" was some eight or ten cars (freight cars) filled with I don't know what, and with a lot of soldiers on top of them. The rear car was a "caboose" if you know what that is,—a sort of baggage car with a cooking stove in it and closets or compartments at the ends, for the use of engineers, conductors, etc., who live on the road. The fire in the stove was acceptable this cold, rainy day, both to "Uncle Billy" and his numerous and dashing retinue,—what *we* lacked in numbers being made up by half a dozen or more others—railroad men, one or two officers (lieutenants), etc., who were also going down. Two hours or less brought us to this lovely spot, which is as much of a town as a railroad depot, a "hotel" and three or four houses can make it. At this point the branch road to Rome leaves the main Atlanta Railroad. All round the little plain on which stand the aforesaid houses, and across which the railroad runs are elevations, hardly hills save one of them on the North; and on this plain are now also huts, log houses, etc., constructed for soldiers. How many or few tents dot the plain or are scattered over the hills is of no consequence, for if there were ever so many tonight they might all be struck by breakfast time tomorrow. We are at the Post Commandant's Quarters, in a one-story double frame house facing the railroad track but some distance from it across the plain,—which distance implied a comfortable walk through the mud of last night's and today's rain.

A propos to mud and what not, I have come to the comfortable conclusion since hearing yesterday of Forrest's performances at Johnsonville, that the "Belle Peoria," the Government boat on which my horse, servant, and all my and his horse equipments, including my riding-boots, were shipped—either reached that place just in time to be captured or, if luckily too slow for that, may have got the news and turned back. In either case the said articles are not available to the undersigned for *this* campaign anyhow. "Sich is life," especially in war-time. I sincerely hope the rebs have not got hold of Ellis, for even if they did not murder him he is very apt to be a good deal less of a free colored pusson in their hands than when he contracted with me at $20 per month. I don't much think I shall see him again, and my little investment in his charge, say about $325, including cash handed him, is "gone up." Now tell me . . . if Forrest and his rebels "gobble" my worldly effects on the Tennessee River, under the laws of war, why haven't I a right to make righteous restitution out of Forrest's constituents and supporters on the Chattahoochee or the—well, say the Savannah or the Mobile or the Cooper and Ashley Rivers, under the laws of war also,—if I get a chance? Not that I would "confiscate" a horse or any other such like thing—not for the world, even if you hadn't made me promise so and so. I would remark, however, that horses are contraband of war by all international codes.

Perhaps you would like to know about this house, by the way, where I am writing in the room which Col. Somebody, Post Commandant, has kindly set apart for the General, and which I share tonight on the latter's

invitation. Who was, or may conceive him or herself
now still to be the lawful owner, I am entirely unable
to say; and as the Colonel—who being in quite undis-
puted possession is *prima facie* the owner,—has been
here but a short time, I am afraid he is equally ill informed, and so I haven't inquired.

I have seen but one of the denizens of this village or
ex-village since I came. That was a little woman of six
or seven years, who came into the yard as I stood on
the front porch, and was slowly making her way into
the hall, looking askance at me meanwhile. I asked her
in a pleasant way what she wanted. She replied, apparently without any fear, and with a touching child-
like assurance, that her Mother had sent her to get a
safe-guard. I turned her over to the Colonel, who gave
or promised to give her one. I wonder whether her father is in Hood's army. Possibly he may be of that
courageous class of Southern patriots hereabouts who
frequent convenient positions along the railroad—like
one near Rome, which the General pointed out to me
as we passed it—whence they fire into the trains.
Wouldn't they have been too happy, if they had only
known it, to send a few bullets after that tall man with
a black wool hat,—not braided nor tasselled who sat in
that "caboose" by the stove, wrapped in his blue overcoat, and in his thoughts which I can very certainly
say were not "blue" at all, any more than were the
telegrams he sent hence this evening. . . .

I hope such gossip as I scribble off may be at least
better than nothing; you will remember that my range
of topics is not extensive at best, and what I am most
interested in I can say nothing about, though it would
be of the highest interest to you.

Since I wrote the above my seat at the table has been
occupied for more than half an hour by the telegrapher
who attends the General taking down dispatches from
his dictation. If you could read these you would have

some idea both of the magnitude of the area over which his thoughts, plans, precautions, previsions, range, and of—what is to me—the wonderful range, celerity, and vigor of those thoughts. If ever a "live man" has commanded any of our armies, he is one. I do not wonder that Uncle E. called him "my glorious friend Sherman."

The information tonight is all *good*. Hood—or rather Beauregard—is evidently aware (though not to the full extent) of the danger of the bold game he is playing, and is taking precautions, which, while precautions in one sense, necessarily damage him. Meanwhile other people are taking precautions too. I repeat that you need not be concerned at anything they may do before you—and they—hear from this quarter. So far as Missouri is concerned, indeed, the late trouble is over and movements in your part of the country will soon show it. A telegram from Grant tonight plumply indorses Gen. S's plans (already communicated to him fully) and this with express mention of and reference to all that Hood is attempting.

I have been writing at intervals, and have been most of the evening listening to the General's talk about both military and other matters. Nothing can be more direct, incisive, or clear than his way of talking and referring as he has done to his former campaigns and mentioning many incidents of them, and alluding also to many other matters of interest; you may suppose I enjoy it. I asked his staff at Rome whether he was for Lincoln or McClellan. None of them knew; he has never said, and quietly ignores all discussion of either. But from a few words he said to me tonight,—not in any sense of a "political" character, however,—and which he prefaced, no one else being in the room, by saying "Now that we are alone I'll tell you," etc., etc.,—I have no hesitation in concluding that he is not a votary of "little Mac." This for your personal—satisfaction?

Pray don't think me likely to turn Boswell to any man's Johnson. My "chief" occupies a position and has already done things which certainly invest him with more than ordinary interest; and he impresses me as a man of power more than any man I remember. Not general intellectual power, not Websterian, but the sort of power which a flash of lightning suggests,—as clear, as intense, and as rapid. Yet with all his vigor, his Atlanta campaign showed, as his conversation and dispatches do, abundant caution and the most careful forethought. Without any signs of arrogance, he has complete confidence in himself and—as he told me tonight he said to Grant at Vicksburg when the latter sent him out to beat off Jo Johnston's army advancing to raise the siege, warning him at the same time against J. as a most wily and dangerous adversary—"give me" said S., "men enough and time to look over the ground and I'm not afraid of the d—l." He had two days to reconnoitre and spent nearly forty hours of them in the saddle; when Johnston arrived the fords were left open for him to cross and attack—and he declined battle. The next step, as you may remember, was that Sherman pushed Johnston all the way to Jackson, and had finally to give up the chase for want of water, the rebels having spoiled all the ponds by driving cattle into them and shooting them there, and our men breaking down and giving out on the road from this cause and the summer heat.

By the way, I made some allusion to Fullerton. The General remembered him and asked who he was, etc. I told what I knew of him. "He stands very high," he replied—"Howard* wanted him with him very much." —It is 10 P.M.—and the General is in bed and asleep. I must close this and do likewise. We may be here long enough for me to write again. . . .

                                                    H.

* Maj. Gen. Oliver Otis Howard.

IN THE FIELD KINGSTON, GA. November 4, 1864

Friday Evening 8 P.M.

I wish I could send you a picture of the scene in front
of our Headquarters tonight,—a picture that you could
hear as well as see,—as it was for an hour or so after
dark. One of the brigade bands came over to serenade
the General, who is passionately fond of music, as is
also Gen. Barry, who I find [is] a brother flutist somewhat after my style "only better." It was rather a picturesque scene, and a very pleasant one, in spite of a
few drops of rain towards the close. The house is a one
story double frame house, with a small porch in front
of the main hall, and looks northward across the plain
I spoke of in a former letter hence, towards the railroad track, some 150 to 200 yards off, the interval being
open save a few trees in and in front of the yard. On
the left of the house are pitched the tents occupied by
the staff, in a row,—some half a dozen, the General and
several of the staff being quartered in the house, where
we also take our meals. In front of each tent blazed a
fire, built of logs, brush, rails and whatever comes
handy—whose combined glare lit up the foreground
and alternately illumined and deepened the shadows
among the branches of the trees, and lit up the darkness
of the plain, disclosing also the presence of knots and
groups of the men who had followed the band over to
hear the music. At and between the fires, and on the
little porch, and in front or just within the tents were
standing or sitting the staff and other officers, enjoying
the music,—not in parade dress though in uniform, and
bearing unequivocal tokens of the mud which hereabouts doth abound; while in the rear of the line of our
tents and fires flashed up now and then the glare and
half-lurid smoke of the servants' fires, while in the intervals of the tents their dark figures now and then
intercepted the light as they moved about or drew near
to listen. Around and against the horizon duskily rose
the outlines of the low hills which surround this lo-

cality, sparkling with distant camp fires—no matter
how many, but enough to add a feature to the scene. It
was something worth seeing and which I shall remember as one of my earlier sights of camp-life,—though I
shall doubtless see many more such. The music was excellent,—the leader of the band playing the cornet admirably and the time and harmony both being capitally
kept. I am told however that there are two better bands
now in Atlanta, belonging to the 2ᵈ Massachusetts and
another Massachusetts regiment kept up by subscrip-
tion among the officers, as the Government very properly no longer allows—or at least provides—regimental
bands. These two are said to be expert bands.

By tomorrow we hope to welcome another courier
now on the way from Nashville and who will surely
bring me letters from home. . . . As I wrote you, on
the march there will be little opportunity to write letters, let alone send them, as you will understand in due
time. For the present we are here, when the time comes
we go.

I have even more reason today than at any time since
I came, so far as it is possible to judge, and so far as
the General's opinion is worth anything, to tell you not
to be concerned at Hood or Beauregard's movements.
The information received this evening tends to show
that B. has crossed only one corps on his pontoon
bridge between Colbert and Muscle Shoals on the Tennessee River, and is moving the balance of his army
westward and towards Corinth. So much the better. If
this means that he has either for the time or permanently abandoned his promised invasion of Middle Tennessee, and is now making for the ''Western Dees-
trict,'' as the Tennessee people used to call it, possibly
to attack Memphis, possibly to besiege Columbus and
threaten Paducah,—it means nothing that will do *him*
any good, no matter how promising his plans seem to
him. He may take Memphis if he likes so far as any
permanent good to him or damage to us can possibly

result from it. He could not hold it if he did, and if he ravishes that country he will—like Price,* only more so,—only be plundering his own friends as much as ours. Such things do not permanently affect the war, unless by them also vital lines of communication are destroyed, or cardinal strategic points taken *and held.* Bragg marched a large army to within sight of the Ohio River, clear across Kentucky,—and what did he effect by it save the destruction of property it caused? Sherman's raid last year to Meridian had for its object the cutting and permanent injury of the Mobile & Ohio Railroad, among other things,—which was thoroughly done for 100 miles,—and Beauregard is today weakened in his present movement by the results, for though the rebels are using the road again, it is only patched up and is not half as available for supplies etc. as it was and should be.

Meanwhile our Chief's plans are matured and his preparations rapidly completing for *his* future work, which includes sundry things. I wrote at his dictation last evening a long telegram to Halleck, sent in cypher, which gave, in a masterly way for its lucidity and comprehensive brevity—a *résumé* of the situation all round and of his own intentions and dispositions with reference to it. If the "Republican" has or has had any doleful articles about "the rebel invasion of Tennessee," one perusal of that telegram would set your mind at rest so far as the success or significance of that "invasion" is concerned. I have already told you, I believe, that a telegram from Grant two nights ago squarely indorsed Sherman's plans. We can afford to "discount *that* paper."

The General had a long chat with me about his old friends in St. Louis, asking particularly after many of them by name—including Maj. Turner, Col. Campbell, Lucas, Gantt, Stickney, Mrs. Keim and Mrs. Beaumont,

* Maj. Gen. Sterling Price, C.S.A., commanding Confederate troops in Missouri early in the war.

Dr. J. B. Johnson, Dr. Pope, Dick January, L. A. Benoist, and numerous others of his old business associates
whom I do not recall,—Mrs. M. McPherson, by the way,
was another, and he spoke with evident pleasure of a
letter of congratulation McPherson wrote him on the
fall of Atlanta. They may talk—the rebels and their
friends—about "the brute Sherman," and to them
while in arms against the Government they may be
sure he will be nothing but a minister of wrath and vengeance, and of absolute destruction so far as the military power of the rebels and everything that is or can
be used to maintain it is concerned. But as an individual and to individuals he is a straightforward, simple, kind-hearted, nay warm-hearted man, thoughtful
and considerate of the feelings and scrupulously just
and careful of the rights of others. I know this for I
have already had unexepected opportunities of seeing
it, in even trifling matters. His manner is off-hand,
often almost blunt, but even in apparently harsh military measures there is often a reason not visible on the
surface but founded in as much good feeling as good
sense. He ordered the establishment of an "*Indiana*
State Sanitary Agent," opened in Atlanta after its
fall, with a big sign hung out, etc., to be summarily
closed, the goods turned over to the U. S. Quartermaster to be distributed among *all* the soldiers and
strictly accounted for, and a sergeant and private
whom the Agent had got detailed to keep shop for him
while he went home to get more goods, were ordered
back to duty. Presently came a peremptory dispatch
from Secretary Stanton (based of course upon the
Sanitary Agent's story of his wrongs) requiring a
categorical answer as to what he did this for, and why
the Agent of the State of Indiana was expelled from
Atlanta, etc., etc. "I told him why,"—said the General,
relating the story to me—"told him I hadn't any *Indiana army* down there but a U. S. army—that I had already authorized two Sanitary Agents, one of the U. S.

GENERAL SHERMAN

and one of the Western Sanitary Commission,—that I wasn't going to have any man come there to make distinctions among my men, and that while I was ready and willing to receive all anybody chose to give and would see that it was distributed fairly among them all *pro rata,* either among the well or the sick as they directed, I wouldn't have one man nursed because he was from Indiana and his next neighbor left to long and pine for what *he* couldn't get because he was from Ohio. And that was the last I ever heard from Mr. Secretary Stanton about State Sanitary Agents." *Toujours perdrix,* and I shall bore you with my *General.* But you see . . . precious little *here* is there to talk about else that is not contraband. I might describe my associates, but that would not be very interesting to you who never heard nor care to hear of them. I do not care to write about the signs of desolation one meets now and then,—sad but unavoidable necessities of war, for which the rebels and not we are responsible, and which will end at once whenever they lay down their arms, and neither can nor *ought* to end sooner. General Sherman is perfectly right,—the only possible way to end this unhappy and dreadful conflict, in whose horrors, though he is Providentially a chief actor, no man is further from finding any pleasure, is to make it *terrible beyond endurance.* I mean what I say, and now that I have shown my willingness to take my full share of all it involves,—Heaven knows not because I desire waste or desolation but because there is no other road to peace,—you must not find fault with me for saying so. Our enemies have shown themselves *devils* in the spirit which ever began this most unprovoked and inexcusable rebellion, and which animates its last utterance in Jeff. Davis' speech at Columbia, S. C., Oct. 4th, —and there is nothing for it but "to fight the devil with fire." Not with wanton barbarity nor with useless destruction; but it is neither barbarous nor useless but just and indispensable to utterly destroy everything, no matter whose, or what, or whom, that does or can uphold, sustain or encourage this gigantic crime. There is no peace else for this generation or the next. I hope you have seen and carefully read that speech of Jeff Davis, or if not that you will do so. Compare it with Sherman's letter to the Mayor of Atlanta, which I enclose to you. J. D. never uttered a more wanton and shameless falsehood,—and that is saying a good deal, —than when he told his rebel subjects that "their government had from the first uniformly tried every means to avoid war,"—or words to that effect. It is amazing, astounding that the arch-conspirator who himself inspired and directed act after act of *open war* upon the U. S. Government during the ten weeks *before Mr. Lincoln was inaugurated,*—for if the seizure by armed men in the name of an independent Sovereign Power so-called, of forts, arsenals, stores and munitions, the capture and detention as *prisoners of war* of U. S. troops, etc., etc., were not acts of war it would not be easy to define what are such—should have had the hardihood to make such an assertion.

This issue is exactly the one which Gen. Sherman makes in all he has to say or write about the rebellion, and I never saw a man more utterly possessed with the conviction of the infinite wrong and crime of its very existence. He says he don't care for any of the "side issues" the rebels and their friends have made since then with Mr. Lincoln—the question is to him as another letter of his, yet unpublished, puts it, "the simplest thing in the world—You have undertaken to rebel against and destroy the Government,—you must stop that and return to your obedience to its laws, or else the Government must destroy you." This is the substance —not the precise words.

Before we left Rome the General said to me, *à propos* to I forget what, that when he heard I wanted to leave my home, with the position, etc., etc., I had there, and enter the service, he "thought it was a strange

freak.'' I was surprised at this, and told him so, adding
—''an expression in one of your own letters, Sir, about
men's showing that they could fight as well as talk for
their country,—though it by no means originated certainly helped on my purpose.'' I then added that the
reason I wished to enter the service was simply that I
could not stay at home and let other men do the fighting
and run the risks while I was safely making money and
enjoying the fruit of their toils; that I had been long
restless and dissatisfied about it, and would have entered the army long ago, if I could have earlier seen my
way honorably to leave or lay aside private trusts of
importance to others which had been committed to me;
that when I did see my way out of these, I did at once
apply for an appointment stipulating however for two
things,—*first* that it should be one whose duties I could
reasonably expect to perform in the absence of military education and experience and in performing them
to render some real service to the cause,—*second* that
these duties should be ''at the front,'' and that having
as I hoped obtained the fulfillment of these conditions,
I was very sure that I should hereafter be able to respect myself for at least having tried to do my duty.
He replied, very earnestly, ''that's the right spirit, Sir,
—that's right; and if all the able-bodied men in this
country who are between say 18 and 45 years of age,—
that's my age, Sir, I'm about 45,—would act on that
view of it, we could finish this war, Sir, in three months,
—yes, Sir, in three months!''

You asked me . . . to write you after I left home,
why I entered the service, so that you could have it to
show to our boy, from his father, hereafter. I had forgotten that I promised to do so till since I began this
letter,—or rather never thought of it before when I happened to be writing to you. I have mentioned this conversation which was accidental and wholly unexpected
to me, as perhaps as good a way as any of doing it.

Of course, as yet I have seen no real ''soldiering,''

though in a fair way to see it soon. I am very glad of this preliminary opportunity which these few days of quiet give me, to get somewhat fitted to my place and those with whom I am to be, especially my "Chief" himself, as Kelton calls him. Pretty soon it will begin in earnest; and I would rather be with this Commander during the next six months, for divers reasons, than with any other General or on any other campaign in the war. Next summer you will know why.

I telegraphed to Nashville yesterday to know whether Forrest captured the "Belle Peoria"—the boat on which my horse and servant were shipped from home— and was answered thence today that he had not. Whether they will get to Nashville in time to reach me, and can be forwarded, is still a question. I did right, however, in buying the one and employing the other, whether they come or not. . . .

Gen. Sherman asked me this evening, if I happened to be writing to any of his old friends to give them his kindest remembrance,—and added, "when you write to your wife, give her my love—I never had the pleasure of knowing her but I have often heard of her."

Please say to Mr. Yeatman—to whom do not fail to say how warmly the General spoke in praise of his devotion to the cause, his judicious and quiet way of managing and the good he has done,—that I shall certainly try to write him if possible before we leave here, and that I believe in Sherman as a General *most thoroughly* and find my relations with him all I could wish. Tell him also not to take any extra trouble about sending stores, etc., beyond Chattanooga after this. . . .

IN THE FIELD, KINGSTON, GA—November 9, 1864

I dare say you are tired of seeing this date, as I am a little tired of writing it; and impatience of our inaction—I mean the comparative inaction of our immediate circle—is manifested privately by most of those here. However, though we are quiet others are moving and all will be in due time.

Shepley* writes me, (Nov[r] 3[d], received today) that considerable fear is felt in military circles lest Sherman should have to abandon Atlanta. I supposed Forrest's performances and Hood's "invasion of Tennessee" would produce such feelings—naturally enough; and it was to meet them that I wrote and have been writing in confident general terms what, if I could give you the particulars of, you would see was *all so*. I have said nothing but what was fully justified by the detailed information here, and I trust you will not allow any panic stories of rebels on either side of our lines nor any apparently reasonable anxiety in military or any other circles to trouble you on our account. I mean exactly what I say—I am not talking to keep up your spirits, but because I *know* the precautions taken, the preparations made and the operations in progress. There is *far* less uncertainty about the coming winter, so far as is possible for human sagacity to see, than there was all last spring; and I admit uncertainty at all only to the extent inseparable from human foresight. . . .

We must both soon at least acquiesce in not hearing from each other for a time, as I have repeatedly written. I am ashamed, or I would be, to complain of what I shall endure only as one of thousands of those around me. But it will not be for long, and it is in a glorious cause. For myself, ten times over I would not refuse the sacrifice: it only troubles me for you. . . .

By the way, you may see a picture of that serenade in "Harper's Weekly" yet—Davis,† their Artist, is here, and has promised to send a sketch of it from the description I gave him of the scene. He finished today and sent off a sketch begun some time ago of "Union

---

* John R. Shepley, a St. Louis friend, in later life a distinguished lawyer.

† Theodore R. Davis, frequently mentioned hereafter.

Refugees going North from Kingston"—a very good
one. He draws well, and faithfully.

.   .   .   .

The horse I was lucky enough to buy is an excellent
one, already acclimated and well tried,—and a good-
looking one beside. All the staff tell me I got a bargain.
As to a servant I am unable yet to get one, but share
the services of Capt. Nichols'* boy,—Capt. N. sharing
my tent.

Gen. Ewing's brother "Charley"†—Lieutenant Col.
and Inspector General—has rejoined the staff, and we
are good friends. I find Gen. Barry a most agreeable
acquaintance,—a gentleman of cultivated tastes, and
a *soldier;* and he, as all, are most frank and courteous
to me. Gen. Barry said to me very emphatically last
evening that Sherman came the nearest to his idea of
a General of all he had seen during the war,—"and you
know I have seen several of them";—viz: Halleck,
McClellan, and for a month or so, Grant. I believe him;
so think all this army too.

I continue perfectly well,—never was better nor felt
better,—notwithstanding the rains almost all the time
since I joined. Tonight we had a heavy shower with
wind, which had like to have capsized our tent. I have
not had a cold and consider myself initiated.

I enclose another photograph, also with an autograph endorsed, taken in September last at Atlanta, on
one of the defensive works of the city. You will find the
names in pencil on the back, corresponding with the
numbers at foot. Barry and Sherman are in the foreground. Beckwith‡ and Poe§ are now at Atlanta; Dr.
Kittoe has been relieved at his own request and gone
North; and there is another A.D.C.—Capt. Auden-

* George Ward Nichols, aide on Gen. Sherman's staff.
† Col. Charles Ewing, a brother of Mrs. Sherman.
‡ Amos Beckwith (later Brig. Gen.), Chief, Commissary of Subsistence.
§ Col. O. M. Poe, Chief Engineer.

ried,* who, as also Marshall† and Baylor,‡ are on
Barry's staff not properly on ours, though Barry is
himself one of the General's staff, as Chief of Artillery.
Barry and his staff have their mess separate,—the rest
of us mess with the General. I send this photograph to
you, but unless you wish to keep it you can give it to
Margie from me. I send you also the General's letter
to me in reply to mine, which followed me back here
and which you may as well put with your autographs.
It will have a special interest hereafter—be sure of
that. Sherman has done great things, but he has not yet
filled his place in this war or in this country,—mark
the prediction. I cannot tell you how fortunate I consider myself to have stepped into this position at this
time. What came to me without effort on my part and
certainly without claim or desert of it has been refused
to others many times. I wrote the other day at his dictation a very civil but flat refusal of an application for a
staff position with him made by an old friend of his
backed by the official request of the Consul General of
Italy and the strong recommendation of Gen. Robt Anderson, in behalf of an Italian Chevalier, formerly a
Major and on the staff of Gen. Cialdini in the Gaeta
campaign. I shall endeavor to persuade the General
that he did not make a mistake. . . .

It is very late and I must close this. No more courier
from Nashville hither after today—but I must have at
least one precious letter from you on the way. If possible I will telegraph you as already advised—any simple message will mean that *we are off* and all well,
whether it says that or not for I may not find it best to
say that. These "mysteries" are not idle; it is of great
importance that Hood and Beauregard should know as
little as possible of any movement or even the fact of it,
—not more at this than at all times—and a message can

* Joseph C. Audenried.
† Capt. John E. Marshall.
‡ Col. Thomas G. Baylor, Chief of Ordnance.

be stolen from the wires and yet go on them too. All important telegrams go in cypher; and none but military telegrams can go in that now anywhere in this country, if known to be cypher. . . .

H.

IN THE FIELD, KINGSTON, GA. November 10 1864
(Thursday 10 A.M.)

I wrote you a letter last night—under divers interruptions,—which goes by courier today. I embrace the opportunity of sending a few lines more by Maj. McDonald who goes up on same train, within an hour, direct for St. Louis. I have nothing special to add to what I have already written, only to send you something at the last moment for writing to say that everything and everybody is well. The rains seem to have ended,—last night's storm winding up with a bracing wind from the N.W., and this morning being bright and beautiful. We hope this means just what the General has been desiring,—that the fall rains should come all together, early in November, and give us fine weather for some weeks, which is what we want *now*. Last night's telegraphic news from above is all good, and the reasons for confidence and high spirits heretofore alluded to all continue. The election is over, the troops all paid up, their sanitary condition—I use the words of the Medical Inspector in answer to my inquiry day before yesterday—"is *splendid*," and their spirit and confidence never higher. What is before us, I repeat, is attended with less uncertainty and more promise of ultimate result than *anything yet done,* save so far as the latter prepared for this. Disregard all croakers, panic-makers and retailers of rebel alarms. Pay no attention to anything apparently discouraging that you may hear *of us* until you hear *from us;* and I imply that you may hear such things for reasons which before long will develop themselves. Remember that what is now to be done has been fully planned and prepared for, that Grant endorses it and Sherman is bound to carry it through; and believe my assurance that I consider myself *most fortunate* in every respect, so far as any service I could take part in is concerned, to be exactly where I am.

Humanly speaking, and in every human probability, the next few weeks must have a powerful effect for good on our cause, with less risk of injury to it than has attended any similar contingency. And may God defend the right. I am writing in the General's room, at a little table in one corner, he sitting on a sofa next to it writing *his* last letters for the present on a blank book on his knee,—the inevitable segar in mouth, and that black wool hat on his head. It seems to be understood that I have rather the special entrée of this room and use of this table. I have just finished sundry orders to be telegraphed to various Commanders, which could be substantially condensed in one word of two syllables, and a word which soldiers love. . . .

IN THE FIELD, KINGSTON, GA. November 11th 1864
Friday Night

Our last courier did go up yesterday, and by him I sent letters; and by same train went Maj. McDonald (not in the service now) by whom I sent a line to Lubke* inclosing a letter to you. Tonight, just as the final preparations to move are completing, Gen. Barry is forced to leave us and go to the rear by an attack of erysipelas which after several days' indisposition has fairly broken out on him—to his and our great regret. I send this to be mailed at Nashville or Chattanooga by Capt. Marshall who accompanies Gen. B. . . .

Rome was abandoned last night and today by our forces, and all buildings in it of use to the enemy were destroyed. No private residences were burned nor was there any violence done to the people. This was the or-

* George W. Lubke, later Judge of St. Louis Circuit Court, in whose hands Hitchcock had left his law business.

der and Gen. Corse* (of Iowa,—the hero of the fight at
Allatoona last month) today answered my express inquiry by the assurance that it was strictly obeyed under his personal supervision. Probably Hood will begin
now to understand Sherman's plans—in part. The
rebel papers will claim, of course, that Sherman is being *forced* to evacuate this and that, etc., etc. *Pay no
attention,* I repeat, to any of these things, and be under
no concern for Sherman. He never was further from
defeat nor were J. D.'s predictions and promises ever
further from fulfilment. Our men are in the finest condition and spirits; everything useless and cumbersome
has gone back, and early in the morning *we are off*. The
weather is cool, bright and beautiful and the moonlight
tonight lovely.—Our last courier down is on the way
and should have been here before now; he left Nashville Wednesday. I have delayed this line hoping to acknowledge one more letter from you—I have received
but one, of October 30, since I left,—but must close
without it. I am in perfect health, and so far as we are
concerned here in the fullest confidence and good spirits, as are all. . . .

IN THE FIELD, KINGSTON, GA. November 11th 1864
Friday Night—11³⁰′ P.M.

I am sure you will smile at my many "last words"
before we start,—but I say to myself that it will be a
pleasant smile. I wrote you already tonight a hasty little note to go by Capt. Marshall's hands, who goes to
the rear with Gen. Barry. Since then, *at last* the courier
has come. . . .

By the way, it quite made me smile, your saying that
I no doubt knew so and so from the papers. I have seen
two St. Louis papers, I believe, since I left home. Lubke
wrote me that the "Union" noticed my appointment
etc. the day after I left, and that he sent me a copy—

* Brig. Gen. J. M. Corse.

but it has not nor will reach me, and if there was anything "cordial" in the notice, I hope *you* were flattered by it as much as I'm sure I would have been, else it was thrown away. Some few numbers of some New York and Cincinnati papers have found their way here, but that is all. I shall know how to value newspapers and some other elements of civilization *hereafter.* . . .

I confess it went a little hard with me to have that box of mess supplies stopped at Nashville;—one day earlier there and it would have come through by this very courier. It would have been very acceptable all round. So too my riding boots, and horse equipments, to say nothing of the horse,—but it's no use nor sense either to fret about it, nor have I. I had a scare last week by the way; I thought I had lost $250.00 which I had got changed into large bills and put in a letter envelope in inside vest pocket. I had placed it in my valise, however, and it slipped under some other things where I found it. It was two days, however, before I found it, having looked in the valise at first where I thought I remembered placing it and really had—and not till I determined to re-search the whole valise did it turn up. . . .

Dispatches received (in cipher) by the General since I began this, indicate that Hood (or Beauregard) has thrown two corps across the Tennessee River at Florence; that the Mobile & Ohio Railroad is to be his line of supplies, and that he needs supplies, clothing, etc., very badly, but has to bring them the last fifteen miles to Corinth by wagons, the railroad being still never fully repaired. It is the talk in Hood's camp, as reported by two of our men, escaped prisoners, that he will move on Nashville. I doubt it; but if he does, he will find more men ready to meet him in the open field than he dare attack, to say nothing of fortifications on the way which he cannot take. I reckon he had a lesson at Allatoona last month how forts can be defended. . . . As to my own health and spirits, my entire satis-

faction with my position—more than that, indeed,—
and the way I find my experience of camp-life so far
agrees with me, I have been really rejoiced that I could
write thus; and you know you can always trust what I
say. I was interrupted at the above,* and have since
written for the General two long dispatches to go in
cypher, one to Nashville and one to Washington,—
which if you could read you would not only understand
my confidence but also see the real meaning of divers
things which you will soon hear of. There will be a com-
motion in Beauregard's camp, and you may next hear
of him as rushing back and when you do, or if he is insane enough still to advance into Tennessee, either one,
look out for Thomas' movements; and then you will begin to hear rebel lies about Sherman's "desperate
situation," very likely, the only truth in which will be
that *he* will no longer use railroad or telegraph. For
the rest, you must be a little patient, but not despond-
ent, for *there is not nor will be any reason for that
whatever.* . . . It is past 1 A.M. and as we breakfast at
6 o'clock and probably march as soon after that as the
trains can be started—*wagon-trains,* now, remember,
—I might as well go to my tent, don't you think?—I am
glad to hear they gave Mr. Nichols a call and hope you
will find pleasure in his preaching and comfort too as
I think you will. . . .   H.

I cannot telegraph from Atlanta; we shall not protect nor use the wires probably after tomorrow. But
remember, this is voluntary, and for a purpose. There
is not a single Corps of rebel soldiers in Georgia today,
and but a few hundred in all. Breckinridge, on his way
from West Virginia, it is said, will get "mashed up"
unless *very* discreet in his valor.†

* In the passage omitted on the preceding page.
† Enclosed in this letter was the following paragraph, clipped from a
newspaper, and doubtless meant to speak for Hitchcock's own feelings
as the great march began:
"Feeling to its full extent the probability that I may not return from

the path of duty on which I have entered—if it please God that it be so —I can say with truth that I have entered on the career of danger with no ambitious aspirations, nor with the idea that I am fitted by nature or experience to be of any important service to the government, but in obedience to the call of duty demanding every citizen to contribute what he could in means, labor or life to sustain the government of his country; a sacrifice made, too, the more willingly by me when I consider how singularly benefited I have been by the institutions of this land, and that up to this time all the blessings of life have been showered upon me beyond what falls usually to the lot of man.''

CAMPAIGN DIARY

KINGSTON, GA. November 11/64.

TOMORROW morning we set out on a campaign which will be remembered. God grant it aid to bring to a speedy end this terrible and lamentable war!

B[rig.] G[en.] Corse joined us today from Rome,—burned last night all mills, R.R. buildings, storehouses, etc., of use to enemy. Tells me special care taken to prevent outrages and destruction of any dwellings, and heard nor knew of any; save that one house across river accidentally burned. No violence to any citizen that he knows of. Heartily glad of it. The necessary and legitimate destruction of war is bad enough.

C's command march in in splendid looks and spirits (XV⁴).* "This regiment the heroes of Allatoona—that, of etc., etc." Also come refugees, white and black, with ox-carts, pack-mules, etc., and little nigs sprawling on top. Poor people! Sad enough!

Immense train northward,—guns, stores, sick and wounded, and refugees. *Plenty of well men and necessaries left,* though. South Georgia has lost 20 thousand people!

Hired Aleck† this P.M.—seems simple, honest fellow. Has wife, Laura, mother, Amy, and three children, to whom devoted. They go North tomorrow: gave him time to arrange for them tonight. Told him if he served faithfully would try and help them hereafter. What a lie his anxious care shows it, that "negroes have no family affection."—Poor fellow—"One touch of nature makes the whole world kin."

---

* Fifteenth Corps, Fourth Division—a form of notation used elsewhere in the diaries.

† Hitchcock's negro orderly.

MARIETTA, GA. November 13/64
Sunday

Two days march to this, one more to Atlanta.

November 12—Up at 5½ A.M., off ¼ before 7. While getting ready Aleck *non est* and "Button" not saddled. Ran over to stable, angry. "Aleck been here, Major,— gone over dar"—viz: to R.R. depot. Next minute A. comes running, breathless, traces of tears—"Been over to see my Wife and Mother on de cars, Sir—gwine to Chattanooga." H. H. disarmed, "Well, A., hurry up now."

Rode steadily 12 miles; at Carterville by 11 A.M. Stopped there two hours; passed three *last* R.R. trains at Etowah Bridge. "Button" scared at second—otherwise did well all day. H. H. very lucky to get him. Weather superb, roads mostly good. Usually first Sherman alone, but often this and that alongside, and H. H. sometimes. When not silent, very pleasant—points out *lines,* etc. . . . Here still few people too late for last train. Hard case of "Ala. guide," family just brought in from twenty-eight miles out—too late. Col. Spencer (1st Ala. regiment) says helped on board last train all here then, some 400. P.M. Passed Allatoona. Sherman mad at man slow to answer *where Corse.* What a gallant defense he made! Wild region—rebs swarmed up ravines all round. Fort hardly anything—pluck all. Kenesaw in distance, and signal thence Sherman—Beyond Allatoona and across A. creek, stopped at Corse's Headquarters camp—about nineteen or twenty miles march, by 5 P.M. Beautiful site, on gentle declivity, creek at foot, pine woods in rear. Most hospitably received—Carper,* Captain and Assistant Adjutant General, provided capital supper, with luxury of hard-boiled eggs, fresh milk, and butter: our train not up till late in night and not unloaded. Six of staff slept under *hospital fly,* H. H. on bed of pine boughs under blanket. Capt. Ludlow furnished plenty hospital blankets.—

* Leo Carper.

N.B. *Always* carry at least one good blanket on saddle, with rubber coat: *Never* sleep at rear of large tent with fire 20 feet distant and wind on back under edge of canvas.—Night lovely, clear, and full moon: but cold. This my first ride for years, of ½ mile: tired, but not exhausted, nor very sore. Knees felt most—stirrups little short. Rode on McClellan saddle, *on the tree,* borrowed of Nichols.

Sunday, November 13/64

Up and off by 7 A.M. Superb morning—sun just up: quite cold, but cape sufficient. Slept well, save waked by cold air till rolled up in blanket. Waked by reveille bugles at 5 A.M.—one after another, very pretty. Manuel gave us breakfast—*onions* good as ever. All in good spirits and chatty—Sherman. Passed line of works, easily tell whose, for rebs ditch on North and own on South side. Amazing campaign through this wild country. Road often through dense woods, close underbrush and between hills. Part of way were between Corse and J. E. Smith,* XV³, and almost expected bushwhackers. . . . Forgot—as we left Carterville, (12th) two of Spencer's men met us with captured guerrilla—citizen's dress but having *Spencer rifle:* evidently taken from our Headquarters' guard captured (9th) near Kingston.

Passed Kenesaw by 10 A.M., or near it. Such lines as rebs had! Begun on top of mountain and ran down the whole side and across our road and beyond. Approaching K. pointed out—Sherman—where battery on summit shelled hotly one day when he [was] on open space in range: also where he went beyond lines with small party,—"had to *git*"—fired on. "This the hardest place of all. J[ohnston] could look into camps and see every regiment move. At last personally found weak point two miles and more to right—carried it.

* Brig. Gen. John E. Smith, commanding Third Division, Fifteenth Corps.

One day felt sure R. would leave that night. Got up before day, fixed telescope on stand, watched top of Kenesaw—daylight, and no reb there. Presently one U.* cautiously crept up,—looked—rose, waved hat, then another came," etc., etc. Well told.

Forgot—Allatoona was impregnable to us in June, but came by Dallas and *turned it*. Also—when near Allatoona saw signal flags waving on Kenesaw.—Keen eyes, Sherman!

In Marietta by 11 or 12 M. Entering square, saw our men with fire engine front of Court House, pumping hard, and man inside with hose. Stopped an hour or so at large hotel on Public Square—furniture gone, but house not vandalized. Fires appear sundry places, and *again* in Court House, and at last this breaks out, and fairly burning. All our staff, and all other officers I heard, regret and condemn. Inquired—Nobody knew how set on fire: but found that Kilpatrick's† aid, Capt. J. S. McRea, *had three times put it out* and tried hard to save it: but 'twas kindled in the lathes under the plaster and 'twas no use. This soon blazed furiously, and this set other buildings on fire, across the street, and opposite hotel. Elsewhere on Square large stores etc., begun to burn, and spread. Large buildings opposite left of hotel showed smoke. This was put out by Maj. McCoy‡ of our staff, and was saved. Found that up to this morning there were guards around these buildings, but they had gone on with column, and thus in unguarded interval fire was set *without orders*. But Gen. S. ordered burning of large steam mill—found 'twas done, Col. E.§ and H. H. going to see "connections" and save neighboring buildings.

When Court House fairly broke out, H. H. remarked —" 'Twill burn down, Sir." "Yes, can't be stopped."

---

* "R" and "U" evidently indicate "Rebel" and "Union."

† Brig. Gen. Judson Kilpatrick, commanding the cavalry division of Sherman's army, a division responsible for much destruction of property.

‡ Maj. James Culbertson McCoy.

§ Presumably Col. Charles Ewing.

"Was it your intention?" "Can't save it—I've seen more of this sort of thing than you." "Certainly, Sir." Went out then together to house (at head of street on left of hotel, or right as you face it) taken for Headquarters.—Passing some soldiers—"There," said Sherman, "are the men who do this. Set as many guards as you please, they will slip in and set fire. That Court House was put out—no use—dare say whole town will burn, at least the business part. I never ordered burning of any dwelling—didn't order this, but can't be helped. I say *Jeff. Davis burnt them.*" H. H.: "Pardon, but if liberty, spoke because anxious you not be blamed for what you did not order." "Well, I suppose I'll have to bear it." H. H. has said all he could to restrain this destruction, and is not guilty of any, even what is *legitimate* by laws of war. What a sad and fearful necessity—how terrible the guilt of those who forced this war and its unavoidable horrors! But there is no help for it. It is war now that it may not be war *always.* God send us peace—but there is no peace save in *complete submission to the Government:* and this seems impossible save through the terrors of war.

Forgot—had long chat with T. R. Davis *en route:* regular Bohemian: but he refused post of artist to Hayes' Artic Expedition because pay too small to support Mother. . . .

Dined with Capt. Cole, Nichols, Dayton,* Audenried, at Mrs. H.—Union woman. Husband conscripted two years past by rebs and all but six weeks in hospital— *consumptive.* Quiet and ladylike. Neighbor Y very bitter rebel, *Northern woman,* from Penna. (Paid for dinner per Cole—$1 each: "Come back to tea.") U. soldier at Y's, hurt on Railroad. "Life not worth 10¢ after 'army leaves.' "—What are ours worth but with army?

P.M. General and staff rode out to K[ilpatrick]'s

* Major Lewis M. Dayton, aide-de-camp and acting adjutant-general on Sherman's staff.

review of *part* of his cavalry, on large field N. of town,
but in sight: beautiful place, ¼ to ½ mile long, on and
between two gentle slopes, over ¼ mile across. Splendid sight. Troops in fine order, well mounted, *vets:*
cavalry, mounted infantry, and artillery—no matter
how many. General received by K. and staff,—K. su-
perbly mounted and looks the "bold and gay dragoon."
Music fine. General, etc., rode clear round (long ride,
even at a gallop) and uproarious cheers from men; he
got excited, *waved hat,* etc. Then took position and
whole command filed by at trot—thought they never
would get done. Ground, display, weather all superb
for picture—glad to see Davis in rear sketching. To
look *forward* only fine show: but a mile off on the right
lay Marietta, from which rose heavy columns black
smoke and lurid flame—terrible commentary on this
display and its real meaning. Thought of Xerxes, etc.

So *our* Sabbath passed—strange enough, sad enough
to me, and many thoughts of the dear ones at home. At
least I am here for *duty* and with as religious a sense
of its necessity as though in church at home.

At night, for a while, E[wing], Davis, and McCoy, in
N[ichol]s' and my room. They sung songs—very good
any other evening. I sat face in hands and thought of
the hymns the dear home voices were singing then: till,
not to be noticed, I looked up, and sat quietly. E. and
D. left for pigeons. We sat talking and sung sacred airs
and "America," etc. Later had Sherman there! Very
sociable,—discussed men. Says *'twas false* that F. P.
B[lair]* to blame on July 22, '64—"He was not responsible for a life lost that day—he did all any man
could, and was there because ordered by McPherson."†
Says F. B. brave, cool and of ability: but "loose and
scattering": compared him unfavorably with Mower‡

* Maj. Gen. Francis P. Blair, who had joined Sherman's army in June
and commanded his Seventeenth Corps.
† Maj. Gen. James B. McPherson, killed July 22, 1864, during siege of
Atlanta.
‡ Maj. Gen. Joseph A. Mower.

as to thorough acquaintance with his corps, its position, wants, etc. But does B. *justice.* . . .

Glad to find self much less tired and sore than expected from riding. To sleep *in a house,* bare, seems a luxury.

ATLANTA, GA. November 15/64

Arrived yesterday by noon: spent 1½ days—leave early in the morning, and fairly embark on a dangerous campaign.

Rode from Marietta to Atlanta, eighteen or twenty miles in 4½ hours—steady gait. Weather and roads good: trip very interesting. General often points out scenes of fight. July 20th, 22d, 28th, etc. Here was Hooker's front, there Schofield's, etc. Rebel works south of Chattahoochee very strong—*double abattis,* one line stakes in ground, one of trees with sharpened branches. "Displayed here but crossed above. J[ohnston] thought I would sit down this side and rest, then try to cross: but I crossed first, *then* rested." *En route,* we pass miles of troops on march, or resting, and long lines of trains: *an army moving.* Curiously they look at him, whisper name along ranks, and watch movements. No cheers from *vets*—he don't like it. (N.B. His story told H. H. at Kingston about Lincoln's visit to his brigade camp S. of Potomac, after Bull Run—L's little speech "better luck, etc.—Col. S. don't like cheers—I do, etc.—what can I do for you?" Mutinous A.Q.M. complains, "Col. S. said he'd shoot me, etc."—Answer (stage whisper) "Well, the fact is, *I really believe he would.*") But the new ones cheer, and even vets sometimes, *for him.* What tremendous defences of Atlanta the rebs had! Forts, breast-works, ditches, *chevaux-de-frise* (saw them) and stockade on flank, unapproachable by musketry and protected by ground, etc., from artillery.

Entered Atlanta before noon, train far behind: went

to Judge Lyon's fine house,—large double brick, very handsome: same Headquarters as before.

Met Col. Beckwith, Ch.C.S.,—plain, rough, vigorous, indefatigable—largely entitled to credit of Atlanta campaign as to commissary supplies. Army of 120,000 never on half rations! B. gave us lunch, very welcome.

Met also Gen. Easton,* C.Q.M., and Capt. O. M. Poe, Ch.Eng. Poe this A.M. *rammed down* big stone and brick depot, no fire or powder applied. N.B. Saw at Kingston joint letter of E. and B. to General, recommending that the destruction here be specially in Poe's charge—"to prevent irregularities, he having reliable men under him." So ordered at once by telegraph.

Rode by the depot ruins in entering town: *perfect smash.* The big Railroad bridge—very fine, on several stone piers over the Chattahoochee—was destroyed early today, before we got there: we crossed on Poe's truss bridge.

Haven't seen fifteen citizens here—all soldiers, and *plenty of them.* Even part of an army of 120,000 men makes a big show: some corps are outside of the city, some below, some above, camped or arriving.

Discussion at lunch about destruction, retaliation, etc. Even McCoy was warmed up, and Col. E. boiled over in recalling the summons of the reb. commander to our men at Resaca, and at Dalton, and at Tilton, "to surrender, or *no prisoners would be taken.*" None were taken, nor those places either. But I don't wonder that such things infuriate our men.

Today (15th) the destruction fairly commenced, though yesterday some large buildings were destroyed. Capt. Poe has charge. Orders are to destroy all R.R. depots, large R.R., etc., warehouses, machine shops, etc., including all buildings of use to enemy: but no *dwellings* to be injured. This P.M. the torch applied, also sundry buildings blown up, with shells inside—

---

* Bvt. Brig. Gen. (later Maj. Gen.) Langdon C. Easton.

heavy explosion, sundry lesser ones for several minutes following. Clouds of heavy smoke rise and hang like pall over doomed city.

At night, the grandest and most awful scene. Our Headquarters are on high ground: on same ridge, across street, next block east, is Court House: on parallel ridge, say 200 yards north, valley between, runs "Whitehall St." (principal business street) with fine blocks of warehouses, etc., running E. to and by R.R. depots, etc. From our rear and E. windows, ⅓ of horizon shows immense and raging fires, lighting up whole heavens—probably, says Sherman, visible at Griffin, fifty miles off. First bursts of smoke, dense, black volumes, then tongues of flame, then huge waves of fire roll up into the sky: presently the skeletons of great warehouses stand out in relief against and amidst sheets of roaring, blazing, furious flames,—then the angry waves roll less high, and are of deeper color, then sink and cease, and only the fierce glow from the bare and blackened walls, etc. Now and then are heavy explosions, and as one fire sinks another rises, further along the horizon, till for say ⅓ of the circle, N.E. and E. of us, and some on the N.W., it is a line of fire and smoke, lurid, angry, dreadful to look upon. Went down to the corner and looked out over where the R.R. depots were—all covered with smoking and still blazing ruins. But was rejoiced to find on the way that sentries were posted in front of the two churches near our Headquarters, with orders so strict that on returning with other officers he would not let us go *by it* on the sidewalk, but ordered us out into the street: and soon after did same to two or three others going down cross street along west side of church. This is right. I note these and preceding facts because Gen. S. will hereafter be charged with indiscriminate burning, which is not true. His orders are to destroy only such buildings as are used or useful for war purposes, whether for producing, storing, or transporting materials, etc., of war: but

all others are to be spared, and *no dwelling touched*.
He talked to me again today about this, apparently because of the evidently painful impression I received at
Marietta. Said nothing like excuse, but simply explained the facts. At table he remarked—"this city has
done and contributed probably more to carry on and
sustain the war than any other, save perhaps Richmond. We have been fighting *Atlanta* all the time, in
the past: have been capturing guns, wagons, etc., etc.,
marked *'Atlanta'* and made here, all the time: and
now since they have been doing so much to destroy us
and our Government we have to destroy them, at least
enough to prevent any more of that."

I knew also (for I wrote it at his dictation) that his
special field order* covering the general disposition
and action of all the troops on this campaign, expressly
defines and limits the discretion of A[rmy] C[orps]
Com[mande]rs to whom *alone* is committed the question of destruction,—making same depend on the conduct of the inhabitants of the country: and all private
soldiers are expressly forbidden *to enter any* house
even to forage.

Saw Poe's men at work yesterday with his new con-
trivance for quickly tearing up R.R'd tracks: simply
a large iron hook, hung on a chain whose other end has
a ring to insert a crow-bar or other lever. The hook is
caught on the inside of the rails, but supported against
the outside, at the ring and end of lever. With these,
the heaviest rails are easily and quickly turned over.
As we came here yesterday from Marietta, every foot
of the R.R'd had been torn up, ties piled and fired, and
the rails, or nine in ten of them, bent and twisted out
of shape. Gen. S. says the rebs now have no place save
Tredegar Works near Richmond at which all sorts of
rails are made, etc.

As I write, 11.30 P.M. the fires are pretty much burnt
out, and from my 2d story (S.W.) window I can no

---

* No. 120, dated "In the Field, Kingston, Nov. 9, 1864."

longer see the glare in the sky. No dwelling has been touched, nor the Court House, nor any church. The Masonic Hall is spared. The only danger yet is from stragglers and teamsters, after the guards are withdrawn, which they must be tomorrow. I see plainly how true it is that "those are the men who do these things."

Quite a feature tonight was a serenade (early) by the splendid band formerly of 33d Mass. Vols.—now a brigade band. Always will the Miserere in "Trovatore" carry me back to this night's scenes and sounds. This band is celebrated, as also that of the 2d Mass., now kept up by the officers.

We start tomorrow at 6: 30 A.M. for the seashore. The movement commenced today—XV, XVII, and XX,* Howard south and K[ilpatrick] dashing ahead. Perhaps the rebs will be puzzled to guess where the blow will fall.

This campaign will be no joke in *any* point of view— but if successful, as we believe and expect, a splendid one now and hereafter. Doubtless it will be death to those of us who may fall into their hands—but if so, 'twill cost them dear.

Cannot keep awake and write more or more fully: so now to rest, and then for action! God grant us safe and speedy deliverance and speedy and *permanent* peace.

IN THE FIELD
November 16/64

First day's march out:
  "Latimer's X Roads"   7 : 30 P.M.

Decidedly "in the field" and on the march. Left Atlanta about 7 A.M., weather fine for marching—

---

* Sherman's army was divided for this march into a right and left wing, commanded respectively by Maj. Gens. O. O. Howard and H. W. Slocum. The Fifteenth Corps (Maj. Gen. P. J. Osterhaus commanding) and Seventeenth (Maj. Gen. F. P. Blair commanding) made up the right wing. The Twentieth Corps (Brig. Gen. A. S. Williams commanding), with the Fourteenth (Major Gen. Jefferson C. Davis commanding), made up the left wing. The cavalry, under Gen. Kilpatrick, was held separate.

cloudy, but not threatening, air hardly cool. Going out of town, passed through burnt district, still smoking. Saw no dwelling destroyed, and outside of central business part of town comparatively little damage. Should say ¼ of area of town destroyed, but this the largest and best built business part.

Passed through and along—000 [*sic*] men, chiefly XIV. Struck with fine appearance and elastic step and bearing of the troops. At head of one brigade the old 79th Pa. band was playing same quick-step as at Kingston serenade. One fellow very drunk, sitting on ground as we passed troops at a rest or halt. Cursed General loudly, evidently for drunken brag: General rode quietly by him, not ten ft. off—heard all—no notice. Followed R.R. (Augusta) six miles to Decatur. Crossed part of battle ground of 22d July and right by ruins of large house from behind which rebs "poured" to assault. Further on, splendid works, with ditch, abattis, etc., made by 23d Corps at our left when army returned to Atlanta after Jonesboro' fight.

Halted at Decatur half an hour, in yard of comfortable looking house: only women and children visible. No time to look at town—did not see any special marks of war in passing through. Servants began to chase chickens—matron remonstrated. Baylor buys her out at $1 per pair. . . .

At Decatur we bore off S.E. on rather narrow road to this point. Country almost all thickly wooded on both sides, and rolling, with two or three hills to *descend,* luckily. Thick undergrowth and small timber: now and then clearings and fields, few houses, fewer people. Troops and trains before and behind us all day —we passing and halting more than once. Absorbed in thought, silent, Sherman, but always pleasant reply when addressed. Weather perfect, little or no sun,— roads in fine order, but often broken and rough, and evidently by-roads. Halted two hours nearly at house six miles from Decatur, General took nap. Old man (sick, they said) three daughters, sundry children. The women good-looking, sat at front door with us, talked very civilly. One about thirty to thirty-two—husband went to our lines, thinks in our army, watched our troops (passing) for him: quiet, good-natured. One, say twenty to twenty-four, quite pretty, blue eyes, "golden hair," very pretty complexion for Georgia, sat in door nursing infant and talking. Husband (rebel) wounded last April at Buzzard Roost—came home and died. T'other younger and unmarried. Say that father "never was in favor of the war—voted against it—but never took part—didn't know who was right. Mighty few of the people about here were in favor of the war, but their leaders told them they ought to do so and so, and they done it." Manner and tone very simple and earnest, and I am sure sincere: no fear nor cringing.

Marched on till 4 P.M. then halted and camped. Just before this—say ½ mile or so, passed very good frame house on roadside, with cabins, barns, outhouses,—evidently well to do. Not a soul visible as we passed. But at supper found that Sherman had stopped and had chat with negro man now *in possession*—intelligent fellow. Says Master in war at *"Champ Case"*: that he used to think himself worth $100,000. Two best "boys" ran off to "Yanks," and he heard that one of them was killed at Jonesboro: understood the Y's at Jonesboro made the negro soldiers go in front, and so they were either shot in front by the rebs or from behind by the Yanks if they failed to go on. It is part of the rebel system to lie thus, it seems. Our servants will help dispel these stories, and must, says Sherman.

Our tents pitched S. of road on hillside, in young orchard,—open field, but good rail fences *when we came*. Gentle slopes to road on both sides, near woods, and with spring in rear on left, and small "spring branch" crossing road. We are behind —— brigade: others followed us for three hours, but at last column halted by

darkness and in camp all round. As I write, in my tent
—book on knee, sitting on bed of blankets on *pine
boughs* (too much trouble to open cot—mem. no more
cots, I think) the sounds of camp are all around. My
tent (with G.W.N.) next left of General's, and till a
few minutes ago he and Dr. Moore* and others sat
chatting at camp fire in front, telling stories, etc., I
hearing as well as writing. From the road for a time
came sounds of troops passing, then bugle "halt,"—
cries and oaths of teamsters,—and then "tattoo"
beats, far and near, and now the voices of men, laughing, talking, and shouting to mules, etc., etc.

As we passed Latimer's house (above noted) not a
straggler from the ranks going by. I rejoiced that
though deserted, it escaped. Since we camped, before
dark, first a thick smoke, then ruddy glow over tree
tops, now a lesser one, signals its destruction by those
behind us. Probably some soldier discovered its master's whereabouts also, and so goodbye to his house.
Sorry for it—yet who can be surprised, and how to help
it? Two minutes' work of one unnoticed straggler.
Talked with Ewing,—condemned it as against "Special Field Order No. 120"—he agrees, but says impossible to control unless by power to kill for it, vested
with General in the field, and that now all such things
must first go to Washington, and there they refuse to
sanction punishment by death. It is a great mistake.
Such "mercy" damages *us*.

Had quite warm discussion with Dayton (Capt. and
A. D. C.) this morning en route: I advocating our self-
restraint, "laws of war" etc., etc., he contending we
should do whatever and as bad as the rebs, even to
scalping. His view not important, save as *typical*.

No straggling today in the brigades and divisions
we saw. Not a sign of an enemy. Flankers thrown out
now and then, but few,—often thought, *if they but
knew it,* and when and where to do it, what one volley

* Surgeon John Moore, of Sherman's staff.

from the thick underbrush would or *could* do! Saw distant smokes to right and left—b^{ds} muc olsdn adra woh, S*[herman]—Tonight, says Sherman, "Three days more clear and don't care!"

Nichols, Verplanck,† and Audenried, all complain tonight of fatigue from today's march. I am delighted to find I do not feel it at all—perfectly good for ten miles more when we halted. Fairly initiated, I think, to march, horse, and camp, and have got off with not ⅓ of expected fatigue, etc., etc.

How dangers, etc., dwindle on approach! I begin by conversation, etc., to get an actual idea of battles, etc., especially as I go over their recent scenes. I do not fear losing my self-possession in any fight. I am only concerned in case of wayside attacks, bushwhackers, etc. I confess I don't want to encounter these or *an ambush*. Probably will not—but may.

Camp tonight is seventeen miles from Atlanta, made in about six hours' marching time, much delayed all the way by troops.

ON RAILROAD 1 MILE W. OF YELLOW RIVER
November 17/64 8 P.M.

Second day out

Up at 4 A.M.—marched fourteen or fifteen miles—in camp at 4 P.M. in a field 150 to 200 yards from railroad, and 1 mile from Y. River.

Breakfast *over* by 5:20 A.M., the Quartermaster having called us all about 4 o'clock. As Nichols and I sat discussing theology, Swedenborg, etc., by the camp fire last night till 11 P.M., long after everybody else was asleep, this was not acceptable to us, but his growls on being wakened put me in a good humor. Our train started by sun-rise, and kept ahead of us all day. We did not start till 7 A.M.—waiting for XIV. Marched three miles to town of Lithonia, on the railroad, halted

---

* Clearly so written—in cipher?
† Lieut. Abram G. Verplanck, New York Volunteers.

say an hour: troops busy destroying track. Capt. Poe's hooks enable a few men to do pretty much upsetting. Track here laid on sleepers above ties. Saw nothing damaged by the railroad, but tonight Poe reports railroad depot was burned at L. and sparks set fire to and destroyed some two or three dwellings. Merely bending rails in ordinary way, by piling ties, laying rails across, and allowing their own weight at ends to bend them, thus ∧, is not effectual. If thus merely bent, they can be restored by reverse process. But if *twisted,* even a little, they are ruined and must be rerolled. Poe has provided wrenches with which his pioneers very quickly and effectually do this—one man at each end of a rail, with a wrench, twisting, or rather pulling in opposite directions, and thus twisting the heated middle.

While at Lithonia, Capt. Cole (—th Wisconsin) of Signal Corps, with three men, went 1½ miles to top of granite hill N.E. of town, say 400 feet high: saw smoke say 12 miles to North—supposed to be H.W.S. (Maj. G) XX:* no other sign, or appearance of any enemy.

From Lithonia followed railroad—partly on the track, partly over roads, seven miles to Conyers: halted 1½ hours at Mrs. Scott's—widow, say thirty-five, civil and disposed to talk. She told Audenried that at Atlanta we had shot, burned and drowned negroes, old and young, drove men into houses and burned them, etc., etc.: first said she believed it, then admitted she did not, but said they wanted the negroes to believe it.

Here and hereabouts "liberally foraged" as per order:† got potatoes (sweet), fodder, chickens, etc., troops busy at R.R. track,—whole line in smoke and

---

* Maj. Gen. H. W. Slocum, commanding left wing, of which the Twentieth Corps was a part.

† "The army will forage liberally during the march": Sherman's Special Field Order No. 120. This statement was followed by instructions for the organization of foraging parties by the Brigade Commanders, and strict injunctions against the entering of dwellings and committing of trespass by soldiers.

blaze. No other damage done that I saw or heard of then, but tonight it is stated depot or R.R. buildings burned. Before we left five stout negro men came together to where we were, desiring to "volunteer" and go along. Two were single—no, three: these Col. Beckwith engaged as teamsters: told the others they might follow if they chose but not their families, and advised to stay with them for the present. No telegraph line along this railroad but two or three remains of old poles. All noticed that E. of Lithonia the R.R. track was in excellent order. T rails, *evidently new* or not over a year old. Yet no train has run W. of Yellow R. since July 22, '64 when Garrard's* cavalry burned the Yellow River railroad bridge, not since rebuilt.

Granite formation, soil red clay W. of Lithonia, but now becomes partly sandy, and symptoms of the bad white clay which makes the worst mud. Country rolling, much better improved than yesterday: frequent clearings and good farms—timber, oak and pine: often dense growth. Came on four or five miles from Conyers, to where camp already selected and tents pitched —beautiful camp-ground in large open field, on very gentle slope, pine woods in rear on crest.

Weather today has been perfect,—signs of rain last night all gone, sky clear, sun bright and almost warm: roads in best order. Such weather, says Sherman, over tomorrow puts us over Yellow River & R.[?], which below from Ocmulgee[?], and also puts OOH XV XVII† across Ocmulgee and all on ridge on table-land, and then *don't care for rain*. Troops with us in best spirits,—no sign of enemy, all well so far. Got at Conyers Augusta papers to and including 13th inst.— articles show no suspicion of our plans, etc., and lies and brag bigger than ever. Georgia Legislature is in session at Milledgeville. Jeff D's message in full—how

* Brig. Gen. Kenner Garrard.

† Maj. Gen. O. O. Howard, with the Fifteenth and Seventeenth Army Corps.

he does lie about Sherman, and about *their* "successes" in Alabama, Georgia, Mississippi, etc! He lies worst of all about treatment of prisoners held by us.

Very jolly to send train ahead and find tents pitched and dinner nearly ready on reaching camp. Ordered Aleck never to unpack cot in fine weather—prefer bed of blankets on pine boughs on dry ground: cot very well when it rains. Plenty of forage along road, corn, fodder, finest sweet potatoes, pigs, chickens, etc. Passed troops all day, some on march, some destroying railroad thoroughly. Two cotton gins on roadside burned, and pile of cotton with one, also burned. Houses in Conyers look comfortable for Georgia village, and sundry good ones along road. Soldiers foraging all along, but only for *forage*—no violence so far as I saw or hear. Laughable to see pigs in feed troughs behind wagons, chickens swinging to knapsacks. Saw some few men— almost all women and children, at front door or gate. Whites look sullen—darkies pleased. At Conyers, Mrs. S. told me "C.S.A." currency is at *27 for 1* in gold *26* for silver. She says the niggers are the only free ones now—whites all slaves, "in our country and yours too."

At dusk troops at work on railroad came on track in front of our camp, and worked at it till 7:30 P.M.— tore up, piled ties, and burnt. Line of fires on track for ½ mile or more visible—striking sight, men all in high spirits.

McCoy sent for *negro* resident, for General to inquire about roads and bridges. "Don't want white man," says Sherman. Very intelligent old fellow came, long talk with General at camp fire. "When the Yanks far off, our people very brave—women and children whip 'em—but come close and den how dey does *git up and dust.*" "Many a dark population has worked on dat railroad—contractor for dis section *whipped some of 'em to death*—buried over in dose woods." Evidently the negro knew what lies the reb stories about us are. Sherman polite and explained "free if you choose and deserve it. Go when you like,—we don't force any to be soldiers—pay wages, and will pay you if you *choose to come:* but as *you* have family, better stay now and have general concert and leave hereafter. *But don't hurt your masters or their families*—we don't want that."

Smoke to North of us. General thinks it H.W.S. XX —hope he has not let us pass him.

Am somewhat tired from loss of sleep last night and march today. Cup of *tea* tonight very refreshing—better than coffee. Our canned milk all gone two days ago: but we shall now have plenty of sweet potatoes, "shote," chickens, etc.: and plenty of corn and fodder for horses. We *can* live, spite of J.D. and his lying prophecies in "Message."—Our friends at home will soon begin to hear of us. . . . Sorry enough am I for the women here and their anxiety and terror—though I must say they show very little *fear* of us. Good story about woman hiding cotton yarns from expected Yanks *in barn,* barn burnt. Yank soldier fished out her yarns for her from ruins and gave them to her.

As to the men, I am not sorry for them, and so long as the destruction is not wanton, nor unoffending persons injured,—of which I hear of no instance,—the rest is inevitable and necessary to end the war.

It is surely not possible that this is to be a sample of our march. Some fighting is looked for—at least from cavalry on flanks. But we learn of no bodies of troops save small ones and they are gone down to Griffin, and Kilpatrick will have them to look after.

CAMP AT JUDGE HARRIS' "QUARTERS" AND FARM AT X RDS 1½ MILES FROM "ULCOFAU" RIVER.

Friday, November 18/64

Third day out

Marched only about eight miles today, having two rivers to cross. Weather cloudy and threatening rain all day, but no rain fell and now no matter. "This is the perfection of campaigning," said the General today, "such weather and such roads as this." It suits H. H.— all fatigue is gone, and I could easily go twenty-five miles per day to judge from my good spirits, good appetite and sound sleep. Next time I shall know how to prepare for it.

This morning we left the railroad trending S.E. to objective point. XX will finish it beyond this as far as intended. Sent train ahead and we started between seven and eight. Reaching Yellow River found pontoons down and troops, etc., crossing. This is a small stream say —— feet wide, but quite deep though fordable. Banks here steep and crossing bad. Bridge had been destroyed—railroad. Another bridge, three miles below, said to be standing, we did not go to. Crossed on our canvas pontoons. Cattle are the most trying things for pontoon bridge, apt to crowd and rush. Our droves were crossed slowly but without trouble.

Before reaching river, stopped little while at Rev. Mr. Gray's—Baptist preacher. Old lady, say forty-five to fifty, nice-looking daughter of seventeen, and sundry younger ones, sat with us on porch. Soldiers passing with forage, chickens, pigs, etc. Evidently bitter rebel, but civil enough, and talked quietly. Never saw Yankee soldiers before "except prisoners passing." Like a woman, that!

From Yellow River say 1½ miles to "Ulcofauhatchee" River, usually called "Ulcofau" pronounced Álcovă. Crossed this without delay or interruption on common bridge.

Between these rivers passed through Covington, quite a town, though as the General passed quickly through one side of it, saw very little of it. While passing through town, young man in rebel uniform rode up and with us as we turned into main road leading out. Reported to General, "was wounded at Spottsylvania, here on sick leave, and have been ordered to report to you." Reply instant "Ewing, take his parole," and they rode off. But the parole is worthless though duly taken. E. says there is a mighty pretty girl where he stays. Parole probably welcome: private, good-looking fellow.

It turned out that the good people of Covington got up a deputation of citizens to meet their distinguished visitor ("brute Sherman") and to offer him all sorts of supplies, etc.: but he did not go through the principal street and they missed him and he them. One lady, I hear, had a fine dinner ready for him, which he did not hear of—but Capt. Cole (signal officer) did and went there and kindly partook. Must ask C. about it.

Stopped for the day at the farm of Judge Harris, say 1½ miles from Covington, south of Ulcofau River. He and family reside in the town: has only his "quarters" on the farm: is a "heavy man" (as our intelligent contraband last night called it), has quite a farm, and said to have sixty or more slaves. Number of log and frame buildings on farm,—chief, a large double log cabin with hall. When we got there found advance guard halted, men lying and sitting along road, very jolly, and with cups, canteens, etc., rapidly being filled with *sorghum molasses,* of which large *trough* full in one house. As we rode up by them, one wag with face upturned and buried all but eyes in cup of molasses seeing General cried out *at him*—"Forage liberally!" (extract from Special Field Order No. 120) and general laughter thereat, but General sober as a judge.

Went in and took possession—train up after a while, tents pitched in yard and lot across road. Plenty of forage, poultry, hogs, etc., and "foraged liberally." Camps all round us and frequent shots round through the woods, each the death knell of some luckless secesh pig or rebel fowl.

We had hardly got into the yard when four or five stout negro men appeared, who had skedaddled this morning early from their "kind masters" four or five

miles off to join and go with us. Quizzed them a little
about how we treat negroes. Asked them if they knew
how the negroes fared at Atlanta. "Oh, yes, white folks
tole us you burned the men in the houses and drowned
the women and children." "Well, did you believe it?"
"No, Sir!! We didn't believe it—we has faith in you!"
One very black, but very quick and manly fellow, a
model, physically, and "driver" for his "ky-ind master," though the youngest (say twenty-five to thirty),
was the leading spirit. I asked him why he came to us—
how he knew he would not be worse off. "I was bound
to come, Sah,—good trade or bad trade, I'se bound to
risk it." (H. H.) "But did you not hear all the terrible
things we did at Atlanta, to the negroes there?" "Yes,
Sir, but I didn't believe it"—and then added "Dey
don't think nothing 'bout here of tying up a feller and
givin' him 200 or 300 *with the strap.*" Another of them
explained his presence by his having heard "the white
folks" last night talking about the Yankee's approach,
and their own intention to run off all their negroes this
morning down to Macon and thence to Florida (!). He
was ordered to have the horses, etc., all harnessed up
early this morning; but instead rose *very* early and
came over to the Yanks himself. It is most striking and
touching, the faith in us these people show.

But the best case yet is old "Uncle Stephen," one of
the Harris negroes, with whom the General had a long
talk this P.M. I sat by and was equally amused at the
shrewd, frank, easy way the questions were put, and
his views, etc., explained by the General, and the really
dignified but simple and manly way the old darkey answered. After diverse inquiries about roads, distances,
etc., answered without hesitation, though sometimes
"don't know," General said—"Well, now, old man,
what do you think about the war?" "Well, Sir, I've
thought a great deal about it,—till I hardly does know
what to think." (S) "Well, but you do think something
about it—come, now, tell me just what you think—don't

be afraid, we are friends." "Well, Sir, what I think
about it, is this—it's mighty distressin' this war, but
it 'pears to me like *the right thing couldn't be done*
without it." The old fellow hit it, exactly. The General
has a capital way of talking to these people,—frank,
pleasant and unaffected, without being familiar, and
they respond with a mingled respect and confidence
which shows how well he understands them. He talks
in the same simple, clear way to all: tells them the war
is because their masters refused to obey the laws, and
must be *made to:* that we are their friends, that they
are free if they choose, and that the able-bodied men
among them who *choose to* may go with us, or those
who choose may stay with their masters. ("I *don't*
choose *dat* den!" said one steady-looking old fellow
today, who came with old Stephen). He always explains
that *freedom* means not being free to work or not as
they please, but freedom to work for themselves—freedom from being bought and sold,—freedom to acquire
and own property, bring up their children respectably
and be secure in enjoyment of personal and family
rights. As to their families he tells them we cannot now
take care of these, nor take them with us, and advises
those who have families to stay with them yet awhile
and do the best they can: and repeatedly has—in a
quiet way but emphatically—discountenanced any violence to their masters. Indeed I have seen no evidence
of any vindictive feeling among them—but *universal*
hope and longing for freedom. As to their being made
soldiers, he always explains that this must be wholly
voluntary on their part, and that in this army we have
no negro soldiers, though elsewhere we have: that
among our people, some are in favor of and others opposed to it, but that the Government will receive as
soldiers all who wish to enlist:—and the nearest he has
come to persuading them to this was his saying today
to Stephen and others around, "Those of you who deserve to be free and wish to be, will certainly be free,

and will no longer be sold like cattle, nor see their
families separated and sold: but we think that any man,
black or white, who wants his freedom, and is able to
fight for it, ought to be willing to do so." They assented
very heartily to this. It is amusing to see how desper-
ately the rebs have been lying to their slaves about us,
and what a failure it is. The darkies receive it all very
gravely, and then run away and join us and tell us
about it, and beg to go along with the Yanks. In fact,
they threaten already to become a serious impediment
to the column.

The 79th Pennsylvania (now Brigade) band came to
our Headquarters tonight and serenaded the General.
All the darkies turned out, little and big, men, women
and children, and listened with evident delight, keeping
time with feet, hands, head and body, many of them.

Judge Harris is a prominent man hereabouts. Nichols had a long talk with his negro driver and came back
full of indignation. The women say that their master,
though an elderly man, and with a family, obliges them
to submit to him, and *straps* them if they refuse. One
fine looking old darky has but one leg: his story, confirmed by the others, is that the white women shot him
—years ago—deliberately, first picking a quarrel about
the way he planted some potatoes, and so he lost his
leg.

Rebel mail captured and brought to General—turned
over to me. Only one letter of interest—from a "young
lady" (Miss Izora M. Fair) of Oxford,—a little town
four or five miles hence, north of Covington—to Gov.
Brown, detailing a visit she made to Atlanta recently,
disguised as a country negress: face stained with wal-
nuts and hair "frizzed." She was fired at by our pickets (this before we left the city) then taken to quarters
of guard—heard and reports a conversation, etc.

By another letter, same mail, from a lady in Oxford,
it seems Miss F's performance was severely criticized
by her female rebel friends.

The General sent a party to Oxford this P.M. to find and bring her to him "on foot": "I don't mean to hurt her, but will give her a scare," he said to me. But she was *non est*. From other letters it is evident they suppose us aiming at *Augusta*. They will know tomorrow when the heads of *three columns* begin to converge on *Milledgeville*. So far, we met no enemy nor any interruptions: troops in fine condition and spirits, forage, etc., now plenty, and all goes well, and I hear of no outrages. But some of our stragglers were shot today by citizens or scouts—served 'em right.

CAMP 7 MILES FROM NEWBORN ON THE
"EATONTON FACTORY ROAD"

Fourth day out.   Saturday, November 19/64. 10 P.M.

Marched today 15½ miles by Capt. O. M. Poe's odometer: left Harris Farm at 8 A.M. (our party) and overtook train in camp 4½ P.M. having halted over two hours at Newborn. Heavy mist and clouds all morning—some rain during day, windy and rainy tonight. It is not favorable to much writing, to sit on one's "bed" (blankets or straw on the ground) with a valise top for desk, and one candle.

Was waked at 5:30 A.M.—lay awhile listening to the heavy rain pattering on the tent-fly—jolly to sleep by, and hard to get up out of the warm blankets. Waited awhile after breakfast for middle division of Corps to pass, and J. C. Davis* to come up.—All his transportation, trains, beef cattle, etc., safely crossed both rivers yesterday, though B's Division camped west of the Ulcofau. This morning all are across and we now go S.E. down the ridge between "Little River" and "Murder Creek": our last night's camp being fifty miles from Milledgeville: an easy four days' march *for us*. This will bring us to M. on the 7th day, as arranged at Atlanta. As to movements *after that*—J.D.

* Maj. Gen. Jeff. C. Davis, commanding Fourteenth Corps.

will know them soon enough; but I am satisfied with
what the General explained today to me of his plans in
any one of several contingencies. An Augusta paper
of 16th received yeserday,—soundly berates the Legislature now in session at M[illedgeville] for discussing
adjournment because of *small-pox.* We had a good
laugh over it. Last night I read to him A. H. Stephens's
most remarkable letter to "Senator" Sumner of Loui-
siana, dated November 5/64, and sent by A.H.S. to the
Augusta *Constitutionalist,* in which we received it.
What an electioneering document for Lincoln, had it
been published North before the election! As it is, it
will utterly destroy the remnant of the "Peace party"
with us who are not real rebels and in favor of separation *per se:* and will seat "old Abe" more firmly than
ever. One paragraph in that letter completely vindi-
cates the Emancipation policy of the Government with
all but real pro-slavery men. The General was greatly
interested, but made few or no comments. I remarked
on A.H.S.'s idea that *separation* would secure "permanent peace," and his talk about the "ultimate, absolute sovereignty of the States." Said the General,
"Stephens is crazy on the States Rights question. This
war is on our part a war *against anarchy.*" This is his
frequent and favorite expression, and intense conviction. He got into a talking mood afterwards by the
camp-fire, spoke of his plans, though not so fully as
when we were alone (Nichols having joined us there)
and said among other things, "I wish they were separated from us and a foreign Government—we'd *whale*
'em then all the time."

Nothing exciting today: no enemy nor opposition.
By 11 or 12 o'clock we reached Newborn,—halted till
after 2 P.M.,—stopped at house of John W. Pitts, a re-
tired merchant, queer old cock,—who laid out the village, containing twelve or fifteen houses, and gave
away lots to settlers. Got up an Academy, gave it ap-

paratus, had quarrels and a schism, and himself built, etc., another (frame building) Academy.

Sat by while General gave *him* a talk, admirably conceived and put, alike to impress with the hopelessness and the wrong of their course. P. assented to everything—says he predicted all the consequences, etc., etc., —and declared the Southern people deserved it all and more. Our soldiers were taking his fodder, fowls, mules, etc., right before his eyes. He said it was all right, "he knew the laws of war," etc. Curious old gent. He is down on *lawyers,* gave us copies of an amusing pamphlet he wrote and published in 1843, advocating the exclusion of all *lawyers* from legislature and abolishment of *fees.*

It seems our march today was wholly unexpected, though it was known we were on the march—but it was supposed to Augusta. Sherman's plans are splendid.

The men are foraging and straggling, I am sorry to say, a good deal. At and near every farmhouse we hear constant shooting—of pigs and chickens. No sign of an enemy. It is reported tonight that two of our men were killed today, and three wounded, all accidentally, by these shots. I remarked to the General something about the straggling. He answered, "I have been three years fighting stragglers, and they are harder to conquer than the enemy." The real fault lies with regimental and company officers. Sherman's orders are explicit to prevent this, and today Audenried, Beckwith, McCoy and other officers did their best to stop it. Several men were arrested for entering houses in Newborn—but it is impossible to wholly prevent it. I am very glad, however, having particularly inquired, to find that so far as I can learn there have been no dwellings burned nor violence even offered to any one. *Foraging,* by proper parties,—for which Special Field Order No. 120 expressly provides, and positively prohibits any others from it,—is all right.

Mr. Pitts told us today that the Confederates were a

great deal worse than our men, that they pillaged and plundered everybody, and the inhabitants dreaded their coming.

Our camp is again charmingly situated, in an open field. Three signal rockets sent up tonight for Howard's benefit: we are now approaching him. A light towards south supposed to be his camp-fires near Monticello.—My candle is expiring.

CAMP 1 MILE NORTH OF EDENTON
FACTORY (THAT WAS)
Sunday Night: November 20/64. 8:30 P.M.

Fifth day out

Left camp between 7 and 8 A.M.: marched about fifteen miles; *we* reaching camp ground by 3¼ P.M.— train up about 5 P.M. Ugly weather all day—heavy clouds, some rain, sullen mist and fog all round horizon, and rain again tonight: but roads today not so bad as expected. Soil mixture of red clay and sand: country rolling, some pretty bad hills, not very: still between Little River and Murder Creek. No enemy yet, nor sign of any one near us.

I have observed closely so far as I could, and repeatedly inquired of the staff of XIV: I cannot learn of any outrage to the person of any one, nor the burning of any dwelling. It is impossible to prevent straggling—I now see why and how: equally so to enforce literally the Special Field Order No. 120 prohibiting soldiers from entering houses. To do so would require a guard for every house, and we *cannot* stop for that. Col. McClurg,* (J. C. D[avis]'s A.A.G.) assured me today that he knew of no outrage, etc.: and told of J.C.D.'s lighting on two soldiers just coming out of a house, each with a *dress* in hand. He arrested both, turned them over to his Provost Marshal, and presently each was tied and walking behind a wagon, *wearing his dress*

* Alexander C. McClurg.

with "stolen" marked on it, amid shouts of laughter from comrades. Good! McClurg, by the way, is a very gentlemanly nice fellow. Yesterday as we passed one house, the yard full of soldiers, pigs, chickens, cattle, and fodder rapidly disappearing, an elderly lady seeing Gen. S. pass, ran out to gate and begged for a guard. General answered, not roughly but firmly, couldn't do it, army was marching and couldn't stop men: but she could apply to Gen. D[avis] as he came by, etc. At night as he sat by camp fire, I only near him, he said, "I'll have to harden my heart to these things. That poor woman today—how could I help her? There's no help for it. The soldiers will take all she has. Jeff Davis is responsible for all this:" etc., etc. I confess I see no help for it. It is—or was—implied in the damnable conspiracy which brought on this war. Either we must acknowledge the "C.S.A." or we must conquer them: to conquer, we must make war, and it must *be* war, it must bring destruction and desolation, it must make the innocent suffer as well as the guilty, it must involve plundering, burning, killing. Else it is worse than a sham.—Shall we then quit and acknowledge the C.S.A.? No, for that is simply to ensure the same thing hereafter, for separation means *ceaseless war*. God help us!

This is a country which has never before felt the woes which they have long helped inflict on others. Abundant forage, crops fine and just gathered—frequent large farms and comfortable or wealthy proprietors: *all the men,* almost, in the rebel army. Large numbers of cattle, mules, etc., picked up, "acquired" the phrase is, today: some fine ones. J.C.D. says he has not yet killed one beef out of the droves we brought along. At every farm house is plenty of corn, stacks of fodder, vats, etc.: plenty *till this army* has passed. One Lieutenant of Escort with small party went across Little River today and returned this evening with eleven mules and six horses; met no enemy. He went off eight or ten miles, returned after dark: General begun to fear was ambushed. Reports meeting Slocum's command. They are (advance) at Edenton tonight—three miles east of Edenton Factory. Their stragglers "all over the country."

We passed "Shady Dale" this A.M.—not a town or village but the farm of one man, containing 7,600 acres —250 negroes. An old man, Mr. Whitfield, worth (before the war) a million. We are told he left yesterday or this morning, having collected his horses and mules and ordering the negroes to bring them along. But the darkies wouldn't follow him, and instead they remained with the stock and joined the Yanks in high glee. So it is everywhere.

Stopped for lunch at house of Mrs. Farrar, six miles N. of E[denton] Factory. Mrs. F. at home—young woman, would be pretty if less slatternly. Never saw a Yankee farmer's wife but would be ashamed to look so. Yet he has a good place, probably twenty negroes, certainly I saw "quarters" for so many or more. *He* is at Milledgeville—"gone there last week to help in the breastworks, and to fight," said the darkies. Mrs. F. said he was in the rebel army *from choice*—the first woman who has not declared her husband was forced to go. General talked to her in his usual strain—kind tone, but declaring that unless they obey laws all will be utterly ruined, etc.

The negroes here (F.'s) say they have been habitually punished by flogging not only with strap, but with hand-saws and paddles with holes—and salt put in the wounds. They also told us of a famous "track-hound" (blood-hound) at the next house, nearby, used to hunt runaways. As we went by that house, Nichols had gone there (by General's permission) and had the hound shot by a soldier: he was a large red dog: we heard the shot and the dog's dying howls. N. says the darkies there were in great glee over it. No wonder.

The negroes tell us the rebs will give battle at Mill-

edgeville, and have been fortifying it "ever since two
years ago." If they do, their State militia will find our
veterans *tough foes.* I don't think the General expects
them to fight there. Artillery was heard this evening,
far to the S. and S.W.—probably Kilpatrick near
Macon. We hear of our troops at Monticello, eight or
ten miles south—supposed to be OOH XV.* Our camp
is on west of a broad hillock, 200 yards from main
road, and N. of it. On similar hills around, glimmer
through the mist and rain many XIV camp fires, and
music of band at tattoo ¼ mile off. very pleasant. I did
a very foolish thing when we reached camp ground,
which Capt. A. had been sent ahead to select:—train
not up, felt tired, lay down on grass (wet) and took a
nap till waked by light rain on my face. Have not
caught cold though—never was in better health, and
don't feel half as tired tonight after the day's ride as
used to at home after an hour's walk.

Camp is on Mr. ——'s place, wife and child at home,
he is in the rebel army, she says "conscripted." She
too appealed to General—had plenty, now soldiers taking everything. He told Col. Beckwith to give her something to eat. It does seem terribly hard. But how is it
with those whom her husband is fighting? And if he
was really conscripted—why didn't he and the Union
men of Georgia in 1860-61 then fight those who "bullied
them into secession"? They and their families must
pay the penalty—no help for it.

Saw one house, perhaps two, but think 'twas same
one seen from different points—in flames, probably one
mile south of road. Looked like gin house: not dwelling,
so far as could judge. This the only fire since we left
railroad—Except as follows:

General sent Capt. Poe (Ch. Engineer) ahead to
burn Edenton Cotton Factory, which he did, also say
100 bales cotton. 'Twas quite a good factory—say 500
spindles, and employed thirty to forty operators, girls

* Gen. Howard and the Fifteenth Corps.

and women. They begged to spare it, but it came within
the policy and order to destroy whatever is of use to
an adverse army. Rebs left the village, a small one, as
our men approached: tried to burn the bridge, but we
got possession in time. Tomorrow General will meet
Slocum at the Factory or at Edenton. Our camp tonight
is only twenty-three miles from Milledgeville, and two
days left of "schedule time." We have made about
seventy-five miles from Atlanta: more supplies on
hand now than when we started. Animals in good condition or *replaced by better*—men in fine spirits. "Button" does finely. Candle in socket—rains heavily—
Goodnight.

AT MR. VAUN'S* HOUSE—ON ROAD
2 MILES BELOW STANFORDSVILLE,
PUTNAM CO. GA.

Sixth day out   Monday Night, November 21/64

Horrible weather and bad roads—very bad. Our luck
for the last forty-eight hours in these respects has
changed. Roads yesterday rather bad: but last night's
rain made them infinitely worse today. We were delayed this morning till 11 A.M. before starting from
last night's Headquarters, though tents were struck,
etc., by 8 o'clock. Dismal sky and steady rain, and the
wagons of advance brigade standing still in front of
house where General waited for Davis to come up—in
rear of which we had camped. At last we get off, floun-
dered through heavy clay mud, under rain sometimes
heavy, sometimes drizzling, threading our way through
and by wagons laboring along, up hill and down, or
stuck fast. No wonder the weather is such an element
in warfare. *A propos,* last night Capt. Poe (who was
there) defended McClellan against censure for not following up battle of Malvern Hill on this very ground:
says the men were without any rations, and were in
mud a foot deep. I saw ruts today fully 18 to 24 inches

---

* In Sherman's *Memoirs* (II, 184) this name appears as *Vann.*

deep through stiff heavy red clay, some half liquefied, some like wax, or thickened molasses. It was bad enough riding through it on a good horse: what must it be to march afoot, or to drive heavy teams. The bad weather which we escaped W. of the Yellow and Ulcofau River has caught us at the worst point of the divide west of Little River. But this P.M. the wind changed to N.W. and turned cold, and though it was disagreeable riding, the rain still falling somewhat, the clouds began to break. Tonight some stars are out, wind still blowing, and good promise of clear day tomorrow.

Our party made in all but six or eight miles today. Tonight we stop at home of Mr. Vaun, nearly half way from Stanfordsville to Clopton's Mills and about four miles S. of crossing of "Murder Creek": XIV not all over Murder Creek, crossing very bad: no camp near us tonight. Nichols suggests as I write that guerrillas would make a rich haul here if they only knew it. Possibly the fact that he and I occupy the main front room downstairs, through which such gentry would enter, suggested it to him. Stopped for lunch two hours at house of Mrs. —— just this side of Murder Creek. Her husband also in the rebel army and like all the rest (except little Mrs. F. yesterday) "was *forced* to go." She said "he never was in favor of war," etc., etc.—Pity these men didn't *act* like men when they might—but they all lay it on their "leading men"—say "they made them do it!" *Delirant reges,—plectuntur Achivi"*: but in '61 the poor miserable fools thought it was they who were the kings, and Cotton king of all.

Saw a very smart negro woman at that (lunch) house, who had a child, almost white, by her master. Didn't hear her talk much, but Beckwith, Nichols, *et al.* talked with her—smart as a steel trap. She hid and fed three of our men, escaped prisoners: knew about Burnside, McClellan, and Sherman, also the fall of Atlanta, and even the recent unsuccessful rebel attack there. They pointed out Gen. S. to her in the door of the house

—they were in an outbuilding. "Dar's de man dat rules de world!" she exclaimed. She was about twenty-five, a common hand, negro brogue strong, but very quick and smart. Spoke most bitterly of her mistress, who she says has treated her most cruelly. Mistress never had a child: *Sarah and Hagar case* only worse. Mistress about forty-five or fifty, heavy sort of woman, sullen and slow, but civil to us: was in great trouble about "perishing." Soldiers "foraged liberally"—took all her peanuts drying on roof of shed: and, as we left the house, after riding some distance, saw her barn, old and rickety, on fire. Think it caught from fire made near it by soldiers to warm themselves. Little or no shooting today—orders out forbidding. (These memoranda are not intended to chronicle the general movements of even this column, much less whole army. By "we" I mean only our party—the General, staff, and escort. The movements of troops I leave for the Reports hereafter.)

It is terribly hard case for this man Vaun. He owns mills near here on Murder Creek ("Vaun's" on map) seems a quiet, clever man, a Virginian, but lived in Georgia twenty years, and here since fall of '60. Says father-in-law lives 1½ miles below, and lost two sons in rebel army. Says this was strong Union County and sent Union delegates to State Convention: had good deal of talk with General tonight, whose frank outspoken way, not heartless, but terribly straightforward, seems to make great impression,—wish I could note it fully. V. says Legislature adjourned last week; "did hope they would do something for peace."

I am bound to say, while I deplore this necessity daily and cannot bear to see the soldiers swarm as they do through fields and yards,—I do believe it *is* a necessity. Nothing *can* end this war but some demonstration of their helplessness, and the miserable inability of J.D. to protect them,—with the understanding also that with the submission of their "leaders" and people to

the laws, peace will come. If they do still hold out,—
then the only alternative is to destroy or remove them.
It is evident General believes the latter—indeed he
says so. General advised V. very kindly (in tone) to
bring all he could, of corn, wheat, etc., into *his house,*
for safety from the soldiers: gave him to understand
they would take all that lay around loose: gave him
sacks to put his wheat in, etc., V. says all the men hereabouts are hiding out,—were told we would take them
prisoners, etc.,—he concluded to stay at home—"told
wife thought you civilized, etc."—Evidently this movement has created a fearful panic ahead. V. says "you
cover a belt sixty miles wide." He heard cannon yesterday: *possibly* Kilpatrick has taken Macon!—Dr.
Vaughn's [*sic:* previously *Mr. Vaun*] losses partly con-
sole me for these people's spoliation, aside from laws
of war. Wind high and cold tonight.

Howell Cobb's Plantation*

10 Miles W. of Milledgeville, Ga.

Seventh day out   Tuesday, November 22/64

Cleared up cold this morning—freezing wind all
night and very cold. Cold wind all day—some sunshine.
Roads much better, but very bad places, and slow
marching. Made twelve miles in all.

Not so much shooting on the flanks today, but soldiers all the time out "foraging" and straggling. To a
novice there seems much more of this than consistent
with good discipline.

Stopped at Gen. Morgan's† Headquarters to lunch.
Morgan is an odd genius—said to be excellent officer
and disciplinarian. H. H. sat an hour by Jeff. C.
D[avis] and General, by camp fire, eyes full of smoke

---

* Howell Cobb of Georgia had served as Speaker of the U. S. House
of Representatives and Secretary of the Treasury under President Buchanan. He held a commission as Major-General in the Confederate army.

† Brig. Gen. James D. Morgan, commanding one of the three divisions
of the Fourteenth Corps.

and back chilled by wind, listening to army reminiscences. . . .

About 4 P.M. General and party *ahead of advance division,* General selected queer place for camp—exposed to wind, *in ploughed field,* etc.: general grumbling by Staff. Presently came orders for horses to go forward to house further on. Rode there—found it Howell Cobb's plantation, deserted by owner and able-bodied hands three days ago, and all moveable supplies taken. Plenty left—fodder, corn, oats, bin full of peanuts,—twenty sacks fine salt—500 gallons or more of sorghum molasses. Took possession and lodged there.

Old darkey came to see "Mr. Sherman"—scared to death—"thought he was to be killed"—"Dis Mr. Sherman?" "Master, please give me dat light"—takes candle and surveys General trembling all over. "Well —well—and dis is Mr. Sherman! I shan't git done bein' skeered all day tomorrow!" General talked kindly—reassured him, etc. It seems that after Stoneman's* raid a party of rebs went round among the negroes, *disguised as Feds,* coaxed them to leave, etc., and when they got as many as they could *committed,* revealed themselves and flogged the poor deluded negroes almost to death. This one was in deadly terror when he came in—thought he would be killed anyhow—and if it *was* Mr. Sherman, that he and his men were savages. Same stories of our cruelty, burning negroes alive, etc., at Atlanta, have been told these negroes. What fools the rebs are!

General told all the darkies to help themselves as well as the soldiers, to the supplies found here, and ordered the balance burned. I don't feel much troubled about the destruction of H.C.'s property—one of the *head devils.* This plantation is about 6000 acres, and worked 100 hands. They left here the aged, decrepit

* George Stoneman (later Maj. Gen.), who had commanded a cavalry raid south from Atlanta in July and August to Macon and Andersonville, ending in his capture.

Hd Qrs 14
Howell Cobb's Plantation
10 miles W. of Milledgeville, Ga.
Tuesday ~~Monday~~ November 22 /64

Cleared up cold this morning — freezing wind all night & very cold. Cold wind all day—some sunshine. Roads much better, but many bad places, & slow marching. Made 12 miles in all.

Not so much shooting on the flanks today, but soldiers all the time out "foraging" & straggling. To a novice there seems much more of this than consistent with good discipline.

Stopped at Gen. Morgan's Hd Qrs to lunch. Morgan is an odd genius — said to be excellent officer & disciplinarian. Hd. out an hour by Jeff. C. D. and Genl., by camp fire, eyes full of smoke & back chilled by wind, listening to army reminiscences. Discussed sundries — Chas. Anderson, smart, & [sprightly,] but no soldier:

— About 4½ P.M. Genl. & party ahead of advance division, — Genl. selected green place for camp — exposed to wind, in ploughed field &c: general grumbling by Staff. Presently came orders for horses to go forward to house further on. Rode then — found it Howell Cobb's plantation, deserted by owners & able bodied hands 3 days ago, & all movable supplies taken. Plenty left — fodder, corn, oats, bin full of peanuts, — 20 sacks fine salt — 500 gals. or more of sorghum molasses. — Took possession & lodged there.

— Old darkey came to see "Mr. Thomman" — scared to death — "thought he was to be killed" — "Dis Mr. Thomman?" — "Masta, please give me dat light" — takes candle & surveys Genl., trembling all over. "Dah — well — and dis is "Mr. Thomman! — "I shan't git over him skeered all day tomorrow"! — Genl. talked kindly, — re-assured him &c. It seems that after Stoneman's raid a party of rebs went round among the negroes, dispersed as Feds. — wanted them to leave &c, & when they got as many as they could committed, revealed themselves &

35

FACSIMILE PAGE OF MAJOR HITCHCOCK'S DIARY

and young negroes—some forty in all, Nichols says: I did not go to the cabins—too cold and hungry. The chief building is a big log cabin, no hall, divided by mean board partitions into four rooms: one at each end, one rear, and one cut off gallery. No Northern farm owner would allow his agent or farmer to have such. No thrift or neatness about the place: sundry rude log cabins for storehouses, mean rail fences— everything shabby: old negroes wretchedly dressed. H.C. has four or five other plantations, and 500 to 600 negroes in all.

Tonight our lieutenant commanding escort went eight miles to visit rich rebel uncle, who, when he hid in woods because Union man and was about to leave country, refused him a blanket. Now he returns an officer with Sherman. Says uncle and all terribly scared— "S. greatest general and meanest man in world." Same old darkey as above belongs to this uncle—when he saw Snelling,* fell on his knees and hugged his feet and legs—"God A'mighty bless you, Mas' Dave!" *One* Union family, Banks: ordered protected by Sherman.†

MILLEDGEVILLE, GA.

Eighth day out   Wednesday, November 23/64

"First act of drama well played, General!" "Yes, sir, the first act is played." General and staff started by 8 A.M.—rode slowly with column five miles,—met courier from Kilpatrick at Milledgeville asking to see him, rode in thence at gallop. Forgot to note yesterday received message from K. announcing entire success and arrival at Gordon; fight with Wheeler‡ at Lovejoy's and whipped him, retaking two 3-inch guns lost by

* The stop at Howell Cobb's plantation is described in Sherman's *Memoirs* (II, 185-186). On an earlier page (31) Lieut. Snelling is mentioned as commanding "a small company of irregular Alabama cavalry . . . used mostly as orderlies and couriers."

† Sherman's *Memoirs* (II, 188) describes the flight of the Governor and Legislature of Georgia on the approach of the Union troops.

‡ Lieut. Gen. Joseph Wheeler, C.S.A.

Sherman; rode within one mile of Macon, fought 4000 cavalry and 5000 infantry, got into Fort Hawkins but couldn't hold it, etc., etc. K. met us this morning outside of town and rode in: at bridge troops drawn up, grand reception, colors dipped, cheers, music,—all the horses scared and *Button* disgraced himself jumping and rearing like mad, but soon subdued. Passed groves of pine cut down for works and abattis—not used: also very strong works partly built across road. Just as well they were given up. General and staff entered Milledgeville at head of troops with band, etc., without show of resistance. Best way for *them,* sure!

Town prettily situated, not large, some very good dwellings. State House, arsenal, Governor's Mansion, all fine, also hotel, good large building.

General at once besieged about cotton—lectured Mr. Compton *et al,* then agreed not to order cotton burned if bond given, etc. H. H. ordered to draw bond,—did so. Before bond finished one party had 270 bales cotton burned,—*not by order,* and guard sent by Slocum to save it came too late. Too bad. These men, principal citizens, say "C.S.A. played out." Old Jew (E. Waitzfelder) says all want peace, but want slaves, etc. Told him *too late.*

Railroad depot and bridge burned this P.M. Guards stationed all over town at dwellings. State House occupied by Col. Hawley* (3d Wis.), Provost Marshal. Never was talk of burning State House—some doubted General would do it: but he says *not.* It would have been wrong and a blunder.

Had a talk with Jeff. C. Davis and Slocum today about discipline, etc. They both condemn this straggling and burning, etc. J.C.D. says the belief in the army is that General S. favors and desires it, and one man when arrested told his officer so. I am bound to say I think Sherman lacking in enforcing discipline. Brilliant and daring, fertile, rapid and terrible, he does not

---

* Later Bvt. Brig. Gen. William Hawley.

seem to me *to carry out things* in this respect. Staff organization not systematic nor thorough—not as well selected as ought to be. Major General Commanding Division of Mississippi should have best staff army can afford—he has not.

Talk with Col. Hawley about burning State House. H. H. denounced the idea. Hawley agreed in general ideas—argued that State House used for C.S.A. purposes, but declared that 3d Wisconsin kept strict roll call at any halt—three men court-martialed today for straggling, etc. I do not see why this army cannot be kept in better trim as to stragglers. I am much dissatisfied with this.

Ewing gave H. H. one package tobacco "acquired at State House." H. H. took it supposing it public stores for legislature. Mr. Wright says taken last evening from his store: H. H. returned it to him: others laugh at this. I have not taken nor received nor shall I, one cent's worth from anybody, other than my share of the subsistence gathered for the mess. Can't help that.

Kilpatrick tells me (and reports to General) that the rebs *killed after surrender* the prisoners they took from him, except four who took oath of allegiance to C.S.A. If this proves true Sherman will retaliate, *and we must not be taken prisoners*. I confess I don't expect any mercy if captured: and the worst of it is that the "foraging" or pillaging of our men is bound to bring this about. It is all wrong. Certainly the laws of war allow of damage enough being done to teach a terrible lesson, and that lesson must be taught: it is unavoidable and right. But I would find a way to stop anything beyond. Today I passed a store, empty, deserted, paper, empty boxes, etc., scattered about—some soldiers in and around it. Heard one (I thought) ask a negro for some matches. "What you want with matches?" said I. "I asked for *tobacco*," said he. I believe he lied, and at any rate told them if any burning was done except by order, somebody would hang

for it. They took it quietly. This P.M. a number of our
officers went to State House and held a mock legislature. I was named to draw up resolutions, etc., but was
luckily busy drawing bond for cotton, etc. Glad of it.
From what I hear it was pretty flat and not very creditable—though no harm done.* I am very anxious to
see and know Gen. Howard and talk to him freely about
all these things. Yet his Report today mentions "with
regret" just such outrages by his men as what I condemn and deplore. Certainly an army is a terrible engine and hard to control. And J.D. & Co. *are* primarily
responsible for all this!

In Camp ¼ Mile of Gum Creek
W. Edge of Washington Co. Ga.

Ninth day out   Thursday Night, November 24/64

This is Thanksgiving Day at home. God hasten the
day when we shall all unite, North and South, East and
West, in heartfelt thanksgiving for Peace and Victory
over these accursed rebel leaders!

Our party left Milledgeville about 10 A.M. marched
thirteen miles without halt—stopped a while near W.
bank of "Gum Creek." Dayton went ahead to locate
camp, with order to find house if possible, as train far
to rear. "Forward" and crossing creek we came to
house of old lady of sixty-five, with unmarried daughter of thirty-five, fat, not fair, but good face. She was
at gate as we rode up, evidently frightened but trying
to conceal it. General went in, soon reassured her. During evening talked with both. Husband dead, no son or
brother in the war—"glad of it—always opposed the
war, etc., this all the good it does me." Old lady in
great trouble about pigs and chickens, corn, fodder, etc.
Dayton civil at first—then "Better be quiet, we'll do
all we can, soldiers will probably take all your neigh-

---

* Sherman in his *Memoirs* (II, 190) wrote of this mock Legislature:
"I was not present at these frolics, but heard of them at the time and
enjoyed the joke."

bors' and yours too." Rascals *borrowed* all her pots
and kettles, even tea-kettle. Hope she'll get them—
can't tell who it was. We gave them supper, none of
theirs as it happened. Guard over well—permission to
draw water for themselves. Daughter says, "I shall
sleep a heap better tonight than last night—they said
you all would burn our house over our heads—kept me
awake all night." Old lady found out Dr. Moore bachelor—began to praise daughter "powerful fast knitter,
—could keep a bachelor's ankles mighty warm"—also
asked if we had brought any pi-anners along,—says
daughter can play mighty well. Old lady much pleased
with Dr.'s praise of homespun dress. "I've made thirteen dresses like that since the war." Daughter says
never expected to wear homespun: calico $100 per
yard. Showed them U.S. notes for first time, never saw
any.

If one stopped to think over all the losses or estimated all the real anxiety and suffering caused by the
simple march of an army like this, it would be sad
enough. But it's no use. *We* have met as yet no enemy,
and no opposition. The "levy en masse" don't take
place here, for the men are all gone. True it is, as the
General said to me the other day, "Pierce the *shell* of
the C.S.A. and it's all hollow inside." Yet such a march
as this, the mere fact of it, is bound to have a powerful
influence of itself: it shows the real hopelessness of
their "cause" first to those who suffer, and to the people of "The South," and then to all the world. However, wait till it ends all right.

Today the second Act of the drama began. Two
Corps united at Milledgeville, and now diverge again—
XIV by upper road, we by southern: Howard goes east
from Gordon, destroying railroads—*all* concentrate by
26th at ——. Meanwhile K. starts on independent but
important auxiliary raid, cavalry, light. Of this more
anon: it promises splendid results. Capt. Audenried
left us today to go with him.

My bright boy Aleck managed yesterday to lose my blue Mackinaw blankets, which I had given him to carry on his horse. He had Nichols' horse (blind) to lead—couldn't lead, tried to drive him—put on him his saddle with my blanket,—horse started off,—A. got off his horse and left him, to catch t'other on foot—lost both horses and blankets! The fool seems so distressed, I can't scold. But a good double Mackinaw blanket is a bad loss.

Weather today superb,—clear bright blue sky, air bracing and rather cold,—roads in excellent order. Near Milledgeville some steep hills, and road narrow, but last seven or eight miles road sandy, country better. We are now in the regular pine region: dense growth of pines on all sides, save where cleared: but several large farms, and big corn fields not yet gathered, that is, *not this morning.*

We are now with XX and Slocum: Williams* in command of Corps,—Jackson, Geary and Ward of Divisions.†

At one point today we overtook Geary's division where large open space one side of road on top of hill. Suddenly troops deployed off road in three lines of battle. H. H. near General who exclaimed—"What, they are coming into line!" Turn of road and bushes etc. ahead shut out view. H. H. thought for a moment that troops formed to advance or resist attack, though wondered to hear no skirmishing. General rode forward with staff, and presently the *stacked arms* of first line showed it was a halt to rest. But for five minutes H. H. expected a fight "then and there."—Knows now how the *expectation* feels.

General lodges tonight in house, we camp in yard around it. Our tent (N[ichols] and H. H.) is pitched in front of house, and in front of it is big fire, by whose

* Brig. Gen. Alpheus S. Williams.

† Brig. Gens. Nathaniel J. Jackson, John White Geary, and William T. Ward.

light I write this. Scene all round is striking. Across the road directly front of house, and on both sides of house, is pine forest, dense shadows, sombre growth. Gen. Slocum's tents are pitched across the road: and one division camps all around us: camp fires light up the open sky in rear of house: horses picketed in yard: sentry pacing before fence—heard his sharp "halt! who goes there?" just now. Camp sounds all round—voices in conversation in other tents—braying of mule now and then, lowing of cattle, occasional shout of soldier in the woods. Our big droves of cattle provoke frequent remarks by natives. They are larger now than when we left Atlanta.

This evening old lady quite in good spirits and friendly, though now and then complains lost everything—will perish: daughter reproves her and excuses to us. Poor woman, I don't blame her.—She (old lady) says we are "all gentlemen" viz: the officers. Asked H. H. confidentially "what road you all go in the morning?" (H. H.) after grave reflection—"Really, Madam, I suppose we'll have to go on the road *that runs by your house*—I see no other." Old lady "saw it" and dried up. If it were not so serious to these people, there would be many funny things and they are so anyhow.—Strange thing this life!

My health perfect, thank God: didn't feel today's ride in the least except a splendid appetite for supper. We start by 6 A.M. tomorrow, to get our train up before dark—it was four hours behind us today.

CAMP NEAR (W. OF) BUFFALO CREEK
6 MILES W. OF SANDERSVILLE, GA.

Tenth day out   November 25/64

Made only seven or eight miles today, thanks to rebs who have burnt bridge ahead of us over Buffalo Creek. From this on we shall be impeded and harassed and have skirmishing every day—and also from this out there will be houses burned—I *guess*.

Left Mrs. Greer's by 6:30 A.M.—up at 4 A.M. and breakfast by 5 o'clock—before day. Before we left, General ordered Ewing to pay old lady $50 Confederate money for the trouble we had personally given: not for army's foraging of course. E. did so. I gave daughter also $5 in U.S. notes on my own account. A younger daughter, eighteen or nineteen, good rebel, was quite sharp on us—"had no right to punish helpless women who had never done anything, etc., etc." I asked her where her young men friends were gone. "In the army." (H. H.) "You have or had influence with them —did you ever use it to keep them at home?" She admitted she had not, and that if they hadn't gone to the war, women would have called them cowards, etc., etc. "Then you have done all you could to help the war, and have not done what you could to prevent it."

Soon learned on the road that bridge or bridges over Buffalo Creek burned: a troublesome place, swampy, creek spreads, really nine successive short bridges. Sent forward Capt. Poe to repair: halted four hours at deserted house W. of creek meanwhile. Two or three stories about who burned bridge—negroes said done by this man, others by party from Sandersville. General very angry at it, no wonder. Wind cold, sky cloudy, fire comfortable as we sat or lay down by side of road waiting. H. H. and Ewing got to talk about proposed burning of this house—quite a good one, two story frame with several out-houses, cabins, etc., etc. Good blacksmith shop with very good set carpenter's tools. Ewing was for burning house. H. H. opposed it without evidence that owner had burned or helped burn bridge. If he did, all right, but no reasonable certainty of it yet. General was sitting near, unobserved by H. H., but, as usual—for nothing escapes him—heard and noticed conversation. Presently he broke in "In war everything is right which prevents anything. If bridges are burned I have a right to burn all houses near it." (H. H.) "Beg pardon, General, but what I was contending for *with Col. E.* was that indiscriminate punishment was not just—and that there ought to be good reason for connecting this man with the burning of the bridges before burning his house.'' (General) ''Well, let him look to his own people, if they find that their burning bridges only destroys their own citizens' houses they'll stop it,'' etc.

I shall quit discussing this matter. I am but a staff officer, to obey orders. To volunteer advice to General I have neither right nor duty, and 'tis but policy also to wait till asked. I have not volunteered any to *him,* but even to discuss or criticize his actions is not my place, and would only weaken my influence hereafter. No doubt to a certain extent he was right—some things can be reached only in that way—hence it is right to retaliate for murder of prisoners by killing in return etc., etc. But war is war, and a horrible necessity at best: yet when forced on us as this war is, there is no help but to make it so terrible that when peace comes it will *last.*

Poe rebuilt the bridges rapidly and well, and the whole delay was only about four hours, though it delayed our entry into Sandersville till tomorrow instead of today. Learned that rebel cavalry were on t'other side and a few shots exchanged at first but no harm done. Crossed on bridge about 2 P.M. Spreads into a swamp, two hundred yards or more wide: dense growth on either side, and ground low some distance beyond. While waiting for bridge heard number of distant cannon shots—some thought it north of us, some south. Strangely deceptive and uncertain, it seems: depends on weather and atmosphere how far artillery audible— sometimes over forty miles, sometimes not audible three miles. General opinion Howard (XV XVII)— fighting south of us.

Within three or four miles of Sandersville General halted at house by road—large double log house, people well off, sundry large stacks of fodder in yard,—cotton

screw, "quarters," etc. In house found old lady, say
sixty, and young woman with two or three little children. Old lady—both indeed—in great distress, crying,
lamenting, etc. General much worried by it: old lady
evidently religious woman,—"hoped the Lord would
reward us all according to our deeds—very hard for
poor old woman to have all she had taken," etc., etc.
So it is. Soldiers swarmed in yard,—upset beehive,
took out honeycomb with bees swarming all round as
coolly as if so many flies,—stacks of fodder quickly
transferred to wagons—how much or how little left, I
don't know. General ordered cotton screw-press burnt,
soon done: but no soldier entered house while we were
there, and the two feather-beds lying on boards in yard
not disturbed. General had intended to stop at house,
but old lady's lamentations made him go a little further and camp in field. If she had only known it the best
thing for her was to beg him to stay there. We were all
glad of it—tents in a good field are better than any
house on a march, above all a house with women in it
crying, etc. I was afraid the house would be set fire to
by some scoundrelly straggler, but it was not. We had
a fine camp—near the wood, on brow of a hill sloping
to rear,—open and level where we camp, dense pine
growth in rear. Colonel asked leave to send band (2d
Mass) and gave General very pretty serenade. This
part of a campaign,—life in open air, riding daily, and
tent life, is very jolly: don't wonder men like it. Col.
Howard,* from Gen. Howard, overtook us tonight—
left Gordon early this A.M. came *via* Milledgeville *41
miles ride* and joined us by 7 P.M. Reached Milledgeville just in time to cross on bridge with our rear guard
before it was burned. Says State House and Governor's
Mansion all safe (glad of it) and people of the town
say Yankees treated them much better than expected.
Better than some of them deserved, say I. Forgot to
note fact before that General spared one man's cotton

---

* Gen. O. O. Howard's younger brother, Charles H. Howard.

who has been engaged in running blockade from
Georgia into Tennessee. *Captured letters,* etc., sent to
rear by Dayton from Kingston prove this.—D. remembered name and *recognized his signature* as soon as he
saw the bond given at Milledgeville. He talked as
smooth as oil. While we were still at old lady's house
and just about to leave, an order came back from troops
on road in front for section of artillery "forward
double quick." General and staff followed. Soon came
up in rear of advance brigade deployed in line of battle on both sides of road in field, supporting artillery—
no firing yet. Presently Slocum rode back laughing,—
false alarm of rebel cavalry charge. Men went into
camp—glowing big fire in front of tents, pleasant chat,
etc.

SANDERSVILLE, GA.

IN CAMP, IN OPEN FIELD.

Eleventh day out   Saturday, November 26/64

Left camp by 6½ A.M.—Wheeler's cavalry in our
front, undertook to skirmish. Slocum's 1st brigade advanced skirmishers and before long we heard their
firing.

General and staff rode forward—road narrow for
some distance and through pine woods and across low
ground through which ran creek: road full of troops,
wagons, camp followers, had to go slow. Rode with
General and Slocum in ploughed field on right. Road
full of advancing troops, in column by the flank. Ahead
a quarter mile off at first one brigade deployed and advancing rapidly in line of battle: ahead of them our
skirmishers pressing forward at double quick with loud
cheers to and into and through the town, pursuing
Wheeler's men, and constant firing by skirmishers. It
was not a battle,—only skirmish firing, but that pretty
rapid and constant for twenty or thirty minutes. We
followed them into town, rebs not attempting to make
stand: after driving them out of town our men halted
there, and at same moment XIV entered it by N. road,

also skirmishing. As *we* entered town passed church with "Grecian front," and from a distance—cross road—saw a dead rebel lying on the portico. Learned after entering town that rebs fired from street corners, from behind houses, and from second story parapet front of brick Court House, which made quite a good fortification. All our loss I could learn was one killed, eleven wounded.

General and staff came through Square and went to large brick house set back in yard, with large garden in front and on both sides. General told H. H. enter. Went up steps—knocked (door locked)—opened by one of our soldiers in hall just entered from rear. Lady in hall—greatly alarmed—begged protection. H. H. ordered soldier out and assured her General's presence would protect her. "I demand protection *because Gen. S. is a* Catholic."*—"Madam, it's a pity the Catholics in the South have not acted so as to protect themselves." (Heard no more about Catholics).—Owner of house, Dr. Green, gone to Macon; this lady, his sister, old maid, wife there, lady-like but good rebel and rather saucy than wise,—old aunt, apoplectic, had a fit when Wheeler came here, still in bed.

General very angry about firing in streets and from Court House. Came in presently, sat awhile on front steps. Told ladies would protect *them,* but would not give guard, and would burn town for people burning bridge and firing in streets. General staid two or three hours. Mrs. G. at first sharp, and got some short answers, but no rude ones,—afterwards General sat in old lady's room with ladies, and talked long time in casual strain. H. H. sat by enjoying it greatly, and joining in. Mrs. G. softened good deal.—General talks "mighty well"—frank, almost blunt, but capital and always to the point and *never over-bearing* nor rude. Before he came, soldiers in yard and began to plunder negro cabins, etc. H. H. ordered them out and they left

* Gen. Sherman's wife, not he himself, was a Roman Catholic.

sullenly. H. H. had long talk with invalid young man,—
quiet and civil,—full of Southern delusions and evidently astonished by many things I told him. Asked if
we were not very much afraid of the population of our
large cities: if I did not think monarchy best government and ours too weak. H. H. laughed at first part,—
told him in North the intelligent middle class all
through interior of Northern States were our reliance
and our real *people*—none such in South. Agreed old
Government was weak—if strong enough it would have
hung J.D. & Co. at once. Quoted A. H. Stephens on
him as to "folly and crime" of Secession. Told him of
rebel lies about our burning negroes at Atlanta, etc.:
was careful to avoid anything personal, and saw he ap-
preciated it fully.

Hard as it is in detail, I am satisfied that on the
whole Gen. S's idea about the true policy is right. He
has his notions, and often says more than he means, but
I have not seen a man who on the whole I think so near
the right man to end this war. I believe he is the man
who will *do it yet*.

He was much troubled about that old lady last night
and had some coffee and other supplies sent her.

Methodist preacher came to the house today and into
room where General was, to "intercede for women and
children." Loud talker, vulgar fool—seemed to think
he could *talk* General into anything. General bore with
him more than I expected or than he deserved, never
lost his temper, never spoke even angrily, but gave
some hard hits. It seems a Confederate Major Hall
burned the Buffalo Creek bridge, against remonstrance
of citizens—so preacher says. General gave him no
comfort except, "I don't war on women and children,"
etc., and spoke sharply about firing in streets, etc. Finally one of ladies whispered to preacher and he shut
up and left. General told ladies dwellings would not be
burned, but Court House and stores would.

General sent division down to R.R. at Tennille Station—Eddy and Nichols sent with them. Eddy got telegraphic communication with Augusta but line cut above. Brought us back Augusta and Savannah papers. "Gen. Wayne* telegraphs that he has whipped *Kilpatrick's* cavalry division at —— Bridge." How we laughed! K's cavalry never went near there and is now far north of us, en route for ——. But Howard has been delayed by Wayne, and only tonight we learn that he has crossed. *We* go down to the railroad tomorrow, and now will march with "left wing" and Howard. Glad of it.

Col. Howard told us last night that in the fight the other day at Griswoldville (only Walcutt's† brigade engaged on our side, with cavalry on both flanks to support) the rebs were severely punished. Walcutt repulsed them and we buried over three hundred of their dead—and a rebel captain prisoner said they lost 2000 killed and wounded. Our whole loss was about *100*. He says further that some of our men taken prisoners, had their *throats cut* afterwards: this was learned by one or two of them who were not killed by it (throats cut too high up) and though left for dead got into our lines again. And as I write Davis and Nichols have just returned from the town where they have spent the evening at a citizen's house, and say that prisoners taken from Slocum recently were also killed after surrender. This statement comes from Wheeler's men. Yet the wives, etc., of the men who fight in this devilish way "demand protection" and get it. So they ought, but for *our own sake,* not theirs. Am glad to learn that our men have destroyed no building in this town, nor injured any person. But they have "foraged liberally." —General would be justified by laws of war in destroying whole town.—Weather fine for several days, but it will rain soon.

* Brig. Gen. Henry C. Wayne, C.S.A.

† Charles C. Walcutt, brevetted major-general, volunteers, for special gallantry at the battle of Griswoldville.

HEADQUARTERS IN A FIELD
TENNILLE STATION ("No. 13")*
GEORGIA CENTRAL R.RD

Twelfth day   Sunday Night, November 27/64

Marched all of four miles today—from Sandersville to this place. Up at 5:20, breakfast by 6 A.M.: *en route* about 7 A.M. Weather fine, quite heavy fog at sunrise, but low down and promise of fine day fulfilled. As we passed through Sandersville—our camp being north of it, just outside, saw many troops (XIV) moving. General called Poe and ordered Court House burned—we went on. Poe staid and burned it. *No other building in this town* was ordered to be burned, nor was any other burned or injured up to the time Poe left to-day. This was burned expressly because used as a fort to fire from on our men, and the people we saw were so informed. Dare say that vulgar and loquacious preacher will claim the credit of saving the whole town. He did more harm than good.

Ride from Sandersville here through pine forests over sandy road. Beautiful Sabbath morning: air delightful, a little bracing, sky and sunlight lovely as fog melted away: and the quiet of the woods is always soothing. Many thoughts rushed on me as we rode quietly along—so quietly yet on this sad and deadly errand. How can any man engage in a war unless he believes its prosecution a sacred duty! But for this, I could not stay in the service an hour: as it is, I cannot stay out of it. As we passed a house, an old woman came to the gate, evidently to stop the General and of course *to get a guard*. He was on the other side of the road.—I was riding just behind him on her side. If she spoke, it was not audible, and he rode along looking straight forward and *did not see her*.

At this place found R.R. depot, store-houses, etc., in

* The stations on the Georgia Central Railroad are found, in a United States military map published in 1865, to be both named and numbered. Maj. Hitchcock's notation, here and later, accords exactly with the map.

smoking ruins, burned yesterday by XX[1].* Large double frame house with several frame outbuildings besides
cabins, etc., facing R.R. track, say two rods or so from
it. Two or three ladies and some young children only
occupants—sundry negro and yellow girls,—men seem
all gone, white and black. One lady, say forty to forty-
five, but young looking, intelligent and rather ladylike,
but not of same grade as those last night: one younger,
very brunette, more ladylike after decided Southern
style and manner. Both hearty rebs but not insulting.
Gen. Hardee† was here yesterday morning—came up
from Augusta night before on railroad, and Wheeler
also, and Gen. Wayne (Georgia State Militia) who
"whipped Kilpatrick's cavalry division" at Oconee!!
—I learn today from Col. Spencer‡ of our 1st Alabama
cavalry, that the only fight *at all* with our cavalry about
here was with *fifty of his men* who crossed Oconee at
Ball's Ferry in morning of 25th,—held the position all
day,—were two or three times attacked, repulsed rebs
each time, but at night being out of ammunition, and
having lost six killed and fifteen wounded, recrossed
river taking all their wounded. We laugh at these lies
here, but these are all the stories our friends can get
about us now, and with what anxiety do not my dear
ones watch for and perhaps read these things! Forgot
to note last night that N[ichols?] brought back from
here Augusta and Savannah papers of 24th and 25th
containing extracts from our Northern papers. One
was that "a St. Louis telegram states that Gen. Sherman's army in Georgia consists of—etc." It is abomi-
nable. So the *first definite news the rebs had* about this
movement was from the Chicago Times of *November
9th,* a week before it commenced, and which was published in Richmond November 11th or 12th. Up to that

* The reader may remind himself that this notation signifies the First
Division of the Twentieth Corps.
† Lieut. Gen. William J. Hardee, C.S.A., commandant of West Point,
1856-1861.
‡ Col. (later Bvt. Brig. Gen.) George E. Spencer.

time they were completely deceived by the heavy trains
going north from Atlanta (as we knew from other
sources than their papers) and believed S. was really
going to retreat. Hence, no doubt, our first week's unin-
terrupted march. I don't wonder Sherman is "down on
newspaper correspondents": he is perfectly right. He
was very angry at these publications and said last
night he had a great mind to resign as soon as this campaign ended—"it's impossible to carry on war with a
free press." That's *talk* and only means how provoked
he is. No wonder.

A propos to newspapers, two nights ago Schofield*
was discussed at camp fire. General spoke *very highly*
of his ability: in effect gave him the first place in the
Western Army: "more ability than Geo. H. T.!† Has
large brain—larger than T. but not as much the confidence of the troops." I briefly gave *my* idea of the vil-
lanous attacks on Schofield in Missouri by "radicals"
and "Missouri Democrat." General listened with interest—said "I wouldn't take command in Missouri—
if I were there I'd suppress every paper in the State."

Caught cold last night, I think: was quite sick all this
morning. . . . If I could always get a cup of good—
even pretty good—*tea,* I would do very well, but our
tea was little, and is out. Sorry enough I "didn't know
the ropes" before I left home—but it's no use now,
though I might have had that tea and all my supplies,
if I had known, etc., etc. Better luck next time.—"Hard
tack" is *hard,* especially on one's teeth, though otherwise very well. It amuses me to find Dayton, Ewing,
McCoy and all these "vets" no more reconciled to it
after three or four years' acquaintance than I am—
indeed they growl at it more than I. I determined from
the start to growl audibly at nothing, and even to myself as little as possible: good rule, and have kept it.
Can't say I think Manuel so fine a cook as the rest seem

* Maj. Gen. John McA. Schofield.
† Presumably Maj. Gen. G. H. Thomas.

to—though no doubt there are many worse. Had biscuit tonight,—so heavy that even N. criticized them. Had oyster soup—pretty mean. I should be perfectly content with good corn bread—plain "pones," which we have had sometimes, and very good. But this is the land for sweet potatoes—from Covington to Milledgeville. Good story of soldier who "don't touch any but *red* ones now," and scornfully rejected white ones. Accidentally got to talking with brunette lady of the house today about the war, etc. I pity these women sincerely, but curse the miserable "State pride" which blinds them. I believe there is no such contemptible *provincialism* in this world as these people have. It does me good to quote A. H. Stephens' Union speeches to them—and it *hits hard,*—the harder because most politely done, with surprise and regret at his abandonment of principles so admirably and truthfully declared. In our talk today, I alluded to my home in Missouri—"You a Missourian!" with marked uplifting of eyebrows and plainly implying "renegade."—"Yes, by adoption and twelve years' residence,—but my birthplace was Alabama." Still higher went the eyebrows and more unmistakable the air and implied suggestion. "And *for that reason,*" I continued very quietly, "I am in the service, and shall stay in it till this war ends in the destruction of those bad and ambitious men who were willing to ruin my native South for their own aggrandizement. I feel towards J.D. and his co-adjutors exactly as I should towards a band of robbers who by fraud and force had gained possession of my father's house."—I went on to say very kindly that I made great allowance for many whom J.D.'s lying telegrams, artful appeals, etc., also personal and social ties, mistaken "States Rights" ideas, etc., had misled, —etc., etc.—too long to quote. Finally she begun *to cry.* I expressed deepest regret if any word of mine had given pain (I had not said a word in an excited tone, nor alluded to nor addressed *her* as a rebel—carefully avoided it and said that I cared not who or where the rebels were, we were fighting against *anarchy* and in self-preservation)—and that I had discussed it at all only to show her what *we* think is truly being a "Southern man." She disclaimed being offended, etc.: but I quit. If I could transcribe the whole conversation it would show two things as the foundation of *her* rebel feelings—State pride and personal sympathies, to which I might add utter ignorance about "the Yankees."

She told me that till our troops came last night— Gens. Jackson and Williams and their staffs staid here, and both these ladies say were "very gentlemanly"—they were told and believed that all along this march of ours we had burned *all houses,* including residences. I told her that such statements were merely wilful falsehoods: told about Wheeler fighting through streets of Sandersville, and that we had right to burn the town, but had put guards at dwellings, and had burned only the Court House, expressly because *used as a fort.* Told her of stories about our cruelty to negroes at Atlanta, etc.,—she hadn't heard these: I dwelt on the folly of such a course, etc., etc.—This P.M. Corse joined us with his division and now we go with left columns of right wing. Old lady came to house to see General—same one who was at gate this morning: wanted guard, of course: Corse sent one with her and also for neighboring house, where three young ladies—General approving it. It appeared that old lady's husband is in rebel army in Virginia. General commented with some asperity on her husband being there killing our men, while we were called on here to protect his house and family. "But he didn't want to go—they forced him— they conscripted him." "How could they force him," said General, "if he was a brave man? Why didn't he refuse to go—and if he *had* to fight, why must he fight against his country—why not for it?" Same story everywhere—we have met but *one* woman who did not

protest and declare that her husband, son, etc., was
"conscripted" and "forced into the army." What a
confession for these "free and independent Southerners!" or else what liars their women are! Which is it?
I have no doubt they *are forced*. We heard yesterday
of Wheeler's "conscripting" an old man of fifty-six:
and by the way, that preacher yesterday (who did not
pretend to be a Union man) abused Wheeler and "his
gang of horse-thieves" in the handsomest style, and
said they had been going all over these counties, seizing
and stealing horses everywhere and *taking them into
the upper counties and selling them*. Lovely fruits this
"peaceable secession" bears, truly!

Wrote dispatch for General to Howard today directing movements of that army: *for which see reports
hereafter*. General in fine spirits, and well he may be.
He desires nothing better than for Longstreet* (who
it is rumored among these people is already at Augusta
with large force) to come and fight him.—Our next
trouble will be at the crossing of the Ogeechee, where
they are fortifying, etc. *Possibly* they may find a coun-
ter-irritant applied before them. *Nous verrons*.

Received today from Howard the official report
(Gen. Wood's)† of the fight at "Duncan's Farm" near
Griswoldville, on the 22d November, already alluded to.
Our total infantry force engaged was 1500 men (less
than 1550), flanks being guarded by two small regiments cavalry. Rebs had over 5000, chiefly State
troops. They assaulted three times, left 300 dead on
the field, buried by us, and had nearly 1200 more
wounded,—were thoroughly whipped. Our total loss
(per official list by name) of killed, wounded and missing, *was less than 100*. After that Howard's column *was
not attacked again*. Their papers did not mention the
fight up to the 25th and *will not*.

* Lieut. Gen. James Longstreet, C.S.A.
† Brig. Gen. Charles R. Woods. (Hitchcock, generally most accurate,
wrote the name, here and hereafter, *Wood*.)

All our commanders constantly report our troops in the very best spirits and condition, "spoiling for a fight." Our little skirmish yesterday at Sandersville showed it—our infantry *skirmishers* went at Wheeler's *cavalry* at double-quick and with incessant cheers and chased them from the word go. Wheeler had 3000 men, so the citizens all told us, and also had four pieces of artillery, but did not even put these in position, hurrying them off through the town. Meanwhile we are all the time destroying the Georgia Central railroad— tearing up and burning the ties and sleepers and bending and twisting the rails. At Oconee Bridge, twelve miles from here, over two miles of trestle work through swamps on both sides of river have been burned, as well as the bridge, which was a long and important one. Even now it would take three or four months to get this railroad in running order and when we leave it, it will be useless for 1865 anyhow—this Central R.R. *artery* from E. to W.

We left the house above mentioned this afternoon and camped in open field east of it, very large open space,—camps of Corse's men in sight. All hands agree in preferring tents to house,—I hate to be in a town or at a house. I don't wonder at the fascination campaigning has for many men: certainly it is full of an independent and vigorous enjoyment, aside from the darker scenes and sad features of war, which is very fine. Can't say, however, that I should fancy the prospect of three years' campaigning without sight of my precious ones.

This has been as much like Sunday in appearance as any will be in camp—that is, not at all. Sorry for it— nothing to do but keep quiet, for tents not pitched till evening. One learns the value of many things only by losing them. I think I could have listened with more than patience today to even a dull sermon: and how dear the memory of Sabbath rest and quiet at home!

Tomorrow we move early, and (today being *with us*

an interlude, though the columns are again in motion on several roads) tomorrow the second Act of the Drama will be fully under way.

IN THE FIELD—IN CAMP, WASHINGTON CO., GA.

Thirteenth day out

Monday, November 28/64: Left Tennille Station ("No. 13") on Georgia Central railroad early this morning: marched S.E. to X Roads at Widow Peacock's,—thence N.E. (on road from Irwin's X Roads to Louisville) past X Roads at Widow Jordan's, to X Roads at J. C. Moye's,—thence S.E.—about fifteen miles in all. We camp by side of road, in open space with pine woods in immediate rear, and on right of camp a neat frame church. Around us is camped part of F.P.B.'s XVII—Mower's Headquarters (XVII), just ahead of us.

At Tennille yesterday a negro woman told Nichols that not long before some Union prisoners were brought there, well dressed: were abused in word and act, forced to take off their good clothes and exchange for old ones of captors,—"You've worn these long enough": and when she (the negro woman) afterwards gave them some food she was cruelly whipped for it: in proof of which she showed *fresh welts* on her back.

As yesterday and today have inaugurated important movements looking to the probable passage of the Ogeechee by our army, I depart from my rule thus far, in part, and note as follows :*—At Sandersville we with XX met J.C.D. (XIV). Thence XIV moved yesterday direct *via* Davisboro to town of Louisville, about twenty-five miles E.,—part also, light, *via* Fenn's Bridge. Louisville is across Ogeechee. Meanwhile XX Slocum move along and destroy railroad to Station 10: and Howard's, per order sent 27th from Tennille, sends XVII or left column from Irwin's X Roads up "Louis-

---

* See p. 16, *ante*: "I do not expect to deal in predictions," etc.

ville Road" to Moye's, thence by road S.E. and parallel to railroad to point opposite "Station 10"—While XV with whom Howard, move up (N.E.) Louisville Road, part to Widow Peacock's and thence S.E. and part to Widow Jordan's thence S.E., both through "Johnson" (on map) or *Wrightsville* to road from Swainsboro N.E. through Canoochee, etc., with orders to come out also near "Station 10." Thus we approached Ogeechee at two points—one column at Louisville, which is ten to twelve miles *above* railroad Bridge,—and other three columns (including XX on railroad) coming towards railroad Bridge across the Ogeechee which is at Station 10. Meanwhile Kilpatrick has gone far round to the North from Milledgeville *via* Sparta, with orders to chose his own road and strike and cut R.R. at or near *Wainesboro,* between Augusta and Millen,—thence to come down on Millen if possible with *dash* and rescue prisoners and again cut Savannah railroad below Millen.—Thus Hardee's purpose of defending line of Ogeechee and fighting behind fortifications at the R.R. bridge—which General forsaw at *Sandersville,* and which at *Tennille* we were told Hardee had avowed *there*—was to be flanked by XIV movement on Louisville—see map—and at same time Augusta threatened by that movement, while yet the two columns of Army of Tennessee on two lower roads are ready to seize R.R. bridge if Hardee goes to Louisville or elsewhere and also threaten Savannah. And to still more threaten Augusta, and to force back Wheeler's cavalry from our front and flanks, Kilpatrick's swing round is made, at first not known to them, but sure to be soon heard of. The plan seems to me a superb one from every point of view.

At Widow Peacock's (X Roads), say four or five miles from Tennille, we met Blair and staff, with his corps. Also met Corse (XV[4]) just turning down as above indicated. Blair looks remarkably well, looks and is very much better than when I saw him last, in S. H.

Gardner's office in St. Louis. With him were young
Ware, a Lieut., and Phil Tompkins, a Major, on his
staff.*

Weather very pleasant. We have had but one day yet
cold enough to wear cloth overcoat, which was the day
after we left Vaun's, 22d—just after the rain. The day
before, during the rain, my flock (rubber) talma was
comfortable. N.B. The "flock" is *not* waterproof
against steady rain, for mine was wet through that day
on the shoulders, though barely wet through.

Today's march on sandy roads, and through woods
chiefly pine, though as yet we still see oaks and other
trees. Good farms along the travelled roads, and crops
have all been good. We see hardly any cotton,—corn
almost exclusively instead—*for which we are much
obliged*. We often laugh over J.D.'s idea that Sherman's army will be starved out. Never was an army
so bountifully supplied. Blair mentioned to General
(we had already heard of it, but not heretofore noted,
I think) the absurdly desperate stuff in a rebel paper of
20th—viz: that Hood had completely succeeded in
"cutting Sherman's communications," and that S. was
thereby forced to his present "desperate retreat
through Georgia to the sea-coast" with an army of *not
over 25,000 men*(!) and that as he could not march
over ten miles per day (Howard made twenty miles
yesterday) he would inevitably be delayed by burning
bridges, etc., till re-inforcements should come to *destroy him*, etc., etc.—How these wretched lies will re-
bound against their authors! *One wing* of this army
alone is *over*—yes, much, but no matter how much, *over*
25,000 men. We can march twenty miles a day whenever we choose, and do march over fifteen. It is a magnificent army of *veterans*, brimful of spirit and devil-
try, literally "spoiling for a fight," neither knowing
nor caring where they are going, blindly devoted to and

---

* Lieut. William E. Ware and Maj. *Logan* Tompkins were members of
Gen. Blair's staff.

confiding in "the old man," in splendid condition, weeded of all sick, etc., and every man fully understanding that there is no return, nor safety but in fighting through. The fact is our men are reckless, and every place we go to is occupied by scouts and stragglers ahead of the *advance guard*. In this way the army has lost several hundred prisoners, picked up by rebel cavalry in detail. General says "serves 'em right"—"hope they'll shoot 'em."

Per contra Blair tells of letters captured, from Hood's army, showing a wretched state of things. One very well written letter from an *officer* complains bitterly of short supplies and hard marches—says Hood has promised his men not to fight save with odds greatly in their favor (guess he won't fight!), says they have all crossed the Tennessee River—but that Hood's army is in such condition that he was obliged to tell them something of his plans to keep them together, etc. It is amusing to know all these things on both sides and then to read the lying rebel brag in their papers.

Stopped for lunch at J. C. Moye's—old man and old woman: apparently well off, till we came. Plenty of corn, fodder, etc., etc.—but how it goes! Says Wheeler's men passed here Saturday, 26th, going N.E.—probably stragglers, etc. General talked very kindly to him—guard put at home, and no soldiers entered it, nor was anything taken but forage. *That* these people all expect and understand, even the women. They have learned that much from rebel soldiers.

I see, I think, at once, the difference between Blair and Davis as a Corps Commander, which General heretofore mentioned. After supper Blair and G. F. Smith* came over to our Headquarters and visited General—sat by camp-fire,—most agreeable that, (I listened) and General never more pleasant. Certainly General

---

* So written, but probably by mistake for Brig. Gen. Giles A. Smith, commanding a division of the Seventeenth Corps, under Gen. Blair.

Sherman is one of the most entertaining men I ever heard talk,—varied, quick, original, shrewd, full of anecdote, experience and general information. "Carrier pigeons 90 miles."

When they left, General said—"Major, let's take a walk"—and I went with him to Mower's Headquarters. "Mower, you found me asleep today—now I catch you in bed." Sat an hour listening,—most agreeable. I like Mower very much, manners very courteous. General says "M. one of my pets—only one of *young* generals who saw *moral effect* of this movement—brave to a fault," etc. (Memo. "Sorry don't find more young men show *statesmanship* also—Grant and Sheridan fine soldiers, but," etc., etc.)—Sleep on pine branches as usual now.

CAMP IN PINE GROVE NEAR "ROCKY CREEK"
Fourteenth day out GILKESON CO., GA.—November 29/64

Certainly *this* "is the perfection of campaigning." Since we left Sandersville *I* have seen nothing of an enemy. We know, however, that it is dangerous to go off the road or to get either before or behind the army. But no orders nor danger can prevent squads of men going off foraging, and only yesterday a lieutenant and small party were "gobbled" in our rear on the very road *we* had just come over in the morning. And this though it is well understood that to be made prisoner probably means to have one's throat cut at once. But of course I have none of these risks to meet—nor *need* any one. The perfection of this campaign just now consists in our marching through this "pine barrens" country: good (sandy) roads, fine pure air, no difficult hills, trains well up, forage of every kind in *superabundance,* and our camp tonight superb. Tents are pitched in open space in fine grove of large pine trees, no undergrowth, water convenient, clear, and good (as is all the water in this region, even the swamps and ponds)—in our rear, say 100 feet from the tents a

dense growth of young pines, just the place to picket
horses,—the ground covered thick and soft with "pine
straw" and "wire grass,"—so soft that while tents
were being pitched, etc. (train coming up ten minutes
after us) I lay down on it as on a bed and had a jolly
nap. Only one danger from it,—once afire it spreads
and burns like dry prairie grass. It caught just behind
our tents this evening, before supper, while I was
asleep,—and Ewing and the rest had a lively time putting it out, and so went our bucket of water Aleck had
just brought. The threatenings of rain of two days ago
diminished yesterday, though cloudy, and today it
cleared off beautifully—weather so warm that I could
not wear any cape after 10 A.M. Afternoon perfectly
lovely and tonight beautiful starlight: atmosphere
dense and smoke from campfires hangs low.—Have
been out of tent since writing last sentence and strolled
round camp to fix scene in mind,—worth remembering.
Dark outlines of pine trees all round, scattered near
our tents,—clear beautiful starlight above—atmosphere hazy with smoke of our campfires,—smouldering
embers in front of General's tent (next ours) sentry
pacing up and down along front line of tents, say fifteen or twenty paces off, his form and glitter of musket
now and then visible as he passed the red and white
lights Dayton hangs up for sign of our Headquarters—
in rear of our line of tents, large "fly" tent for mess,
and beyond that, among trees, flickers expiring light of
Manuel's camp-fire, around which lie the servants
strown on the soft bed of pine straw, wrapped in blankets, fast asleep.—Still beyond, the dark mass of grove
of young pines, in which horses picketed,—through
which glimmers light from soldiers' camp-fires beyond.
In front here and there at distance glow camp-fires of
one division of Blair's Corps, camped near us, and
from which even this late, (10:30 P.M.) come through
still night air sounds of voices,—soldiers calling, laughing, faint shouts, etc.; while from without the light in

our tent shines through its white canvas walls,—all others dark.

News tonight that Slocum has thrown forward a brigade on the railroad and seized and holds the R.R. bridge across Ogeechee, without resistance. General says our column at Louisville has obliged Hardee to do this—flanked the Ogeechee line,—as he expected. Also news by an old darkey of Kilpatrick being within thirty miles of Augusta and having sharp fight yesterday with Wheeler. This also helped clear them from *our* front—also *as expected*. No news from Davis direct— but General says that Hardee's failure to stand and fight at Ogeechee is a demonstration that XIX is at Louisville. Slocum has been moving along and destroying railroad as ordered during past two days. Meanwhile our southernmost column—Woods' Division, XV —has moved on lower road, S. of us, and Woods sends word tonight that he has headed off fugitives southward and captured *800* horses and mules! So far all looks well.—Even if K[ilpatrick] got worsted yesterday he has Davis' strong support at Louisville to fall back on,—and if Lee has detached even 50,000 men and they appear tomorrow in our front, we are in perfectly good position **—Interrupted here (11 P.M.) by voice outside of orderly armed with dispatches for General inquiring, etc. Took them to General's tent, woke him. Forage, etc., dispatch (from Howard, inclosing his orders to XV and XVII for tomorrow and stating his own Headquarters position, etc.). Wrote and sent off answer. Went back to my tent, presently heard somebody poking round camp-fire—or the smouldering embers of it—outside and saw shadow on my tent. Went out and found General up—"sicut ejus est non"— costume as to lower extremities,—bare feet in slippers, red flannel drawers,—as to upper, woollen shirt, over which his old dressing gown, and blue cloth (½ cloak) cape. He is proverbially the most restless man in the army at night,—never sleeps a night straight through, and frequently comes out and pokes round in this style, disregarding all remonstrance as to taking cold. His staff think that just such a freak at Rome brought on the neuralgia attack in the right arm and shoulder which has been troubling him for a month. Joined him and chatted a while about weather, climate, late hours, etc., etc. Says he always wakes up at 3 or 4 A.M. and can't sleep again till after daylight: and always likes at that hour to be up and about camp—"best time to hear any movement at a distance." He makes up by snatches of sleep in day time. I asked him today if any truth in story of newspapers about two or three soldiers seeing him (unrecognized) lying asleep in fence corner one day on Atlanta campaign, saying "There lies a Major General drunk while we have to fight"— his being waked by approach, hearing remark and answering "No, boys, not drunk, but I was up all last night and need a little sleep." Says incident substantially true,—'twas one hot day last June,—he lay under a tree, tired out, face covered, etc., etc.—rest much same as told. No soldier who ever served under him would—if he recognized him—suggest his being drunk. He has told me that when a brigade commander he invariably posted his own pickets, and went Grand Rounds himself: and some of his old staff speak of having had to go with him on some ticklish rounds at this.

On march today we stopped first a few minutes at Tarver's Mill on Limestone Creek—Blair and staff there also. T. R. Davis took sketch of scene from little elevation to right of road and rear of mill, under branches of fine *live oak tree,* the first I have seen. Mill on creek, dam makes swamp above, with cypress trees in it, from whose branches hung first "Spanish moss" I have seen for years. These pines, cypress, live oak and Spanish moss, are all old friends and bring back my childhood on Mobile Bay.—Quantity of sacks of cornmeal in mill, all rapidly "acquired," and Nichols got two for our mess—bully! "Hard tack" *is hard,* and

I find my teeth tired and sore from it, and am answered that the oldest officers in the service gladly exchange it for soft bread and cornbread when they can. They all abuse hard tack except Gen. S. who says it's finest thing out—*but he eats the other too when on table.*

Stopped for lunch at Tarver's house at X Roads: met Hazen's Division (XV)* which Osterhaus got up on our road by mistake—turned it back. Met Howard and staff at this house. Staid say two hours. Judge Tarver gone from home—man of wealth, fine place,—large, two-story frame house, porch all round, wide hall, etc.—eight or ten rooms on first floor; numerous out-houses, plenty of forage, corn, fodder, etc.—Divers women old and young and some children. One young girl, slight and delicate make, the prettiest I have seen in Georgia,—seventeen or eighteen, dressed in home-spun but if [she had] been brought up in city would be very lady-like and refined looking. Poor girl greatly agitated about soldiers, etc. General told women to get tubs and buckets etc., and save as much provision, meat, etc., as they could and bring it into house—set guard at house. After while H. H. had talk with this girl—she says none of our soldiers rude to them today, but *two* came yesterday (scouts or stragglers) and talked very rough—called her mother (Mrs. T.) "D—n liar" for saying she had seen no rebels pass. H. H. talked very kindly, told her nobody could control *all* stragglers, and if those men could be pointed out would be severely punished, etc., etc. She became quite reassured—talked pleasantly, deplored war, said her father always said it was wrong, etc., etc.—Said we treated them much better than they expected, etc., etc. But neighbors tell us her father (Judge Tarver) was a "very hard man on the poor" and a leading secesh. *Quien sabe?* H. H. went into yard. Negro woman came up. "Please, Sir, soldiers robbing me of all I got, clothes and everything." H. H. went to cabin, found four or five soldiers turning things

* Brig. Gen. William B. Hazen's Division of the Fifteenth Corps.

TARVER'S MILL, GEORGIA.

FROM HARPER'S WEEKLY, JANUARY 7, 1865

over—XV men—ordered them out instantly, all obeyed
at once. One soldier outside said he tried to stop them—
they knew and he knew the order, etc. Howard has issued the severest orders against pillaging, etc. The two
scoundrels who came here yesterday piled up chairs in
the parlor and set them afire,—but went, and the
women put it out. The poor girl could not speak of it
without sobbing: yet another young woman, more stout
and buxom in appearance, was very cheerful about it
all, and "toted" potatoes with great good will. The
fact is the former was worse scared than hurt, though
not strange at all. But she herself said, when I told her
that we did not forbid soldiers taking forage, provisions, etc., because our army must be subsisted, and
their own Government and people insisted on being our
enemies and her father was gone with a militia company to fight and destroy us, etc., etc.—She said they
understood very well the army must have provisions—
they expected *that*. I find from an old darkey here that
a number of Wheeler's men passed here two days ago,
—been scattered, said they were going to rejoin W. at
"Station 10": and *they* took all his horses and mules
as they passed.

We expected to find a poor country on this road—
fairly entered today into the "Pine Barrens" or
"Wiregrass" (region),—so called by these people
from long slender grass, tough woody stem, unfit for
forage ("except for Indian ponies" says General, who
knows all about this country and South Carolina)—
which covers the ground in the pine forests. Today
after leaving Tarver's hardly a tree except pines, extensive forests, gentle undulations, occasional creeks,—
little underbrush except near swamps. But our road
skirts "Williamson Creek Swamp," and every now
and then we pass farms where cornfields have wholly
replaced cotton: and all our wagons are overflowing
with corn and fodder, men on mules and horses loaded

down with bundles of fodder, and even the gun cais-
sons piled up and *hidden* with same.

* *The preceding three pages written November 30
forenoon while halting at a house 2½ miles from River
and 7½ miles from last night's camps. Pontoon train is
passing on to river—foot-bridge having been destroyed.

In Camp on East Bank of Ogeechee River
at "Burton"* or Station 9½

Fifteenth day out

Started at 6½ A.M.—left that "Wiregrass" camp
with real regret—or rather regret that shall not probably again have so complete a specimen of camping
"among the pines." Favored as usual with weather—
smoke of camp fires and morning mist hung heavy, but
followed by beautiful day, too warm to ride with even
cape on. The "wire-grass" (region) *proper* extends
east to the Ogeechee River; rode all morning through
or among pine forests, whose aromatic odor is delightful to me. Here and there crossed little creeks, arms or
tributaries of "Williamson Swamp" on our left. Our
road lay at first S.E. or S.E. by S. for say five miles.
All through this pine country there are better farms
than we expected, and large stores of corn, fodder and
potatoes (sweet), but Lieut. Snelling tells me that this
is true only along the main roads and that off these,
there are either no farms or mere patches cultivated by
the poorer whites, whom he describes as a very inferior
class. S. is the lieutenant† commanding our Headquarters escort (cavalry) and was assigned to that duty for
this trip by Col. Spencer of "1st Alabama Ree-
giment" because he is a native Georgian, "raised"
near Milledgeville. People whom *he* speaks of as *very*
ignorant, etc., certainly cannot be very high in point of
culture or education—"poor white trash."—But he is
cool, quiet and certainly brave. He has repeatedly run

* "Barton" on Military Map.
† See *ante*, p. 85, note.

great risk on this trip, going off on scouting and foraging parties, after horses, etc., with five and ten men. Yesterday morning we thought he was "gone up"; he went off the day before after horses and failed to return, and as we knew rebel cavalry were in the direction he went we began to think they had him. But he turned up at last: had made a long and wide circuit—told me he thought he had ridden nearly fifty miles, and struck the column again ahead of us, being wrongly directed to our Headquarters.—Stopped for lunch today at house where "no man lived for twelve years"—two or three women kept house—neatest place we have seen, though plain enough. Porch in front and primitive wash-stand outdoor at end of it T thus. Halfway of today's ride (which was some ten miles in all) our road turned square to left and thence through thick woods and over swampy ground on narrow road to the river. At the point where the road strikes the river there is an island, though it was hard to tell whether the W. branch of the river was that or a part of the swamp. The scene as we approached the river was the best commentary on the importance attached in army movements to the crossing of rivers. Narrow road, muddy, wet, dense growth of trees and bushes either side, often *blocked* by wagons, footmen and horsemen, General and staff threading way through slowly in single file, often having to stop, etc. Finally worked through to edge of main channel of river—200 feet wide, quite a current—say three or four miles per hour—muddy looking water—but good sloping bank on t'other side at this point, though dense growth of trees above and below. On this island,—whose width don't know, for after crossing short bridge leading to it the road was under water some distance,—I saw the first *palmetto* plants growing. The R.R. bridge is five miles (by railroad—don't know how far by river) above this point,—*that* (R.R. bridge) being at or opposite "Station 10" or "Sevastopol," which we crossed opposite

"Burton" or "Station 9½." It would have been an
ugly business, impossible, in fact, to cross where we
did if Hardee had defended it. A battery on the E.
side would have made havoc of us as we approached
through the woods and swamp. But the *flanking* movement by Louisville (before noted) settled that question
by turning the line of the Ogeechee and so we crossed
without a sign of opposition. There was a foot-bridge
across the main river at the point where we came,
which the rebs *tried* to burn, but only succeeded in
charring the timbers at one or both ends, though fifteen minutes' sensible work would (and did when we
were ready) utterly destroy it. It was easily and
quickly repaired by 1st Alabama cavalry, though a
shackly concern at best—mere planks on frame work,
no sides nor roof, but wide enough for two horses. All
our footmen and mounted were crossed on this, the latter leading their horses,—we included. Meanwhile the
pontoon train were at work (1st Missouri Engineers),
laying pontoon bridge for wagons fifteen or twenty
yards above. It took ten boats, and made bridge (measured) 195 feet long—was laid and ready in 1½ hours,
though much delayed by crowded condition of road on
W. side. Our pontoons are *canvas* boats, made for this
army. Poe says this kind first used in U. S. this year,
by Thomas' army, last summer. Gen. Cullum's india-
rubber (inflated) pontoons don't do—float, etc., well
enough, but very easily punctured, and then collapse.
Watched laying of this bridge—work systematically,
rapidly, and well done. Trains began to cross about 4½
P.M., or between 4 and 4½, and came in one steady
stream till midnight or later. Went down to bank about
9 P.M. and watched them crossing by light of fires on
either side, striking scene, and sounds too. Railroad
here at Station is say 200 to 250 yards from river bank.
Very good brick station house *was*—that is, we shall
say *was* after tomorrow morning—at this point. Sundry log cabins, etc.,—no good houses save one frame,

of "old Johnny Wells," R.R. agent here. Our tents pitched fifty yards from station, front of some cabins. Splendid camp-fire, made of fine new yellow pine R.R. ties taken from pile at Station: they say there are 5000 of these new ties lying along the railroad here. Old man Wells came to see General—sat with us all evening by camp-fire—jolly old brick, great talker, full of jokes, some coarse ones, and mother wit. Never met a man more quick, in his way, in shrewd and odd "points" and laughable sayings. He claims to be utterly opposed to J. D. & Co.—d—ns the lying editors and warlike preachers (all exempt) in heartiest style,—says, as all we have met, almost, that a minority not only did force but *are still forcing* on the war in the South, but that the people "can't help themselves," etc. Odd sayings— "Cut any fool in two pieces and either end of him would know better than that." "Solomon's dog hasn't bit him in more than two places" "I told my wife these preachers said the God of battles was on our side and would be round playing the d—l, but you look for him tonight and he's out hid in the swamp" etc., etc. General talked to him in usual kind off-hand way—promised to save his cotton and barrel of guano, etc.

Here as everywhere same terrible stories and lies have been spread about us—killing everybody—burning *all* houses, including dwellings, etc., etc. Capt. Cole's orderly riding along his horse's foot sunk into ground, and *smash* went a lot of china and crockery buried by an old negro woman. Cole had it taken out— orderly kept some of the plates—returned rest to her, told her safe in house.

General laughed over saying of old darkey at Tennille, "Dem Yanks some of 'em come down here and first burn the depot—den some more come and dey burn de railroad, den some more come and *dey* burn up *de well*—dem Yanks is de most *destructionest* people ever I see."* Got copy of Augusta paper of last Satur-

---

* See Sherman's *Memoirs* (II, 191) for the same anecdote.

day, 26th, ridiculous editorial—"Where is that fellow Sherman anyhow?" Urges rebel General to make the *Oconee* "Sherman's river of Death"; Funny to read this after crossing the *Ogeechee,* and seven days after he crossed the Oconee—both rivers crossed without a shot. Wells says our pontoons over the deepest place in Ogeechee River!

In Camp at J. B. Jones', Near Herndon, Ga.

Sixteenth day out.   December 1/64

Staid at last night's camp till after 10 A.M. today, though train on road by 8½. XVII at work this A.M. destroying R.R. hence back to R.R. bridge and also forward. Fine new ties made very fine material for big fires to bend rails. All trains of XVII, and two divisions crossed Ogeechee last night—this morning pontoon train and 4th division and all men, etc., safely over on road before 9 o'clock.

Weather today perfectly lovely—cloudless sky, air warm, too warm for cape in riding. *We* made only six miles to this place, where Blair also camps his Headquarters—slow progress, troops burning railroad, also outer columns XV and XX moving on Millen by upper roads from Louisville. Howard sends word this A.M. that he captured rebel lieutenant of Wheeler's command yesterday, across river, who says Wheeler told him we had *all* crossed. Lieutenant says he thinks we will meet no serious opposition from here to seacoast, but *there* will find large army and *Lee at its* head.— General does not think Grant will let Lee come or send any heavy force,—wishes he would, so as to have serious fight and whip them badly.

XIV (J.C.D.) and XX (H.W.Sl.) move today on Millen,—XX via Birdsville direct, XIV by roads to north of that, and K[ilpatrick] still further north. Before we left Burton this A.M. saw the foot-bridge *all* on fire, "good"—easily burnt, thanks to quantity of pine boarding lying on river bank, first used to repair bridge

and now to destroy it. Ferguson's brigade of rebel
cavalry were on W. side of river yesterday in our rear,
—dashed at rear guard, some firing and scattered our
men at first, but no harm done. When we left Burton
this A.M. the track there was already destroyed, and
work going on fast: preparing to burn railroad depot.
Up to this point eighty-five miles of Georgia Central
R.R. have been torn up and destroyed, and though
some of it has not been done as thoroughly as desired,
since it is possible to bend back and use some of the
rails, yet many miles of rail have been utterly ruined,
by *twisting* the rails, so as to make them wholly worthless until *re-rolled.**

East of Ogeechee the timber is still largely pine, but
also mixed with oak, etc. The "pine barrens" or "wire-
grass" (region) is bounded E. by Ogeechee. *This*
county (——)† is said to be one of the richest in the
State. Near the river, however, and by the road we
came, near R.R. (S.E.) are still quite thick woods.
Marched (Headquarters) only six or seven miles to
this place,—large farm of Jos. B. Jones, member of
rebel Legislature—owns another near Waynesboro.‡
J.B.J. left here last Sunday for Savannah but left his
family here. Wife sick in bed: infant *four days old,*
eight other children, five girls and two boys, *oldest only
ten or eleven* years old; two sons nearly grown both
absent in "Cadet" corps, rebel army: two children
dead—poor woman has had 13 children, about *one
every year;* next to youngest still an infant 12 months
old!

Smart servant woman, Louisa, talks freely—"light
on her feet anywhere," says Dr. Moore. "I suckled *that*
child, Hattie," said she, "all these children suckled by

* One of Col. Poe's methods of destroying rails was, after ripping
them up, to heat them in the middle over bonfires built of cross-ties, and
twist them round adjacent telegraph poles or tree-trunks. See Sherman's
Memoirs (II, 180).

† Herndon is in Burke County, near the line of Emanuel.

‡ This word is spelled *Wainsboro* in the diary.

colored women.'' Mrs. J. and children and servants all
in terrible fright, expecting to be killed. Louisa says
Jones used to declare he would wade in blood knee-
deep before Yankees come here, etc.; but he ''took an
early start'' four days ago, for Savannah, the brave but
prudent Jones, and left his sick wife and helpless children to the marcy of the horrid Yanks. Gen. S. went—
by permission—into Mrs. J's room, re-assured her, and
before long the poor frightened children whom we
found in tears were talking to him and us like old
friends. If any one thing is more despicable than another in these ''Southern chivalry'' it is the infernal
lies they spread about the ''Yanks,''—our uniform
cruelty, our killing all the women and children, burning
all the houses, forcing the negroes into our army in the
front rank of battle, etc., etc. Everywhere we go we find
these stories have been systematically and persistently
spread and are believed, even by intelligent people. It
is not said that our stragglers do thus and so, but ''Mr.
Sherman'' orders it and his whole army do it; and so
the story—the damnable lie—about our burning negroes at Atlanta. But the whole thing is founded and
built up on lies.

The General, finding that stragglers yesterday and
soldiers today had taken all the potatoes and other provisions, had a supply for the family sent from our own
mess to keep them till we leave and the brave Jones can
return and get more. He is represented to us as a bitter
rebel and a hard, close man. Talking with Louisa today,
I said of course that after we left they would abuse us
as much as if we *had* burned the house. ''It *ought* to be
burned,'' she said bitterly. ''Why?'' said I, surprised,
for she had been showing much affection for the children and no love (and no *fear*) for us. '' 'Cause there
has been so much devilment here, whipping niggers
most to death to make 'em work to pay for it.'' ''Mr. J.
ever whip you?'' ''He never struck me but twenty cuts
since he owned me, these fifteen years,—but he has

whipped plenty of niggers with paddle and strap too, and I seed one whipped *till the flies blowed the blanket he was layin on.''* I learn tonight from Capt. N's boy Sam that she has been inquiring closely of our servants how we treat them and whether she could leave here and go with us,—and how she would be treated. Told him to discourage the idea—we didn't want women to come, and have all along tried—though in vain—to prevent them.

This is a fine place—large three-story double frame house, wide porch three sides, five large rooms and wide hall on first floor, and cupola on top—finest house we have seen yet, and with excellent out-buildings. 'Tis quite new and the servants say *built by a Yankee for Mr. J.* and not yet paid for. He raises cotton on the other plantation—on this, which he has owned ten years has raised no cotton, but corn, peanuts, potatoes, etc. Has in all on both farms some 150 negroes. Kilpatrick must have been on his other place going to Waynesboro. J. is a leading Methodist.

Audenried rejoined us today. Kilpatrick has fulfilled his errand—struck the R.R. at Waynesboro, sent party and burned railroad bridge over Brier Creek, say thirty miles S. of Augusta, and made fires along the track for two miles from Waynesboro. Had some sharp skirmishing and one pretty good fight with Wheeler both going and returning. Says Wheeler's cavalry fought well, made one or two quite desperate charges, but ran up against battery of six guns—and left. Good dodge of K's when attacked in rear in crossing swamp. Two bridges, near each other; K. passed first and left it untouched; passed second, but then took up planks— then halted about 100 yards off and, placing two mounted howitzers in position, loaded to muzzle with canister, waited. W.'s cavalry came on full gallop after "retreating Yanks"—passed first bridge safely—came to second found planks gone, halted, and just then bang went the two howitzers and a shower of canister shot (bullets) sent them whirling back with many empty saddles. Will look over K's report when it comes in. His expedition has fully accomplished what was expected, as herein before indicated,—for he struck R.R. at Waynesboro as ordered, burnt Brier Creek R.R. bridge, and returned with loss of about 100 men in all. He did not make the dash on Millen, because he learned that all our men (prisoners) had already been removed; nor did he strike the road below Millen, that being left optional and to be done if no serious opposition made. The wrecking of railroad at Waynesboro answering every purpose for the present of securing Augusta and Savannah. No doubt we shall soon learn from rebel papers that Wheeler "whipped" Kilpatrick's cavalry division and "drove him back," etc., etc. Just so the brigade in our rear is "driving" our whole army.

Tonight a man named Mallory who lives near here, at or near R.R. station, came to see General and had a talk with him. I . . . didn't hear it, but on General's invitation he took supper with us. Don't like his face—not manly, rather hang-dog and cowed looking. Pretty intelligent man, but evidently in chronic apprehension of rebel conscription. Has been C.S.A. Tax-assessor; says he was worth $50,000 in C.S.A. money yesterday, but broke up now—soldiers came to his house, took all provisions, and *he says* clothing, etc., etc. Not unlikely stragglers did this; it makes me indignant to find how much straggling. Yet the division Commanders are every day tying up and punishing men for straggling, and say authenticated case of pillaging would be most severely punished. Howard's orders make it *death*. Gen. S. has told me more than once that for first two years no man could have done more than he against everything of the sort—has personally beat and kicked men out of yards for merely going inside, etc., etc. His orders for this camapign explicitly cover and prohibit every such case, but it is the Regimental and Company officers who must carry them out, at last. At same time I don't think General would take same trouble now—indeed he admits as much—to hunt out and punish it. Evidently it is a material element in this campaign to produce among the *people of Georgia* a thorough conviction of the personal misery which attends war, and of the utter helplessness and inability of their "rulers," State or Confederate, to protect them. And I am bound to say that I believe more and more that only by this means the war can be ended,—and that *by this means it can*. It is a terrible thing to consume and destroy the sustenance of thousands of people, and most sad and distressing in itself to see and hear the terror and grief of these women and children. But personally they are protected and their dwellings are not destroyed; and if that terror and grief and even want shall help to paralyze their husbands and fathers who are fighting us and *bringing like terror and grief into more innocent homes* in our Border States, and shall help to break up the terrible despotism which—so they all say—"forces them to fight us," even if this can be done only by driving them to despair,—it is mercy in the end. This man Mallory fully confirms all we have heard about the large Union majority in Georgia,—that it was *bullied* into rebellion, by a desperate minority,—that they are now "forced" and dragged into the army,—that a vast majority of them long for peace but dare not say so, etc., etc. He begged us not to allude to his having been at our camp—"They would hang me quick." He gives our *host* Jones a bad name for grinding, swindling, etc.

In Camp Near W. Bank of Buckhead Creek.

— Miles from Millen

Seventeenth day out.   December 2/64

Marched today eleven or twelve miles, leaving Jones' about 8 A.M., stopping ¾ hour to lunch at deserted cabins on road side. Roads good, save that sand sometimes heavy for hauling; weather quite threatening in morning, but slowly cleared off into most lovely day, so warm that I could not wear cape. We have been most highly favored in weather, not a day's rain since 21st November, and but one rainy day on whole trip so far. Heavy rains—even moderate ones—when crossing these rivers, would have been a bad business; especially where XV and XVII (Howard) crossed Oconee. As it was, it was no slight matter to get the trains across the long, swampy bottoms on either side, across which *were* nearly or quite 2½ miles of trestle work, for railroad track, some of it (measured) 18 to 20 feet high. All of that was effectually destroyed. Col. Spencer reported first he had burnt it as it stood—but it being found only burnt in part, along *top,* a force was sent back who *cut down* the trestles, piled them up and burnt them "good."

Before leaving Jones' I passed by side of house, and saw hanging out of dining room windows one of the women house-servants, with whom I had some little talk yesterday—not the one, Louisa, already mentioned, but older, not so smart, but better and kinder face, and evidently one of the kind most trusted, etc., in the South. She is the nurse and servant of Mrs. J. and children particularly. She saluted me very civilly— "Well, Auntie," said I, "we are going now and I dare say you'll all talk about us as hard as ever." "No, Sir, I know *I* won't, *shoo-ah:* I don't lack much of gwine 'long wid you all myself." "Better stay where you are, we don't want women to come with us,—we have long marches to make," etc., etc., "and besides we'll come back again some day." "*Is* you all truly comin' here again, Master?"—and her face fairly lit up: "I'd like mightily to go wid you now, but Mas' Jo (Jones) when he went away last Sunday, he says to me,—'Now, 'Liza, I rely on you to take good care of my little children,' and the pore little things, dey so scared and cry so, dat I don't see how I can leave 'em." (H. H.) "Don't leave

'em—stay where you are. You are free, but you are
better off here than with this army now." I went on to
explain to her that "freedom" meant *not* freedom
from work, but the right to herself and her earnings,
freedom from personal violence, etc., etc., but implied
also good conduct, etc., etc.; all which she assented to
very earnestly—"dat's all just right, Sir": also that
we took with us, or wished to take, none but able-bodied
men who *voluntarily* went. Two words of encourage-
ment from me would have brought her along, in spite
of "the pore chillen" and sick mistress,—and yet she
evidently loved them. Was she "ungrateful"? She was
evidently one of the favorite and trusted servants, was
probably forty years old, was quiet, well-bred in manner, etc.; just the kind to illustrate the beautiful "pa-
triarchal relation." Yet the selfish and cowardly brute
who left her with his sick wife at the mercy of the "van-
dal soldiery" he ran away from would moralize over
the "ingratitude" of her desiring to be no longer his
slave.

Also before we left five or six of the older negro men
belonging to Jones came to see and did see and had a
half hour's talk with "Mr. Sherman." Never was I
more interested. General met them in same frank, off-
hand way, not familiar nor at all forgetting himself,
but putting them at ease at once. Their spokesman was
a man over fifty, tall, fine-looking and really dignified
negro (quite black), remarkably intelligent, and who
"understood himself" very much better than the white
man Mallory who supped with us last night. The rest
were inferior to him—plain common field-hands, who
said very little, only by way of endorsing what he said,
but who fairly drank in all that was said by General.
But their leader spoke with quite remarkable clearness
and great fluency, and used excellent language. He was
explaining to General when I came up why he and his
fellows had concluded they ought *not* to go with our
army, and reasoned it all out "like a lawyer" that what

with the age of them all, and the rheumatics of this one and the lameness of that one, and the families they must leave, it was really better for them to stay where they were. General listened very kindly, told them they were perfectly right and ought to stay—that we forced nobody, only *permitted* the able-bodied, who wished it, to go with us. Much further talk—wish I could note it. General asked why the poor whites who had no niggers were fighting us for the slave-owners. "Because, Sir, when the war broke out, the rich men told 'em dat when they whipped the Yankees they should have land and niggers too." The fellow was perfectly aware of Lincoln's Proclamation and had also heard of Gen. Jackson. He said the niggers never had got the credit they deserved about the battle of New Orleans—that it was a negro who suggested to Gen. Jackson the idea of a breastwork of cotton bales! Gen. S. said to him that J.D. was talking about arming the negroes, "Yes, Sir, we knows dat." "Well, what'll you all do—will you fight against us?" "No, *Sir,*—de day dey gives us arms, *dat day de war ends!*" These were his own words, eagerly spoken—and the rest as eagerly assented. Afterwards he repeated it, "Dat day dis war ends"—and then added, "or in a very few days after, anyhow."

Nothing special on the march today; our party made in all only about six miles. All the XVII crossed Buckhead Creek except about one brigade which remained west of it for rear-guard and as guard for *us*. We rode down to the creek at R.R. bridge; it is about 75 to 100 feet across *there,* quite a deep stream, and quite a current. Approach on this side through thick woods, and the road leading to R.R. bridge (an old one, not now used) low and full of water. Infantry marches across bridge—officers and mule drivers swam their animals—great fun watching them, specially mules, obstinate and unwilling to go in. A mule in swimming tries to keep only ears and *tail* above water; 'tis said that if the water once enters his ears he gives up instantly and drowns.

We then rode back and made camp by side of the road, in a pine grove—*pleasant always*. Meanwhile the Engineers had laid pontoon bridge across creek at crossing (higher up) of a branch road, at narrow spot, not over 60 feet wide, and the trains all cross tonight. Wagon after wagon passes by and in front of our camp, and the shouts of drivers, etc., and voices from the brigade camp near us are our lullaby.

Howard sends today copies of two letters captured, —one from Wheeler's chief surgeon, t'other from one of his staff, both to their wives—The latter (aid) named I think Hudson. They brag of having whipped Kilpatrick and "saved Augusta!" It happens that K. was ordered not to go nearer Augusta than Brier Creek Bridge—which, as ordered, he burned, and came back. But the surgeon also *urges* his wife to sell all her negroes and buy land; says "This people is whipped, and so are the people of Alabama, and will *make peace within a year on the basis of liberating their negroes.*"

IN CAMP "SCARBORO" OR "STATION NO. 7"
ON GEORGIA CENTRAL R.RD.

Eighteenth day out   Saturday, December 3/64.

Made in all today only about eight miles—from camp west of Buckhead Creek to "Station 7" on railroad. Weather fine as ever.

Left camp early, crossed on pontoon bridge. Forgot to note last night that the railroad buildings at *Millen* were visible from R.R. bridge across creek, not far off. The pontoons were laid higher up, at point where creek not over 60 feet wide (took three boats), and were down and bridge finished in forty minutes. All trains passed over last night. At Millen, which we reached before 9 A.M. we halted two or three hours—probably longer. Millen is a point of importance as a railroad centre, and is the place where the Rebs have till *very* lately

kept our men prisoners, i.e., the officers at Millen
proper, the men at a point four or five miles up the railroad, so we are told. But there are hardly any—that is
were hardly any but railroad buildings here. Over the
R.R. track stood *when we came* a really fine frame R.R.
depot,—of which Davis is making a capital sketch for
Harper's Weekly—some 200 feet long, I should judge,
open at the sides, the roof resting on wooden arches
springing longitudinally from wooden columns. On the
E. side of this was a handsome little station house, apparently used for ticket and other offices and perhaps
cold refreshments. I didn't go into it. On west side, facing Stationhouse, say 100 feet off, was large two story
frame hotel, with many rooms, large dining hall, and
quite a number of outbuildings, also a *gasometer* and
gas apparatus in the yard and the house lit with gas.
In front of this was a yard or garden filled with handsome trees, bushes, etc. Further down railroad on
t'other (E) side stood three large frame storehouses,
100 feet deep x 40 to 50 feet wide each, side by side, and
facing and very near R.R. track, and good high board
fences round three sides. They were evidently built and
had been used for Confederate storehouses, and had
contained meat, etc.; but we were told two of them had
been used recently as prisons for our officers; nor were
they particularly objectionable if treatment otherwise
proper. We found XVII men already at work on track,
tearing up, etc. Sat about there till very tired of it. The
hotel was abandoned, of course, all furniture, etc., gone.
They left one or two families of darkies. I saw one old
man, his wife—a middle-aged woman—and sundry colored children. They left also a *crazy white woman* who,
I found, had been living there for several years, fed by
the hotel people for charity, the negro woman said.

I think if I were, etc., etc., I *would* somehow manage
to twist rails as well as merely burn ties—and I would
have my men *all* at work, and better "organized labor." Asked Poe why he didn't speak about it—says

he has—says he offered to take Michigan Engineers (1st reg't) and do as much as is now "done" by a brigade, in *same time,* and much better. But no such order given—only answer "They (XVII) won't do it right." It is too bad; I don't understand it. Ewing was right, it would seem, in telling me at Kingston that General don't persist in having *orders carried clean out.* Is this from the impatience of detail which results partly from natural energy and partly from necessary preoccupation with large matters,—or is it also possibly a sagacious tenderness about being or seeming "fussy," etc.? I can understand that in some things such an idea as last noted is wise in view of general influence over an army, even at the expense of a certain amount of looseness; it is not possible to be always poking up subordinates, without fretting them, and good riders don't jerk a horse every time he stumbles. But that don't explain these things, e.g., straggling, and imperfect destruction of railroads. Both these are important matters, too important to slight for the reason above indicated. Besides, one order giving the superintendence of railroad-burning to Poe, who is a *very* sensible man, judicious and pleasant as well as *thorough,* would fix it all and avoid any appearance of fussiness, etc.—Poe agrees in my comments (of course I said nothing to him about such an order as above) and suggests some apparent lack of that iron will and *persistent* determination which Bragg has. I think it must be this. Far-sighted, sagacious, clear, rapid as lighting, —personally indefatigable, but also something too impatient to see always to execution of orders *in detail.* He ought to have a first rate A.A.G. whom he fully sympathized with and trusted and *liked personally,* as well as officially, who would take it on himself sometimes to fill up this deficiency. Even then there would be occasions when he himself would have to act, and such an A.A.G. would sometimes be in a delicate position. Dayton is not exactly he.

About 10 A.M. the soldiers who were swarming and straggling all round,—including some, it is said, who were once at Millen as prisoners and were rudely refused the privilege of buying a meal at this hotel,—set fire to the hotel in rear, without waiting for orders. It made a roaring big fire, and all our horses which were standing tied to fence a little way above, were very quickly taken across railroad track to yard of house (dwelling) up on a hill to —— of the railroad depot, say 300 yards off, plainly visible from and commanding it. Just as the hotel, or rather the rear building, which was just set afire, got fairly ablaze, somebody suggested that the crazy woman had not been taken out. Capt. Dayton, Lieut. Snelling, and H. H. all at once rushed to the hotel, where soldiers still wandering through rooms—saw one fellow amusing himself knocking off a row of hat hooks fastened to the wall in hall, though sure to be all burned. When told at last that she *had* been taken out, unwilling to leave a doubt, found old darkey and he said so too,—still hunted her and at last found her out in the garden—poor wretch, say fifty years old, coarsely clad, gray haired, wrinkled face, sitting with sad, *set* face, with a large gray "Hong Kong goose" (so they called it—it was some new variety—black streak up neck and on head) standing on her knees, she holding it by a piece of green cloth round its neck, and stroking it and talking softly to herself, the goose caressing her head now and then. Pitiful sight. Snelling came up also just after. Near by was the negro woman, with children, bedding, etc., saved from kitchen, etc. H. H. asked her about crazy woman—says she came from Southern Georgia "ten years ago,"—crazy then, no friends, came on railroad, "these people have let her stay and fed her." I made the darkey promise to see to her and do all she could for her after we leave, and gave her $5 (U.S.) to do with till other help comes. Before this an elderly white man came from house on hill to railroad depot, anxious to see

Gen. Sherman. H. H. finding he wanted "guard" sent him to look for Gen. Blair. Came back, couldn't find him; said he was citizen of Philadelphia, recently came here to look after his son's property—that soldiers had burned one of his negro cabins and were going to burn his house. Told him dwelling was safe, etc., etc. After hotel took fire General and staff all went up to house on hill, and staid there till after 12 M. Found same old man there and found that the negro cabin was burned by order of Gen. Leggett *because* 100 bales of cotton were nicely concealed under it. They had dug a vault underneath,—stowed the cotton there, put a floor over it, filled up twelve to fifteen inches earth over it, then put a second floor over that, being the apparent floor of the cabin. Old man is a German Jew, named Myers,— greatly troubled about cotton, which he says was his son-in-law's, a Prussian. On further talk and pretty sharp cross questioning—which he tried apparently to dodge and made me mad,—I found that this "citizen of Philadelphia" had lived in and claimed to be a citizen of Georgia since April or May, 1861. He said the cotton was bought at seven or eight cents per pound then, and buried for safety, "to make it fire-proof." (It did not prove so). Told him he could not speculate in cotton without taking the risks. The old fellow made me angry by his double stories and evasive answers, and I spoke sharply to him, the only man I have spoken so to in the campaign.

From this house we had fine view of the burning of the R.R. depot, ticket office and storehouses. The depot made a superb fire, even at noonday. Densest black smoke in immense volumes,—then broad sheets of flame licking the shingle roof and pillars, and *sucked* in under the eaves like a sheet of blazing fluid. Davis' sketch shows this very well, but he ought to have made a larger picture and taken in whole scene: smaller building this side of depot, woods all round, troops fil- ing round from destroyed track up road over hill and

past our house, and storehouses also burning near the
R.R. track, to the right. Gen. Howard joined us at this
house and sat some time talking with General and rode
on with us. Mrs. Myers also there, *Frau* of the old Jew,
and much more sense. She took the loss of cotton much
more quietly and tried to stop his ceaseless talk and
protestations. "It's no use to talk—'tis brennin' now."
As usual the soldiers had carried off all provisions and
they said had also entered the house and stolen clothes,
knives and forks, etc.—besides gutting a little frame
store in front of the house, which constituted (with the
hotel) the business portion of the "late town of Millen." There is but one comment on these things; no
need to repeat it. I cannot think there is any sufficient
excuse. Admit (as we must) the difficulty of preventing
all lawlessness in a large army,—especially that of
negroes and camp followers, who *cannot* always be
reached,—yet I am sure that a Headquarters Provost
Marshal, if necessary, with a rigid system of roll-calls
in every company required at any halt—severe punishment inflicted not only on men who straggle but also on
officers who *fail to prevent it,*—and the absolute prohibition and summary punishment even of legitimate foraging except by regular details,—would go far to prevent these outrages. The general orders contemplate
and call for this,—but they are *not enforced,*—at least
not as I think they should and might be. *Per contra* it is
true that real efforts have been and are made by both
Division and regimental Commanders to do this very
thing,—Howard has issued very severe orders against
pillaging, denouncing the punishment of it by death,
and has now several men on trial for it who if convicted
will be shot. Also, it is in fact next to impossible—
obviously so—to catch, or when caught to identify or
convict, the guilty parties. The mischief is *not* done under the eye of officers, and five or ten minutes is long
enough to do irreparable harm.

Left Millen by 12:30 or 1 P.M., satisfied that for the

DESTRUCTION OF MILLEN JUNCTION, GEORGIA, December 3, 1864.

FROM HARPER'S WEEKLY, JANUARY 7, 1865

present anyhow its value as a *R.R. centre* and depot
for provisions is greatly diminished, to say the least.
This is (or rather was) the third place (the fourth) in
this campaign where the rebs were going to fight us—
first Milledgeville,—then the Oconee at Oconee Bridge
(below Milledgeville)—then the Ogeechee,—then Millen. Each time they were *flanked*—and had to "git up
and dust." There was a Y or triangle of R.R. tracks at
Millen, the roads from Savannah, Augusta and Atlanta
(and Macon) all forming junction here. This Georgia
Central R.R. was the best, and the best managed R.R.
in the South, and was the main and vital R.R. connection for Richmond with the fertile districts of Georgia
and Alabama and Mississippi. Its destruction alone is
a terrible blow to J.D. & Co., to say nothing of the
moral effect at home and abroad of such a march as
this through the heart of the "Empire State of the
South." We shall have torn up and destroyed over 100
miles of it, burning long and costly bridges, depot
buildings, new ties and material,—damaging immense
amounts of R.R. iron, and (thanks to Capt. Poe) *completely* destroying many miles of rails which nothing
short of re-rolling can make it possible to use again.
While at Millen General sent courier to XX and received answer from H.W.S. [Gen. Slocum] that all
goes well. Those two columns are moving round N.E.
and outside of us,—we with F.P.B.'s [Blair's] XVII
keeping near and destroying R.R. and they (on two
roads) J.C.D.'s [Davis'] XIV being *outside* with Kilpatrick, to swing round and cover the rest of the peninsula between Ogeechee and Savannah R.R.; while
Howard's right column, XV, goes down W. side of
Ogeechee as far as 2befCbel* to cross and *flank* when
needed. The General's opinion is that the right place
for them to fortify and fight, and when they will probably do it, is at the neck or narrowest part of the peninsula, with "Ogeechee Church" as their westernmost

* Cipher.

point. There we must cross a creek and there they have
the shortest line to hold from river to river. Perhaps
we shall fight them then—*perhaps not.* I think *"not
much."*

Train went ahead and stopped for camp at or near
"Paramore's (Qu: Paramour's?) Hill," but General
came up and day being fine his and Blair's Headquarters came on to this place, though tents had been already pitched at former. At first camp made (Blair's)
saw first wounded man—negro, who went ahead with
party of stragglers to show them house to "forage."
Met fifteen rebs there, our men skedaddled—negro was
shot in back under right shoulder; our men soon ral-
lied, went back, rescued darkey and drove rebs off.
Poor fellow walked into the camp, doctors examined
wound, probably not bad; but that's all I know or probably shall. On the road today passed a squad digging
hole in the ground near road. "Somebody died" was
the brief reply to my question. In the army men "get
used to this."

Camped in front of good dwelling tonight—deserted,
empty. Large pile of R.R. bars near track—suppose
they were destroyed—men at work on railroad. This
evening man came to see General—R.R. Supt. of wood
and water, native here, plain, frank, sensible man.
Same story, house stripped, family left without bread.
General invited him to supper. Confirms stories of utter despotism here—says C.S.A. "gone up," wants to
emigrate, etc. General talked kindly, etc.

> CAMP N.E. OF GEORGIA CENTRAL R.R.
> 1 MILE FROM STATION 5½ AND
> 1 MILE S. OF "PARIS ACADEMY"

Nineteenth day out   Sunday, December 4/64

Left camp 7½ A.M., marched about sixteen miles to
this place, which is on the road running nearest to and
parallel with the Central R.R., and is situate as above,
—just *above* intersection of road leading (N.) to

"Paris Academy," and about six miles above "Halcy-ondale." Roads good generally except some heavy sand, and now and then wet swampy spots, but nothing bad. Trains move very well, animals all in good and most in splendid condition. Abundance of forage—chiefly fodder—hardly ever twenty minutes together out of sight of cornfields, though land is sandy and unpromising. No cotton today, as usual. That monarch is evidently an exile for the present from where he once reigned. Last evening it was cloudy and promised rain, —and there was a light rain during the night; but this morning just after sunrise the clouds melted away before delightful cool N.W. wind—sign of fine weather— and the weather today again has been *perfect;* clear sky, beautiful sunshine, air "neither cool nor warm"— kept my cape strapped on saddle. Certainly one is inclined to think with "old Johnny Wells" at Burton Station, "The Lord must be on the side of the Yankees, he sends them such weather." Our march today was really one half longer than General intended, or than exactly suits his combinations (as I see tonight by putting this and that, etc.), but Blair, instead of halting at Station 6, pushed on to this point, opposite to and one mile W. of Station 5½. I note again that General is very considerate about expressing disapprobation. He don't scold when things don't suit him (though in case of wilful disobedience his anger is fierce) but makes the best of it, simply saying something that a man whose ears are open can understand if he chooses. However, I don't mean that Blair disobeyed orders, or is *to blame;* he had no distinct orders about it.

Lt. Col. Ewing had a disagreeable mishap today, thanks to his own imprudence in carrying a *scalpel* in his (side skirt) coat pocket. Mounting his horse, his skirt doubled under right thigh, handle of scalpel striking saddle, and, bringing down his leg, the point and blade were driven into inner side of his thigh to the bone; one half inch higher, Dr. M. says, would have cut the femoral artery and bled him to death. As it is, he has painful cut and cannot ride his horse tomorrow.

Thanks to "Button's" nonsense, I came near getting hurt today. Riding in narrow road through woods behind a wagon in supply train, my horse scared at a bloody hind quarter of fresh pork hanging behind wagon,—begun to jump, etc., and while I was urging him to pass it, suddenly shied, jumping obliquely up a low bank on the left and dashed forward under and through overhanging branches of small tree on top of bank, festooned with vines. Said branches and vine struck me in the face, eyes, and body, knocked off my cap, and tangled me up "muchly" in about 1¾ seconds, also knocked off my eye glasses and knocked *out* one of them (luckily not one of the eyes). But I kept my seat and reins, and the vine also getting tangled in Button's hind legs he stopped eight or ten feet further on. I had to get off and *cut* away the vines to free him. By the time B. stopped an orderly was on hand who helped, and Aleck also rode up and restrapped blanket which had been almost pulled out of straps on cantle; also Capt. Bachtel.* Luckily I picked up the glass unbroken and have replaced it, and escaped with only a slight contusion of the lip. I have so far escaped all trouble in the riding line, though Button is a little gay and requires watching. He is an excellent and handy horse, and has borne this march—already over 200 miles— admirably. His flanks are a little thinner than at Kingston, but otherwise he is all right. We quarrel a little now and then when he says "trot" and I say "walk," and he is very discontented when I make him go elsewhere than at the head of our little (staff) column,— but the curb rarely fails to quiet or at least conquer him. His pet aversion is fresh or bloody meat, at which he always scares. I confess also to some anxiety about his behavior under fire, for he sometimes jumps at the sound of a gun, even of a musket at a distance, and as

* Capt. Samuel Bachtel, Signal Corps.

he is very hard-mouthed he may give me trouble when it is least convenient. But I reckon I'm master, after all.

Aleck does very well indeed,—losing the blue blanket always excepted. I believe him perfectly honest and well meaning, and am satisfied he is *very* anxious to please me, and he has shown a degree of careful attention and thought I hardly expected. I have rarely had to repeat any direction, and divers little thoughtful things he has done without orders. Nichols rather brags on "Sam," his Milledgeville acquisition, but I think Aleck the better. I was amused at A.'s delighted surprise at the rubber pillow, which I produced three days ago and find a good thing for use.

We stopped for lunch today in a *rice-field* by the road,—the rice all cut, only stubble above ground; the first we have (or I have) seen. General took his noon nap on the ground at foot of pine tree—we sat and lay round, ate lunch and talked.

It is a real effort to keep the run of the days either of the month or the week. For two days I have not kept up this diary (having written the preceding ten pages "nunc pro tunc" tonight)—Friday evening because I sat till late at camp fire, last evening because tired by standing and walking round at Millen, even more than by a long ride; so that today I did not know it was Sunday till towards noon I thought of it. Certainly the army is a bad school for religion, and its dangers, etc., rather harden men than solemnize their thoughts. Take human nature as it is, and this is not at all strange,— sad as it is. For that matter, whether in the army or out of it, *not* the fear of death but the love of God is what makes men Christians.—I would give a great deal if I knew how to stop the profanity I have to hear all the time, as well as some other things. I am much disappointed that Howard is not with this column—but his place is of course with the other, and I have barely seen him when he has come once or twice to advise with the General.

E. and N. had a regular quarrel two days ago. I didn't see it and don't know nor want to know the details. I understand both well enough to know all I want. I have been fortunate enough to make good friends, I believe, of *all* the staff,—at least it seems so from the tone and manner of all—and that by simply avoiding any sort of affectation or "airs," treating all with respect and courtesy, and always receiving the same. I find human nature much the same everywhere, and that petty self-ishness is at the bottom of most disputes among all sorts of men. Here Capt. A. don't speak to Capt. D.— Capt. W. dislikes Capt. D., and has quarreled with him and with Col. E.—and so it goes—though on the whole the unavoidable intercourse of our positions and the presence of the General obliges these boyish "spats" to be kept out of sight. I saw at once, even at Kingston, 1st, that I could easily have trouble with some of my associates if I chose,—2nd, that by the exercise of a little common sense, self-respect, and good temper, I could avoid it—and so far have not had any shadow of it with any of them.

Our camp is again—to my delight—in a pine grove, on ground covered with "pine straw" and some "wire grass." We are just off the road, on the left,—tents pitched as usual in one line, fronting road. We have come today over somewhat undulating country —growth chiefly pine, but also oak and other trees. By the way we passed in a field some fine large mulberry trees, from whose boughs to my surprise hung Spanish moss. General says it is found on all kinds of trees in low and swampy districts. Forgot to say that I brought two *souvenirs* from Millen : a piece of the triple twisted telegraph wire, say eighteen inches long, which I twisted off when our men cut down the poles there, and a little Spanish moss plucked by Capt. Bachtel from a live oak tree overhanging the road just out of Millen as we rode away.

Just here the land lies nearly level, and the camp scene tonight is quite pretty though without any bold features. Three or four fires blazing in front of our tents, the chief a big old pine stump about seven feet high, burning like an altar on top, and round it sat the General with Blair (whose Headquarters are near), on camp chairs, with say a dozen staff officers sitting and lying around it and them. In rear of our tents glow and flicker our mess fires, around which lie and sit the servants; and beyond them thro' the trees can just be seen the horses picketed. Some distance in rear on the right (facing thither) the otherwise deep shade of the pine grove is lit up by the camp fires of our escort,—off to the left, still farther, on a little ridge of open land, the more numerous camp fires of one division of XVII— while directly across the road in front of our tents, sparkle drops of flame scattered all over the large open fields they occupy, across which stand out the dark moving figures of men and horses. Presently up the road come shouting, laughing, singing—as if they were just beginning a holiday—the troops who have been all day hard at work tearing up and destroying the railroad. They file off into their camps, and then the music of a fine band begins to swell upon the air, just far enough off to lose all harshness. They are playing sacred airs—good old hymn tunes—and the first one they play is

—the words to which are;

"Thus far the Lord hath led me on:"

I do not know how they came to select this, perhaps by accident; but it touched me very deeply. God help me to remember that He has indeed thus far led us on,

and that if we go safely through this land, once of
brothers, now of foes, it is of His mercy and not—
Heaven knows—of our desert.

While we thus sat (or *lay*) round the fire, Col. Kirby*
returned from his cavalry reconnoissance down the
road to "4½," some ten miles ahead,—the point where
General has been expecting opposition. He found the
enemy there,—believes from 2000 to 5000, can't say exactly; they have burned the R.R. bridge, but left the
dirt road bridge across the creek standing—are felling
trees and fortifying. He had some skirmishing with
them—was just in time to rescue a body of sixty or
eighty men from XV who had gone ahead under Col.
—— without orders and were fairly surrounded:—lost
one man killed, two mortally wounded, and had a shoulder strap (himself) cut by a ball.

This is as expected. Tomorrow we (with XVII) are
to move to Station 5,—say five miles farther. Blair will
throw forward skirmishers to *feel* and occupy them,
but not make serious attack. *Meanwhile*—plans all laid
for this state of things, to be now rapidly developed
and in fact always being executed. General will not butt
this army against breastworks—"flanking" is better.
Heard from Slocum tonight—XX O.K.—Camps tonight on creek, six miles nearer due N. of "No. 6":
orders sent him to suit this news. If things go right the
rebs will "git up and dust" *again*.

It is past 2 A.M.—but my diary is brought up to date.

"OGEECHEE CHURCH" OR
STATION 4½ GEORGIA CENTRAL R.R.

Twentieth day out   Monday December 5/64.

Left camp between 7 and 8 A.M., troops already in
motion, we riding along slowly. Blair and staff go on
to front to see about enemy and their promised opposition at "4½." Soon after 9 A.M. came to house of Mr.

---

* Dennis T. Kirby, of Gen. Blair's staff.

Morton (or Martin?) on main road, opposite to and E.
of "Station 5," and about five miles from camp of last
night. Just before reaching this place, saw large blaze
and smoke on our right, near road, and found it was a
very good dwelling house burning. Felt very indignant
and grieved, but no use to make comments. But after
reaching Morton's found that said dwelling house belonged to one Mr. Stubbs,—that the said Mr. Stubbs
has regularly kept a pack (five or six) of "trackhounds" and made it a business to hunt negroes with
them, and also to hunt escaped Union prisoners with
them; and he has a reputation of having, by means of
these dogs, prevented the escape of a large number of
our men who got away on one occasion from a R.R.
train, got into the swamps, and were hunted down and
caught. Found further that he was well known by name
and reputation to our troops, who have been inquiring
for him and his house as we came along for two days
past. There is now with us a Colonel who was once
prisoner in Southern Georgia—escaped (last summer)
and got within forty miles of our lines at Atlanta, when
he was caught *by dogs* and taken back to prison; and
this man has sworn that no dog (hound) shall be left
alive on the road he marches on. The troops (strange to
say) sympathize with this man and his feelings, and I
have repeatedly seen dead dogs (just shot) lying by
the roadside and in yards. At one place I am told they
killed five or six full grown dogs and as many more
pups, and to the woman interceding for the latter as
harmless they replied that the pups would soon be dogs
if not killed. Hence Mr. Stubbs' house was burned—by
whom, nobody knows exactly. I have satisfied myself
that he did keep such dogs for the purpose in question
and used them, and I find it difficult to feel any further
sympathy or indignation about it. I can't say it is
"right on general principles"—*but* it "served *him*
right," the scoundrel! Mrs. Morton and one or two
other ladies were at home, all middle-aged or old;

looked sour enough, said little. House very good one,
two-story double frame, with front porch; good out-
buildings, quite a handsome garden in front, plenty of
forage. We stopped here two hours or more to hear
from front at "4½." Wagons coming up were drawn
off, most of first division halted,—some troops sent
down road in addition to skirmishers already gone forward. Sat waiting for what might turn up. General and
staff on piazza talking,—General sometimes looking at
map, and awaiting for news from Blair. Guard was
placed at house and soldiers kept out, but the provisions suffered as usual. Saw bull-dog which had seized
pig by back of neck,—men tried vainly for half hour
to get him off, but neither blows, nor sand in eyes, nor
anything succeeded till water dashed over his head.
Found to my disgust that curb rein of my bridle was
nearly worn out,—already nearly broke in two, close
to bit; not very pleasant when expecting "forward" at
any moment and *possibly* to go near if not under fire
with a hard-mouthed horse who is pretty sure to run
off. No help for it just now though—take the chances.

At last came "Forward!" Troops already have begun to move on, as 2d Division came up from rear to this
point. General and Staff rode on slowly, this about
10:30 to 11 A.M. The main ("old Savannah") road,
on which we were, passes in front and S. of the Morton
house, from which a side road leads off to right about
one mile to Depot or Station "5." The main road here
lies on N. side of R.R. track, having crossed it at or
near "No. 7" and thence run[s] down nearly parallel
to and from half mile to two miles distant,—about one
mile distant at the Morton place, which seems to be the
same designated on the map (our map) as "Halcyon-
dale." Some four miles below this the R.R. road is
crossed by (or crosses) a creek not named on map but
hereabouts called "Little Ogeechee." The main road
crosses R.R. track before reaching this creek, and
afterwards crosses the creek between the railroad and

Ogeechee River and just above a church known as "Ogeechee Church," which gives its name also to the R.R. Station "No. 4½." The rebs *had* determined to stand at Ogeechee Church; had destroyed the R.R. bridge, and had removed some of the planks of the bridge across the creek on the main road, but otherwise left it standing. Going down towards the creek from "No. 5," or Morton's, we passed through a beautiful grove of fine, old live oaks, very large fine trees and very tall, the branches beginning very high up for live oaks. Farther we passed a good looking residence, probably "Armenia" of map, in front of which a beautiful grove of "water oaks," very fine young trees, say twelve to eighteen inches in diameter planted with regularity in rows. Farther on, say ½ mile or ¾ before reaching creek, General was met by officer who reported that *our skirmishers* had taken the rebel fortifications without resistance and found the works there but the birds flown. Stopped in road and took lunch. On one side of road where we stopped (right) was dense woods, full of thickets and underbrush; along the other just there an open field, beyond which also thick woods. General dictated on spot a dispatch to Slocum, recalling previous order to swing his column round by the left and turn this position, and telling him to march forward on Springfield R., and bring up Davis on Savannah Railroad and let us know as soon as practicable how soon left wing can be ready to "march on Savannah."—N.B. It does not follow that Savannah is our "objective point" even from this.

While we were at this point the battery we had passed on road came up and passed us. General said to me, "This is better than having to fight those fellows in these bushes, ain't it?" Going on again we came to the bridge, which was not passable but easily forded the creek, say fifty yards wide, including water on road on E. side—creek proper not very wide but quite a stream. Forded also by the guns. On E. side of creek

found rebs had thrown up earth works on either side of
the road a short distance from the bridge, from which
they could have poured an ugly fire right on the road
and bridge. The works were simply a line of earth and
rails, say three to four feet high, ditch in rear running
some distance from road on either side. Don't think
they had thrown works *across* the road—if they had,
the pioneers had levelled them. They had felled some
trees in the road, already removed. We rode on to
"Ogeechee Church," large plain frame church in grove
of oaks—fine grove for camp and where at first General
ordered camp made, but presently learning of good
house nearby we went there. Found that the house was
a Mr. Loughborough's—a former New Jersey man;
very nice place, house well built and comfortable—high
brick basement, one and a half stories (frame) above
that,—large grounds in front of house, through which
is avenue between two rows of "water-oaks" (a variety of or much resembling the live oak, an evergreen
and handsome tree) some 300 feet or more to front
door. These grounds are planted with thrifty young
fruit trees. Numerous and very good out-buildings, and
sundry log cabins for negroes, of which a number
(women and old men, of course) remained. In one
building found large quantity of *rice,* threshed but not
yet cleaned—several piles and stacks of rice-straw in
yard; also a building (one story, frame) with steam engine and machinery for hulling the rice—engine not
very fine one,—boiler in shed adjoining.

Evidently L. was man of wealth. Inside house everything in dire confusion—bureau drawers pulled out,
furniture upset, books piled and tossed about, house
evidently "ramsacked" as Aleck calls it. Glad to learn
from L.'s servants—all I asked telling the same story—
that *the rebels* did this. L., it seems, left here yesterday (Sunday) after dinner; the main body of rebs
staid, camped in his fields, till daylight this morning—
then left, but their pickets remained, some few at work

near creek, others at the house,—and *these* did the mischief at the house.

It seems our skirmishers came down to the creek and pitched in with a cheer and a volley,—*three shots* fired in return, and the rebs all left, whereupon our fellows walked in and took possession, "nobody hurt." Either one of two reasons is sufficient for this their fifth failure to make a stand; either they had learned that Howard was below them on the W. side of Ogeechee, or they heard that we were advancing on them in three columns down the Peninsula between the River. If they had staid there *we* (XVII) should have amused them for a while, and either Slocum would have gone round them with XX on their right, or Howard would have come up from below—or sent up men enough—to capture them; probably *both*. They *had* to leave. As we came up to L.'s house General turned to me with a smile and said, "Now you undersand what a *flank movement* means." No man in the army is bolder or more rapid and daring than Sherman, whether personally or as a General; but no man is more unwilling to *throw* away his men. I have repeatedly heard him say that the best way, he thought, to win battles was more by the movement of troops than by fighting. On this campaign in particular he has expressed his determination not to damage this army—"it is too valuable." His men all understand this thing in him, and hence their unbounded confidence in him.

We reached this house by noon, and halted and made camp. Tents are pitched along and fronting on the avenue leading from the house. Our mess uses the front parlor for dining room, and Manuel cooks in the kitchen, otherwise we don't use the house. But we decidedly use all the provisions we find, and all forage; and Nichols tonight unearthed in the garden a barrel of sugar, another of molasses, and a quantity of lard, butter, preserves, etc.—all very acceptable. The R.R. runs along directly in front of this house, by the front gate, not ten yards from it, but from the R.R. the house it not visible, though fronting on it, being hid by the avenue of trees. Went with Dr. M. and saw the works thrown up in rear of house—ditches, embankments, trees felled, etc., etc.—a double line, quite a long one, and *would have been troublesome.* These works much better than those near creek but 'twas "hate's labor lost." Flanking is good—very.

LOUGHBOROUGH'S HOUSE—NEAR
"OGEECHEE CHURCH"—"STATION 4½"

Twenty-first day out   Tuesday, December 6/64

Staid here all day today, where we camped last night. Waiting now to bring up, concentrate and arrange all the columns for forward movement. General remarked to me tonight, "I have been dividing my army so long as I knew there could be no serious opposition to either column—now that they must make whatever opposition they can, I concentrate; tomorrow all my columns will be within sound of cannon and in supporting distance."

By dispatches of today we learn that XX's advance is now a little ahead of ours, on the Springfield road and will camp tonight seven miles this side of Springfield; Davis XIV advance was at Buck's P.O. last night and will be tonight at Sister's Ferry on Savannah River, *abreast* of us; ours, XVII, is at Ogeechee Church,—and Howard's, XV, w. of Ogeechee River, is at Branham's Store. Howard has all facilities for crossing the river if necessary, and there is nothing between him and us to interfere, nor can be. Tomorrow we move again "on Savannah." Howard sent five parties down to cut Southern and Gulf R.R. last night. General told me this evening they had returned, finding road too strongly guarded. "They'll let go that road," said he, "when we get to Eden. They guard it because their prisoners are down that road, but they must let go that to concentrate. And so they are in another of the dilemmas of war—if they concentrate for opposition they must give up important points, as they have had to do all along.''

I begin now to understand as never before what a science war is in the hands of a master, and what "strategy" means. We have had an easy march, practically without opposition, *because* our movements have been so directed as to utterly confound the enemy, and to *circumvent* him—literally. They have done exactly right in five times abandoning their purpose to stand and fight,—because each time our position gave us great advantage. The cannonading we heard Sunday forenoon to the South, and which General said then was Kilpatrick, was explained by dispatch from K. received this morning.—He was at Alexander (five or seven miles S.E. of Waynesboro) yesterday A.M. and wrote thence. On Sunday (4th) at 7½ A.M. he *attacked* Wheeler at or near Thomas Station on R.R. (four miles S. of Waynesboro); W. had five pieces artillery and 6000 men, so prisoners said, and had put up a barricade. K. reports that he drove in picket and skirmish line and "rode over his barricades" in thirty minutes —found W's line too long to flank, and so charged on and broke his centre—drove him back in confusion to and beyond Waynesboro and across Brier Creek, four miles north of it,—*again* burned R.R. bridge over Brier Creek "which was imperfectly burned before and was nearly repaired," and which the Colonel of 5th Ohio Cavalry reports was 500 feet long; also burned divers other bridges over Brier Creek above and below R.R., and then not wishing to be too far from main body fell back to Alexander. His (K's) loss in all was about 200 killed and wounded. Thinks W. lost over 500 including considerable number of officers. Says his command somewhat jaded and wants fresh horses from captured stock. General has also heard from Davis, XIV, whose column is outer and rear one, next Savannah River— he has met *no impediment;* Slocum ditto. General has

sent word to S. not to go too fast, nor beyond Springfield tomorrow.

I remember the absolute confidence with which *at
Kingston* General told us we would meet no serious opposition till we got to seaboard or near it, if at all. I
doubted this—did not think it possible—but so it is.
"He was born on Kenesaw."

Barnard, the Photographer, joined us today, and
showed quite a number of photographic views of Atlanta, etc., etc.*—all beautifully taken, also same for
stereoscope. He has "negatives" and *when we stop*
will print copies.

Barnard went, while we were at Millen the other day,
to the *stockade pen* where our men (prisoners) were
kept. It was simply a *pen,* surrounded or made by
stockades—high posts driven into the ground close to
each other,—about 300 yards square; no shelter of any
kind, no shed, nor tent, nor roof whatever, in any
weather. He went into and all over it and examined
closely. Would have photographed it but did not know
of it in time enough. It was about five miles up railroad
from Millen—not at the Junction. There was no spring
nor well nor any water inside the enclosure. He saw
750 graves,—no head board nor other designation save
that each fiftieth grave was so numbered. He heard that
five or six dead bodies of our men were left there *unburied* when they removed the prisoners,—and *he saw
one still lying there, unburied, himself.* He said, after
telling about the place, (at dinner this evening)—"I
used to be very much troubled about the burning of
houses, etc., but after what I have seen I shall not be
much troubled about it." If B. feels so from *seeing* the
prison pen, how do those feel who have suffered in it!
The burned houses, in spite of orders, are the answer.
By the way, the rebel papers republish with great

---

* G. N. Barnard's *Photographic Views of Sherman's Campaigns,* issued soon after the war, preserves these pictures in a folio volume of
remarkable interest.

gusto a long letter from the *National Intelligencer* telling horrible things about the sufferings of the rebel prisoners whom the writer—a woman—saw at the *R.R. depot* at Elmira, N. Y.—their unclothed condition, half-starved or worse, dying off from bad treatment, etc., etc. She does not explain how she got her information. I know that in September last I had a long talk with Dr. Alexander,* Surgeon U.S.A., then on an official tour of inspection of all our military prison depots, and having then recently inspected all but two, and including *all* the important ones, and unless he wilfully lied to me this letter is a tissue of falsehoods. It is rather hard to meet these lies down here copied from our own papers, especially when one has such positive and unimpeachable evidence as Dr. A.'s full statement to me, just after he had made a thorough inspection, officially, under orders which I read, for the very purpose of detecting and preventing any such abuses. A confirmation of his statement was unintentionally given by the announcement I saw recently in a Savannah paper of the receipt there (to fight *us,* by the way!) of 3600 of their men exchanged—"all in good health and condition!" Brilliant thing, that exchange, just *now* and *there!*

Improved this leisure by having Capt. Bachtel's harness-maker make new curb-rein for my bridle, also a pair of martingales; have been using martingales very kindly offered and lent me by Capt. Dayton. What a nuisance it was not to get an article of all my horse equipments! Hope they were not lost. Also had Aleck grease and clean bridle, saddle, etc., etc.—and had all soiled clothes on hand washed and ironed by old ladies of color here. One learns to make the most of such opportunities. Old Mrs. Loughborough returned this P.M. to her mansion, from neighbor's house two miles off whither she had fled Sunday, went to the garden and had dug up a tin box which the darkies say contained "Valuable Papers" and money. I heard of her and saw

* Richard Henry Alexander.

her dress as she passed down the avenue in front of our tent as she left. Don't think she saw or ever asked for the General; nobody interfered with her.

Asked one of the colored women here—twenty-five or thirty, quick and smart, regular Southern Georgia *twang* in her talk,—if anybody near here used to keep dogs. "Yes, Sah, Mr. Stubbs, he kep' dogs." "What did he do with them?" "Catch nigga, Sah, and catch de soldiers dat run away." "What soldiers?" "De soldiers dat they taken prisoners from *oouah*, Sah." "Well, our men burned Mr. Stubbs' house yesterday *for* that." This "oouah" for "you" is new to me— these women all say it, I find.

CAMP OPPOSITE AND TWO MILES
WEST OF "STATION NO. 3" GA. CENTRAL R.RD.

Twenty-second day out   Wednesday, December 7/64

Marched today about fourteen miles (Poe says twelve) from Ogeechee Church, down the road (see map) between R.R. and Ogeechee River. Camp tonight is in pine grove on right of road, just above—say ¼ mile N. of—cross road leading E. to "Guyton" or "Station 3" on R.R. Left Loughborough's house (Ogeechee Church) about 7 A.M., marched steadily till 12 : 30 P.M., through steady rain almost whole time till 11 A.M.—stopped for lunch at house of Mr. Elkins, opposite "Station 4" ("Egypt")—resumed march at 2 P.M., stopped and made camp about 3 : 30 P.M. No opposition to this column today, nor obstacle save that at three places found trees cut down across road in swampy places, which pioneers and 1st Michigan Engineers quickly removed—the two first causing no delay whatever, troops going round, and the trees out of road by the time trains reached there; the third delayed us about thirty minutes.

Yesterday ended the third week of this campaign, during all which time we had but one rainy and two disagreeable days. Last night it rained steadily almost all night (no wind) pattering on the "fly" of your wall tent. Fortunately we are in the *sand country*, where rain has the least effect on the roads. The early part of today's ride was anything but pleasant to me, either a little cold taken last night or something eaten yesterday had quite seriously indisposed me, and I rode along through the rain, now drizzling, now pouring, with a dull headache and tendency to nausea which "Button's" obstinate efforts to trot made worse. But by noon I was much better and tonight am pretty well again. Soon after we started passed a burial party carrying some poor fellow's remains to be interred by the roadside. Perhaps by some once happy fireside his place is now empty forever, and loving eyes will look vainly for his return. Only one more of how many!

I find Mrs. Loughborough did ask for the General yesterday, but Dayton saved him the trouble of telling her that her son was and must remain a prisoner of war. He was one of the militia, I believe,—was taken down in the swamp the day we came here. She asked if she could dig up and take away a box containing papers, etc.—D. said certainly—she did so and left.

About noon today the clouds began to break and this P.M. it was clear—has been clear all day. Tonight, after dark, it suddenly rained quite hard again for a while, and now (9 P.M.) is clear moonlight again. I write in my tent, sitting on the ground, book on campstool, candle on my valise. Nichols is asleep on his mattress (of corn blades covered with blankets).

T. R. Davis ("our own artist on the spot") is finishing his sketches of Madison, Ga., for *Harper's Weekly*, sitting on t'other side of the valise, by the same candle; and we hear the General's voice in his tent reading to Frank Blair his letter to Grant from Kingston, written just before we left there.* Blair's

---

* See Sherman's *Memoirs* (II, 165). The letter, dated Nov. 2, ended with the words, "I am clearly of opinion that the best results will follow my contemplated movement through Georgia."

Headquarters are say 200 yards off in same "neck of
woods." Since we came here has come a messenger
from Slocum, XX, saying that he is at Springfield,
abreast of us, in the middle of the peninsula between
the two rivers. On the road this P.M. came word from
Howard that he would be at (opposite) "Eden" or
"Station 2" on the R.R. today, some ten miles further
down on the W. side of Ogeechee, and would lay his
pontoons and cross there. But the messenger states
that while coming up here he heard cannonading in the
direction of "Station No. 2"—he having crossed the
Ogeechee at Wright's Bridge, higher up. Where Davis
is tonight I haven't heard, but presume he is coming
along all right or I should.

Tomorrow it is expected there will be fighting in our
front,—whether more likely with Slocum's advance or
with Blair's—with whom we are—I am not sure, but
believe the latter. The rebs are reported fortifying in
earnest at some point below "No. 2," and doubtless
will try—or have tried—to keep Howard from crossing. *Nous verrons.*

A rebel paper (Savannah) of 5th inst. contains telegram copied from N.Y. papers that Hood made fierce
attack on Franklin, Tenn., with two corps,—was completely repulsed, lost 6000 killed and wounded and 1000
prisoners,—our loss 500. If anything like this is true
Hood is "gone up." Same paper contains, I am told—
didn't see it—a letter from Milledgeville stating that
while there we gave a grand ball, at which only negro
and mulatto women present—all the white women "of
whatever condition" indignantly refusing to attend.
What do these wretches expect to gain by printing
these dirty lies?

Mrs. Elkins, at whose house we lunched today, was a
regular Georgia woman. Came to gate in great fright,
trying, poor woman, to hide it,—invited General (who
had already dismounted) to come in, and all his officers,
etc. It was quite laughable had her panic not been so

real. Before long she was re-assured. General sent
Audenried with her to smoke house and rescued her
clothes, etc., which she had buried there but which soldiers were rapidly exhuming,—also saved her a quantity of provisions, etc. She "rubs snuff"—"taking
snuff" she says they call it here, and lamented depriva-
tion of good snuff since war—eyes sparkled when Merritt* offered her some—"if she could get good snuff
wouldn't begrudge hardly anything else." Beckwith
adroitly drew from her that her children *eat clay*—
"can't keep 'em from it when they gits old enough to
run about." She knew our friend Stubbs, whose house
was burned on Monday as above noted, and confirmed
the account of his keeping dogs and hunting niggers
with them. She spoke of hunting negroes with dogs as
a customary thing, hereabouts, and said with naïve un-
concern,—"They don't worry 'em much." She was a
woman of thirty-five or so,—sallow, thin featured, but
tolerably good face, ignorant, but apparently a very
honest sort of woman. Says some soldiers came to
house this morning and took her husband off to guide
them to Mr. Moore's house; he had not yet returned
and she was very much alarmed at first lest he had been
shot, till re-assured by General and all of us. She tells
same story about all the men being *forced* to go into
the army who can serve—her husband is old, or disabled, or something,—says they were told before we
came that we had been killing everybody and *burning
every house.* This whole people seem to live on lies. She
has heard that they talk of fighting us below here at
"No. 2" but believes "and hopes" that we shall enter
Savannah without a gun being fired,—and was very
anxious to know of General when he would open the
port and permit trade.

Road today all sandy except where creeks and
swamps cross it,—then muddy and treacherous. There
is a sort of *crust* to the soil, a few inches deep, which

* Capt. Nehemiah Merritt.

bears a moderate weight, but when that is broken through the mud below is very bad and deep. One or two bad places delayed part of corps trains much and had to be "corduroyed." General passed one team stuck fast—sent N. with order to destroy it and move on, but finally 'twas saved. N. said mules go down in mud till it came up *over their backs*. Men in camp across road now shouting, "no bottom!"

CAMP AT X ROADS OPPOSITE TO AND
TWO MILES EAST OF "STATION NO. 2" GA. CENT.

Twenty-third day out   Thursday December 8/64

Left camp about 7 this morning—marched about twelve miles to this place. Camp on roadside opposite church (or school house) across road in pine grove, where are Blair's Headquarters. Weather very fine all day, and beautiful moonlight tonight—lucky 'twas so. Roads today heavy sand and both yesterday and today very bad at swampy places and creek crossings—same thing in fact, for all the creeks seem to spread into swamps. Peculiarity of this soil that it has a sort of upper crust or layer, from four or five to twelve inches thick, beneath which when wagons have worked and cut through it, it is very deep, bad mud, quite like quicksand. The train of one division may get along pretty well over one of these places, but those of the next may (and probably will) cut through the "crust" and go in to the wheel hubs. We have been most fortunate in weather today,—and this P.M. the wind is N.W., which is the best quarter for clear weather.

Mower's division, in rear of XVII, had a hard time yesterday and today both, at some of the swampy crossings. Concurring testimony all along the road from above "No. 4" down to this point—statements of people living along it—fixed a man named Marlow, living down here near "2½" as having been at the head of the party who made the obstructions in yesterday's and today's march—and that he gathered sev-

enty or eighty negroes to do it. His house was today
identified and burned in return for it. We crossed two
or three creeks today, one of them the "Little Ogeechee
River," all bad and swampy, and all obstructed; but
our pioneers and the 1st Michigan Engineers were
ahead and worked hard, and there was little delay.
Stopped at house of Rev. Mr. Heidt—fifty-four years
old, Methodist, very well off, barns, etc., full of all sorts
of forage *when we came.* Fluent talker, pretty shrewd,
but foolish enough to argue with General about importance of *cotton;* General "down on cotton." Dayton
found lot of *rebel cartridges hid in his hen-coop.* General said quietly, "Better look into that, Sir, it may
compromise you." He was badly scared, protested he
knew nothing about it—"Must have been done by your
soldiers." "We don't draw ours from the Macon Arsenal," said D. showing label on packages. He went off,
and came back with cock and bull story about his boy,
etc., etc. General listened, said nothing. When we
joined Blair afterwards, found that B.'s staff wanted
to burn that house, being satisfied that the old fellow
himself had burned the bridge over creek on road
nearby; his negroes declared it, but Blair was not sure
of it, forbid them, and set guard and protected the
house.

Tonight Slocum reported in person to General. His
Headquarters are abreast of us, about one mile east,
and XX well up. He says Davis with XIV, on Savannah R[iver] road has had a very hard time—roads
greatly obstructed at swamps and creeks, of which he
has had more to cross than any of us. But he has
pushed along most vigorously,—marched twenty miles
yesterday. His column has not been attacked. Kilpatrick covers rear. K. has not been attacked since fight
with Wheeler Sunday.

Howard sent General paper of 6th (Savannah).
Telegrams copied from New York papers state that
after Schofield *defeated* Hood's attack on Franklin, he

(S.) fell back to point three miles S. of Nashville, and that there was heavy skirmishing around Nashville. I agree with Howard's note to General—"the account of Schofield's victory is not satisfactory." But Poe, Mc-Coy, and others scout the idea that Nashville is in danger, and say that Thomas has purposely let Hood come so far in order to "ruin" him. Same paper publishes *in full* General Sherman's "Special Field Order No. 120" issued at Kingston giving general directions *about the expedition,* also Gen. Slocum's general order promulgating same. General very much provoked, and quite bitter on newspaper men everywhere. I don't wonder. Nobody has any idea how they got hold of this order—Slocum thinks at Atlanta. This order by the way contains express prohibition of any outrage or violence by soldiers, even in language, etc., and completely shows that Sherman at least, not only did not order but expressly forbid all such—and Slocum's order repeats same and promises severe punishment for such offences. Yet this paper also contains the most atrocious lies about us—tells about a ball we gave at Milledgeville, where all the women were *negroes,* etc., etc. Also an editorial about our men ravishing women there and that one victim had become insane—and the whole article is a most furious appeal to the people of Georgia to destroy these ravishers, etc., etc. These miserable and deluded people read and believe all these stories and the poor women are frightened nearly to death.

Gen. Howard's Headquarters today are at Eden or "Station 2"—two miles due west of us. The cannonading heard in that direction yesterday was *his* guns, driving off rebs who tried to prevent his crossing. They were there in force, but were driven away and went down the R.R. on a train which was lying seven miles below but started up *as soon as our cannon were heard,* and so they left, horse and foot. Howard then crossed without further opposition.

This evening after making camp we heard several distant reports of artillery to the S. or S.W.—though some doubted if it was artillery. Later, Gen. Howard and Col. H. came to our camp with good news. Corse with XV[4] has gone down the road S. from Eden between the Ogeechee and "Little Ogeechee," reached the *Savannah canal,* seized, bridged and crossed it without opposition, and now has his whole division there in a position which they cannot drive him from. He is at a point thirteen miles below "No. 2," and only about twelve miles W. of Savannah. The canal leads directly to the city, and the tow path along it is a first rate road for an army; as is also the plank road near it—see map. This is an important point gained,—was a surprise to the rebs who were expecting to oppose Howard's passage of the Ogeechee lower down—and we learn that they have at once abandoned a strong and well-built line of defensive works reaching from the Little Ogeechee clear across to Savannah, but which Corse has now *passed* on its west, and turned. Their mistake was in stopping it at the Little Ogeechee River, —Corse went down west of there, and between it and the Ogeechee. He did this pursuant to orders from Howard, of the 6th. Meanwhile Osterhaus has been to-day fighting a little with rebs on the W. side of Ogeechee River, who were sent there as a flanking force on S. side of Canoochee River to prevent our crossing there:—a small river which runs eastward into the Ogeechee between "Eden" and the Gulf railroad. Howard ordered Hazen's division of XV to cross Canoochee and go down to Gulf R.R. (running W. from Savannah) and cut it,—and it was this force which was fighting at Canoochee as above. Col. H. says they heard some cannon thence this morning, but it soon ceased and it is supposed our men have crossed Cannoochee and probably by this time reached Gulf R.R.— One of our men, taken prisoner some time ago, who escaped from Savannah, says they sent their prisoners (our men) from Millen to Savannah,—thence recently down the Gulf R.R.—thence back to Savannah,—and now *again down Gulf R.R.* seventy miles to Doctortown. *Possibly,* we may rescue them yet! Tomorrow or next day Davis will cut the Charleston R.R. and within two days we shall know whether Savannah will stand a siege. The distant cannon this evening Howard says were signals from our gun-boats in Ossabaw Sound. So far all goes admirably well. Rebs seem puzzled and act strangely.

CAMP AT "POOLER" OR "STATION No. 1" ON
GEORGIA CENTRAL R.R.—*9 miles from Savannah.*

Twenty-fourth day out   Friday, December 9/64

Left camp this morning at 8 A.M., though we were up before day and breakfast over by sunrise; General waited for advance of XVII to get well under way. Blair's whole corps follow the road leading direct to Savannah, N. of R.R. track, which sweeps round from Station 2, soon after passing that point, and goes direct to Savannah in E.S.E. direction—see map. "Station 2" is about nineteen miles by R.R. from Savannah. Our camp last night was abreast of Station 2, but about two miles E. of it. Our road today first ran S.S.E., some three miles, then E.S.E., swinging round like, but not so much as the R.R. and gradually nearing it. Weather much cooler last night and this morning was cloudy, with raw chilly E. wind, too cold to rain, threatening snow, and has continued raw and ugly all day. We learned today—by testing it—that the rebs had *not* "abandoned their works" in our front as supposed.

Not long after *we* started, while riding along by side of road by trains, heard cannon ahead—four shots at one or two minutes' interval. Rode on some distance— say two miles—more cannon apparently not more than 1½ miles ahead of us;—and the troops which we had overtaken in part began to cheer and push ahead in prospect of a fight. Further on as we (General and

staff) entered large field on left of road, parallel to
which we were riding, say 100 yards from it, more cannon shots ahead, quite near and loud; and for a while
my horse acted like a fool, but finally quieted down.
Rode into the field, when we saw by group of our men
in the road on our right that something was the matter. General and staff rode up to fence along road, and
we found that rebs had *buried torpedoes* in the road,
two of which had exploded, killing one horse which still
lay there, and wounding several men and among them
Lieut. Tupper, Adjt. of 1st Alabama cavalry, who was
lying on roadside a short distance back—his *right foot
torn off* just at or rather just above ankle joint, a piece
of the shell also wounding him higher up below the
knee, and another piece wounding his hand. Poor fellow
lay on the ground, covered all but his face with a blanket, only pale, but without a groan or complaint. Other
torpedoes still lay there, part of one (unexploded) just
visible, the rest still covered with sand as placed by
rebs. Just as we came up a squad of rebel prisoners
arrived under guard, whom Blair had ordered to be
made dig up the rest of the torpedoes. They were
greatly alarmed—no wonder—and two of them begged
Gen. S. very hard to be let off, but of course to no purpose. He told them their people had put these things
there to assassinate our men instead of fighting them
fair, and they must remove them; and if *they* got blown
up he didn't care. He did exactly right. These cowardly
villains call us "barbarous Yankees"—and then adopt
instruments of murder in cold blood where they dare
not stand and fight like men. Torpedoes at the entrance
to a fort are perhaps justifiable, for the fort itself is a
warning. But here they run away, refuse to defend the
road, but leave hidden in an open public road, without
warning or chance of defense, these murderous instruments of assassination—contrary to every rule of civilized warfare. We dismounted in the field and remained
there some time, General waiting for news from the

front, whence we plainly heard not only cannonading but continuous musket shots and the cheers of our skirmishers. The rebel prisoners were ordered into the road and *very carefully*—and without accident—soon uncovered seven more torpedoes—the whole nine having been buried in a line directly across the road, just under the surface, and so arranged as to explode when the friction tube was trod on even by a man's ordinary step. Four of these were simply 12 lb. shells, with a sort of nipple projecting from the fuse-hole; the other three were large copper cylinders, rounded at each end. —I measured one and found it 13 in. long x 7 in. diameter, and at one end were fitted on two brass nuts on which were screwed some sort of friction tube, arranged as above. These would hold four or five lbs. powder and explode with terrible effect. It seems one battalion of 1st Alabama cavalry passed over them *without injury*—but under the second battalion one exploded killing a horse and wounding several men. Blair's Adjt. (Hickenlooper)* then came up, and was stooping over one, scraping dirt away. Tupper joined him, did same a while, then rose, and in stepping back trod on another which burst and *tore off* his foot, etc., as above. Hickenlooper escaped unhurt. Perhaps when we take Savannah the 1st Alabama Cavalry won't make somebody suffer for this! Tupper was a fine officer and his time of service was just expired. These rebs are certainly insane; their torpedoes could at most kill a few of our advance guard—could not possibly delay or interfere with such an army,—and they *know* must inevitably exasperate our men! *Quos Deus vult perdere prius dementat*. But this is Southern "chivalry"—as their lying newspapers probably illustrate "Southern honor"! So at Yorktown, just before they abandoned their works, they put torpedoes all round inside—and so also McClellan compelled his prisoners to dig them

* Col. (later Bvt. Brig. Gen.) Andrew Hickenlooper.

up—so Capt. Poe tells who was then and there on McC's staff.

Just beyond the fields on left and right of road—in former of which we had stopped as above—began a pine forest through which the road ran, and from whence came the cannon and musketry firing we heard. General went forward on foot, presently sent back for staff, and riding 200 or 300 yards forward we came to house on left of road where General had stopped and ordered horses up. General has a way of doing this— halting and dismounting, which staff then do also, handing horse to orderly,—then quietly going ahead on foot without a word to anybody, and we not knowing it unless by watching him. The forest just mentioned— or the point where the thick woods begin again after crossing the field as stated,—is I think about eleven or twelve miles W. by N. or rather N.W. of Savannah, on the "Millen Road" which here lies (see map) on N. side of Georgia Central R.R., and soon after entering it begins one of the swamps around the city which are so important a part of its landward defences. The main road on which our troops (XVII corps) were approach- ing, is carried through this swamp on a causeway, or "pike," a sandy road some forty feet wide, level and good, and kept in good order—apparently built many years ago from size of trees on either side. One division of XVII has gone forward, and Blair and staff with them; rebs had one or two pieces of cannon planted *in the road,* say half a mile beyond the house above men- tioned; on either side of road was regular swamp, pine and cypress trees, miry and wet and sometimes water visible from road, sometimes regular marsh. The can- non we heard were all rebel shots; the musketry (and the cheers) were from our skirmishers thrown out on either side of road and pressing *through the swamp* in mud and water. While at this house saw Adjt. Tupper (who had been brought there in ambulance) lying wait- ing for amputation; came accidentally when group around him lying on table in porch and—without intending it—saw poor fellow's leg, horribly torn and mutilated, raw and bloody end of bone and torn muscles, etc., where torn off. Piece of shell had also run up leg *inside* along the bone, and came out near knee, shattering bone. Leg was soon afterwards amputated above knee—hope he'll recover but doubtful. Two or three other wounded men at same house.

Presently found General had again gone forward down the road on foot, and Dayton after him. I followed at once on foot down road, pretty muddy; about 800 yards further came to first rebel "works" where their cannon had been placed in road but whence they had retreated. "Works" were merely small earth banks running out thirty yards or less into swamp on either side of road. Found General and Dayton here, just arrived—Blair and troops gone ahead and firing of cannon and musketry say half a mile ahead. Orderly gone back for horses and staff, who soon rode up from house. We stopped here for over an hour and lunched. Good advice Kelton gave me—Never leave camp without haversack and *lunch in it*. Nichols laughed at my always carrying mine—said I would soon lay it aside, but I find it worth carrying. But this one is already worse for wear—get one *made* when I get back "to the settlements."

Finally word came back to General that rebs had left "works" ahead of us and given up contesting our passage of the swamp. "Forward!" down the road passed second "works" much better than first,—considerable earth thrown up on both sides of road off into swamp, but no use. Mower had deployed part of his division in skirmish line through swamp and rebs fell back, firing 12 pounders and some shell down road. Blair had an escape today; one 12-lb. shot came down road as he and staff rode forward with troops,—passed directly over Blair's head very little above him, and went through the body of Capt. —— (Mower's Div. 2d Maine) riding behind Blair, also killing an orderly's horse. Killed Capt. —— of course. He was out of his place, his duties were with the train in rear. I was surprised that rebs had made no more effectual defence at this swamp, for it seemed to me an ugly place to pass through; only one road not wide enough to form one company in line of battle, nearly straight, and perfectly open for cannon, and bad swamps with thick woods and brush on both sides and our men forced often to wade through deep mud. General says rebs ought to have made more of it. Our officers say our skirmishers always beat the rebs and that reb troops are inferior to ours in everything except in an *assault,* in which they often show more dash at first.

No further opposition today—firing ceased in front before we left first works. Rode forward to swamp beyond E. end of swamp and found our troops held "Pooler" or "Station 1" on R.R. The dirt road at this point is very near R.R. track—hardly 100 yards N. of it. "Pooler" is simply a small neat station house or *shed,* say fifteen or twenty feet square, by side of track. Our main line formed at this point across R.R. and dirt road, extending longways S. of R.R.—advance line parallel to it 300 or 400 yards ahead. As we came up with main line, which was formed under cover of pine woods—(the swamp ending some distance back)—with open space, field, etc., in their front N. and S., they stacked arms; and forthwith, *without orders,* the men went to work and built barricade all along their line, made of three rows of logs one above another, about four feet high in all, and in front were placed on end, sloping forward from top log, sticks of cord wood of which they found large pile ready cut and corded for R.R. use at the Station. Good defence against musketry —worthless against artillery; done from *habit.* In the beginning of the war our officers and men thought these things cowardly as also to dodge a ball or shell or get behind trees. They know better now, and think men fools and probably cowards who affect to despise these precautions—at least so officers tell me who have been three years in service and been *tested.*

Our camp is on left (N.) of dirt road say 300 yards back of main line of troops,—Blair camps opposite, on right of road. News from Howard tonight that he has pushed 2d division (Corse's) ahead down dirt road between Ogeechee River and "Little Ogeechee" and swung on round up to and on plank road S. of canal— see map. Also has cut "Gulf R.R.," in two or three places. *Two of his officers* alone captured a R.R. train with 25 passengers, among whom R. R. Cuyler, President of Georgia Central R.R. One of the officers came over to our camp and told me—pretty good joke all round, for after capturing it *our* scouts appeared, fired, and they left quick, thinking them rebs. No news from Slocum or Davis tonight, but we heard cannonading from that quarter—possibly similar defence of swamps.

CAMP ON "MILLEN (DIRT) ROAD" (OR "LOUIS-
VILLE ROAD"), ABOUT *5 1/2 miles from*
Savannah. Sat. December 10/64.

Twenty-fifth day out

Didn't march our fifteen miles today, nor ten miles either—if we had, *"Savannah serait prise."* How long will it take us to get over the *last* five of our "300 mile march"?

By special Field Order No. 130, issued this evening, the Corps Commanders are ordered to proceed to *invest* the City of Savannah. Gen. S[locum], XX, to occupy left of line, extending to Savannah River—and Army of Tennessee to occupy right, swinging round to River below city.—Gen. H[oward] also to open communications with the fleet; Capt. O. M. Poe to prepare suitable maps, etc. Thus today may be considered as ending our *march* on this campaign.

I may well thank God for the health and safety which has thus far been my own lot, as well as for the safety of this magnificent army. As these memoranda show, we have been most fortunate in weather—have had but two days of rain, one of cold (not severe) and one or two others only on which the weather was not everything we could wish. The health of the whole army, so far as I can learn, has been unusually good,—and mortality *very* small; my own health, as a general thing, has been perfect, not once unable to ride regularly with the General nor once ever really indisposed, though several times slightly so from cold taken by carelessness. We have escaped more than was thought possible the obstacles which might have been interposed; our infantry has been but once engaged—Howard's column, November 22d, at Griswoldville,—from Atlanta to the immediate vicinity of Savannah, and then *one brigade* of infantry repulsed and terribly punished the rebels. The great object of the *march,*—the destruction of 100 miles of R.R. on the vital chain of rebel communication from E. to W.—has been more than accomplished, and it is shown that a large army can march with impunity through the heart of the richest rebel state, after boldly cutting loose from all its bases, and subsisting on the country. Whether we can take Savannah or not, what is now *done,* and an accomplished fact, is of itself a great and important success, full of significance for the future.

Our supplies are yet hardly drawn on at all, our droves of beef cattle are larger—much larger—than when we left Atlanta; our teams in good condition, and those of XVII corps "traded off" till they have been replaced by very much better ones than Blair started with, which were poor. The men are in the finest spirits, ready for anything "Uncle Billy" orders.

I do not forget, and God knows I am sorry for the people of the regions we have traversed. But I have already noted day by day all that is worth while as to this. Their losses, their terrors (many of which they find and acknowledge to be groundless) their sufferings, all are implied in and inevitable with war—and for this war, not we but *their* "leaders" and their own moral and physical cowardice three years ago are responsible. This Union and its Government must be sustained, at any and every cost; to sustain it, we must war upon and destroy the organized rebel forces,—must cut off their supplies, destroy their communications, and show their white *slaves* (these people say themselves that they are so) their utter inability to resist the power of the U. S. To do this implies and requires these very sufferings, and having thus only the choice of evils—war now so terrible and successful that none can dream of rebellion hereafter, or everlasting war with all these evils magnified a hundred fold hereafter,—we have no other course to take. At least I am glad to remember that I have not only not abused nor insulted a single person, but have repeatedly stopped the depredations of soldiers, and that except the provisions of which I have had my share at the mess table— and which we have good right to take,—I have not "acquired" the value of a pin nor destroyed any private property. . . .

This morning Blair's column advanced on same road by which it has come down to "Pooler" or "Station 1" on Georgia Central R.R., which was the halting place last night. This is called the "Louisville Road" and crosses the Georgia Central R.R. track from N. side to S. side not far below "Pooler." General and Staff left camp about 8 A.M. following 1st (Mower's) division down road which is good, but still wet though not heavy. Weather cloudy, slight, misty rain sometimes, generally disagreeable. Passed eight and seven mile posts, began to hear cannon in our front about 9 A.M. General kept on by side of road to near the five mile post, and stopped at frame house on left of road nearer town than where we are camped tonight.

On the way, riding along with troops passed one house where women at door whose smiling faces didn't

look like rebels. Laughed over exclamations of one at
a soldier on mule with game-cock perched up behind
him.

At house above mentioned General and staff dismounted. The "Louisville (dirt) Road" runs in front
of house,—directly in rear and N. of the house runs
track of Georgia Central R.R.—open fields along road
—by "road" I always mean dirt road—on its left, before and after reaching house, for considerable distance; on right of road for half-mile or more W. of and
before reaching house are thick woods—but beyond
house these woods extend only 100 or 200 yards, then
open space again on right of road, with woods off to
right. General sat some time by fire in yard in front of
house,—several wounded men already brought there
from our troops in front. Our skirmishers were already
pushing ¼ mile or more beyond house across road and
R.R. After a while I found General had walked down
the road (towards City) to where our main line was
being rapidly formed say 100 or 200 yards beyond
house, on right of road. I went after him, got to where
troops were deploying from road into line, on the right
—went ¼ mile and more (on foot) along and to the end
of the line as far as then formed, into the woods—but
couldn't find him. These woods full of bushes and not
pleasant to go through, but dry and free from swamp.
Returned to the house, and found General there. After
twenty or thirty minutes saw General again quietly
start off down the road along which troops had been
steadily passing to the front and deploying on right of
road and now Leggett's division* were coming up and
deploying to left of it. Followed him at once and before
long overtook him, say 100 yards from house. Had
hardly done so when—just after report of cannon
ahead to which I had paid no attention though loud
and near, certainly not over 800 yards off,—saw him
quickly stop, look forward and upwards, and step one

* Brig. Gen. Mortimer D. Leggett's Division of the Seventeenth Corps.

side; at same moment heard loud *rush* and whizzing in air over and in front of us, very like noise of a rocket, understood *that* easily, looked for the shell (as I supposed it) but "couldn't see it"—saw, however, very decided and rapid movements of men near us in and on side of road,—concluded to "git" myself, but no shelter was near, and so, expecting the shell to strike and burst concluded to risk its striking me, but to dodge the *pieces* if possible, and thereupon went down on the sand into a gracefully recumbent posture; the next moment heard the shot strike the ground heavily somewhere near, but "didn't see it" still. Got up at once and walked forward to where General was, who by this time had crossed the road to left side. As I joined him, he said quietly—"This place is not safe, they are firing down the road—we had better go back." So we went back, walking quietly up the side of the road a few steps and then through a field on right of road to the house. As we started I asked him if he wished to know anything from the front—intending, as of course he understood, to go back if he did; but he replied that he did not, and so I *followed* him back. Got back to house, went through yard to R.R. track in rear—found that all our officers had left front yard and were at rear of the house, some near it, and Dayton, Bachtel, and one or two others standing on and looking down the track. Found afterwards that the 32-lb. *solid shot* which had passed over the General and me as above, had struck the ground just beyond us in the road, and "ricocheted" up the road till it came just about in front of the house where some of them were sitting by the fire in the front yard. It occurred to them that the fire was getting uncomfortably warm, and they went back to rear of the house accordingly. Was surprised when General told me as we came back, that it was a solid shot, not a shell; it made such a noise I took the latter for granted. He saw it coming and got on one side of

its line of flight; it passed over me but some distance
above.

Just as we reached R.R. (as above) there was a column of soldiers marching across it (by the flank) two
or three rods further back, going out on left of the
road. General also went on R.R. track and looked down
it, and I did same for a moment, then started off to
yard just beyond house to find my horse and get field
glass out of saddle bags to get a good view of rebel battery said to be on the R.R. track half a mile off. Had
just got off R.R. track and into yard—ten paces—when
another loud report of cannon down the track and the
next moment I saw a solid shot come *ricocheting* up the
R.R., across it obliquely at small angle right by where
General and these officers were still standing on the
track, strike ground just beyond them and bound along
to within a few feet of the column of soldiers crossing
the R.R. The next moment some one said "There's a
man killed" and looking across the track, not over
twenty feet from General there lay dead a negro whom
the shot had struck on back and side of head as it
passed, killing instantly.

The rebs had guns in position—or a battery—not
over half a mile off, looking directly down the straight
R.R. track, which as also the *road* near it, is straight.
Seeing our troops in the road, deploying to right of it
and also to left across R.R., they naturally send some
shot down to stop it—General says 32ˢ because they
ricochet. After these two hints, General wisely concluded to leave, and we all rode back up road ¼ mile
and went off to spot in woods 100 yards to right—Sat
there under trees and lunched, Blair also joining us
presently. While there we heard our friendly gun down
the road fire several times, and once *rifled shell*—so
they all pronounced it—came whizzing over our heads
through the trees and struck and exploded beyond us,
but hurt no one. No attention paid to this chance visitor,
—but after conference over, Blair went back to front,

and General and staff went further up road where our train had been sent. My orderly had taken my horse back there already by mistake, whence I walked back, and thereby came up too late—to my great regret—to ride with General and one or two of staff over across the canal to see Howard. Dayton remained at road, also McCoy, and after hunting round for good place fixed on camping ground still further back up the road on edge of ploughed field on right of road, with woods in our front full of bushes and underbrush. This is the meanest camp-ground we have had in the campaign.

The two immediate questions now are to arrange our lines, and to open communications with the fleet. For the former it is necessary to find where the rebel lines are, all round the city—ascertained by finding out how near we can go to the city on each road without being driven back by their shot. The latter, however, is a vital question, for though we have reached here safely and with supplies on hand, yet these supplies can last but a few days at most and unless we can very soon communicate with the fleet which is awaiting us somewhere near on the coast, this large army will soon begin to be pinched.

Tuesday Night, December 13/64.

Have not kept up daily journal because partly other things have interfered, partly there has been nothing of importance or special interest, till tonight.

Tonight Col. Ewing brought back from beyond the Ogeechee River the glorious news that today at 4½ P.M. the 2d Division, 15th Army Corps, under Gen. Hazen* (*Sherman's own* old Division, formerly the 5th Division of Army of Tennessee) assaulted and carried Fort McAllister, a strong rebel fort on west bank of Ogeechee River, *the* obstacle to our communication with the fleet below. Gen. Sherman, Gen. Howard, Gen. Giles A. Smith and divers other officers including sev-

* Brig. Gen. (later Maj. Gen.) William B. Hazen.

eral of our staff—unhappily *not* including myself—saw the charge and capture from the roof of a mill three miles distant. A general order announcing this vital success, and that our communications with the fleet of Farragut ("and Porter" the order says, but there is no evidence of P.'s being there) are opened, has just been issued and everybody is jubilant,—well we may be. We hear no details but the grand fact was visible. More of this again. I continue *as of yesterday.*

Since Saturday the time has been spent in reconnoitering all round, arranging our lines, feeling the rebs, and trying to find where our fleet was, and to open communications with it. On Sunday morning I rode over with Gen. S., Col. Ewing and Capt. Audenried, and a small escort, to Gen. Slocum's Headquarters on our left, near the Savannah River, where we took lunch and staid nearly all day. General busy consulting with Slocum—of whom he thinks highly—and also with others as to the lines, plans, etc. Nothing special to note. Col. Clinch* (rebel), Aid-de-Camp to Gen. Hardee, and brother of Gen. Robert Anderson's wife, who was taken prisoner among others on a boat captured by our men Saturday evening, had asked to see Gen. Sherman, whom he knew years ago at Charleston. General saw him and gave him the sharpest talk I have heard lately —not personal abuse, but very bitter denunciation of the rebel leaders, and a scathing rebuke to the "Southern gentlemen" who had allowed themselves to be dragged by such men into rebellion. Clinch don't amount to much, and his efforts to parry the points the General made were feeble, even after all allowance for his position. General told him he had kindest feelings for him personally, but having voluntarily entered rebel service and being a prisoner of war he must take the lot of a prisoner,—that he could do nothing for him more than for any other, but he would be treated kindly, etc. Clinch was captured on a steamboat which

* Duncan Lamont Clinch, formerly an officer in the U. S. Army.

left Savannah for Augusta—was stopped opposite our left, first by a small party of our foragers who happened on the river bank, but who were quickly reinforced by more, and then by infantry, when rifles *persuaded* the people on board to come over to our side. The boat was then foolishly burnt by our men.

The rebs were firing cannon along their lines all day, but no particular damage done. No reply from our batteries, which were being got into position to some extent; but the chief thing for the present is to ascertain accurately their lines, get the country and approaches surveyed and mapped, and place our men. Davis' XIV has arrived *via* the "Savannah Road" along the Savannah River, and is to replace Blair's on the left centre, Blair pushing farther to the right, etc. But these details I pass over for divers reasons.

Returning to camp to supper found there Mr. R. R. Cuyler, and his brother Dr. C., both among the prisoners taken on a train on the "Gulf Road" on Friday. Mr. Cuyler is and has been for over twenty years President of the Georgia Central railroad, and a leading R.R. man in Georgia. He is a very intelligent man, remarkably vigorous for his age, sixty-nine, and takes the terrible destruction of his R.R. very philosophically—"fortune of war"—recognizing its destruction as legitimate and necessary for our purpose.

General knew him personally long ago, and had sent for him to Gen. Howard's; received and treated them both very politely—neither having been in C.S.A. service—gave them the best accommodations we could in our camp, and so far from detaining them as prisoners promised them conveyance in the morning to our lines on the west, across the Ogeechee, with a "pass" beyond. Dr. Cuyler is older—seventy-one—much less vigorous, very quiet, and almost sullen. R. R. Cuyler, the General thinks was and—so far as he dares or can be—probably is a Union man. It was very odd to hear Mr. C. ask Gen. S. in the most unconcerned and business-

like way, what portions of the railroad we had destroyed, and to hear Gen. S. detail to him step by step
how much had been burned, how thoroughly the rails
had been torn up, bent and twisted, etc., etc. He is what
is vulgarly called a "regular old brick"—is Mr. C. He
sat with us at the camp-fire till late, though it was not
very pleasant, a raw cold North wind blowing hard and
chilling us through unless well wrapped up. The conversation was quite general. General alluded among
other things to the abusive and lying articles in the
rebel papers, and the falsehoods about the outrages,
murdering of women, burning of dwellings everywhere,
etc., etc., which they are full of. Mr. C. says these things
are not believed in Savannah, and spoke of a letter
from Milledgeville, written thence since we left, and
published in Savannah, in which a more truthful account was given, and one corresponding, he says, to
what Gen. S. told him. By the way, I had a little chat
yesterday with Col. Clinch, who said much the same
thing when I alluded to these falsehoods.

On Monday morning General sent off Dr. and Mr.
Cuyler in an ambulance down to "King's Bridge" on
the Ogeechee, on their way to Macon.

Soon after the General started off to Gen. Howard's
Headquarters eight or ten miles off on the right. As
Ewing, Audenried, and Nichols were going with him,
and he said nothing to me about going, I staid in camp
and wrote up diary for Friday and Saturday, and did
very little else. Rebels firing more or less all day, to
little or no purpose,—haven't heard of anybody being
hit. Our camp is entirely within range of shells from
their battery on the R.R.—the same that sent the 32 lb.
compliments to us the other day,—if they only knew it,
but they don't.

Every now and then we hear the deep tone of those
guns, sometimes quickly followed by the equally loud
explosion of a shell, to front and left of us some hundred yards ahead. Then other guns off to our right and

front, over at the canal; and now others far over to the left, with occasional popping of musketry. Very few guns have been fired on our side—we are not ready. Poe and his engineer officers are busy riding around and preparing maps: the Corps and Division Commanders are getting their troops gradually in front of the rebel lines as far as yet known. Capt. Poe, who was on McClellan's staff all through his campaigns till after his failure to take Richmond, and is a first rate officer, tells me that "these swamps are *ten-fold* worse than the Chickahominy swamps, so much talked of."

The question of our supplies begins to look threatening unless we can very soon communicate with the fleet. There are rations on hand enough to last the *men* for ten days, but the "forage" (fodder, etc.) for the immense number of animals, horses, mules, cattle, etc., daily needed, cannot any longer be had, and the supply of corn and oats we brought is rapidly diminishing. Heard heavy firing today over on our left, at Savannah River. Found it was a little fight between Capt. Winniger's* battery, of *3-inch* rifled guns, six pieces, on river bank, and two rebel gunboats, which with a supply steamer were coming down the river. One of the gunboats, the "Macon," said to be iron-clad,—the other, the "Sampson," not; between them they had six heavy guns, much heavier than W.'s and pitched shot and shell all round him, but only killed two horses, hurting no men. His shells were splendidly thrown,— disabled and captured the supply steamer "Resolute," and *drove the two gunboats back up the river*. On board the captured steamer were six or seven C.S.A. naval officers, besides the crew—all made prisoners. The boat was not seriously injured though disabled for the time —will be in good running order by tomorrow. She is a regular tow-boat, sea-going, like those in N.Y. harbor, and will do us good service. Capt. Winniger—who has already a reputation as an artillery officer—says this is

---

* Spelled *Winnegar* in Sherman's *Memoirs* (II, 338).

the first *naval* engagement he ever took part in, and that he wants more of the same sort. It is rather a hard joke on the rebels that their gunboats with 68 pounders and Blakesly rifle guns, should be driven back by three-inch rifle guns.

Ewing and Audenried came back tonight from Howard's, the General remaining there,—and tell us that an assault on Fort McAllister has been ordered for to-morrow by Hazen's Division of 15th Corps. Immediately on our arrival here the General begun to make every inquiry about this fort, its exact location, strength, etc., etc., but had some trouble in getting it, and I believe only today learned definitely about it. It is a strong fort, built to command the entrance to Ogeechee River, about five miles (so I am told) above its mouth, and has twice successfully resisted the attack of our gunboats. It *must* be taken, for we must communicate without delay with the fleet which is already in Ossabaw Sound; but it is sure, even if we take it, to cost heavily. No little anxiety is expressed here tonight for the result of the assault, and if it succeeds it will add new and splendid honors to this superb army. To take even earthworks, resolutely defended, the history of this war *on both sides* has shown to be next to impossible, as at Fredericksburg, Gettysburg, etc., etc., to say nothing of Hood's bloody defeat at Allatoona, so vital to Sherman's plans. How much less flattering the prospect of infantry alone taking by assault a strong and regularly built *fort,* mounting (it is said) 26 heavy guns, is easy to see. But it has to be done.

The rebs continue to fire today all along the line at intervals, and there is reply to some extent from some of our batteries in position. The menaced attack on our rear is shadowed by the presence of rebel cavalry who have followed us hitherto at a very respectful distance since Kilpatrick whipped Wheeler a week ago at Waynesboro—for last night a party of fifty rebs dashed in on a foraging party in our rear, captured two wagons and some twenty men, though other accounts say only six or seven men. To meet this danger, infantry has been posted in our rear, and a battery of six guns is placed half a mile or more down the Louisville road in rear of our Headquarters.

Had a chat yesterday with Capt. Brady, of 2d New Jersey, who escaped recently (his third escape—was caught twice) from a rebel prison at Columbia, S. Ca. He fully confirms all the stories of bad usage of our prisoners—says they were better off at Columbia than any other place. There they (officers) were in an open field, without any shelter or cover, and not even a stockade round them, the remoteness of the place and almost certainty of recapture being relied on against escapes. Their food was a little cornmeal and some very bad sorghum molasses—no meat. He mentioned by name and with detail two officers who were shot in his immediate presence by the guard, wantonly and without the least pretence of fault—one was sitting by a fire with other prisoners. He himself was once caught by "trackhounds," and told me of one officer who to his knowledge was not only caught but killed by these dogs. I don't wonder at the men killing all the dogs as we marched through—they did right.*

Tuesday Night December 13/64

Ewing and Audenried and also Verplanck and Capt. Poe rode over this morning to join Gen. S. on the right and in hopes to witness the assault on Fort McAllister from a distance. I had a great mind to go, but finally concluded—being free to do either, as the General had sent no instructions to any of us—to go over to Slocum's on our left. I shall never cease to regret the mistake. I found that to get to the mill at King's Bridge whence to see the assault I should have to ride nearly twenty miles round, to avoid a part of the more direct

---

* Such reports as Capt. Brady's throw some light on the situation soon to ensue at Columbia.

road (even that being eleven or twelve miles) which is commanded completely by the rebel batteries, which fire across about 800 yards of open space directly on an open causeway through the swamp. The assault being ordered for 11 A.M., if it came off at all I reasoned would probably be over before we could get there, and we should have the ride and back for nothing. In the meantime there was reason to expect that on our left, only two or three miles from our camp, Slocum would today make a co-operative assault, and perhaps the gunboats would appear again on the river; so I went over there instead—desiring also to learn the meaning of some very heavy firing in that direction late last night. Went over to Slocum's Headquarters, staid till 1 P.M.—nothing done there all morning except the ordinary movements and the usual spiteful firing from the rebel batteries. The firing last night was further down the river, and they did not know at Slocum's what it was. So I came back by 2 P.M. and remained in camp. Between four and five P.M. we heard very heavy firing to the S.W.—evidently a number of miles off—in the direction of Fort McAllister—were satisfied the assault there had been made. It lasted but a little while, not over fifteen or twenty minutes. We waited anxiously enough till tonight, after 9 P.M. when Col. Ewing returned with the news. From the mill they could see (with glasses) our column emerge from the woods in front of the fort—press steadily forward in solid mass without firing a shot, bayonets fixed up the causeway to the "lunette" or outer work, under a heavy and constant cannonade, unfaltering; then the column dashed against and into the lunette, with *all the regimental colors at the front*—some twenty flags in line. Straight forward they pressed on to the main work, the whole column deploying into line on either flank. Presently the head of column seemed to sink down and disappear. The General, says E., had been watching them through his glass with eager anxiety, and visibly excited, but when this apparent hesitation—the sign of ruinous repulse if real—appeared, he took down his glass, as if unable to witness the failure. But Ewing says he himself was satisfied it was only apparent and caused by the ground being lower, just in front,—and sure enough, in a few moments the line was again visible, though enveloped in smoke, still pressing forward, and in another minute had reached and was on the parapet —The Fort was ours! Instantly the whole parapet swarmed with their dark figures, and our flags waved in triumph all along its walls. And then Generals, officers, and orderlies (at the mill) joined in a *yell* of triumph, the General as much excited as any of them, and exclaiming (alluding to that excited old darkey who saw *him* at Howell Cobb's plantation) "I shan't sleep any dis night sure!"

Before the assault was made the General had been communicating by several flags from the roof of the mill with *our ships* in the Sound, eight miles off. They inquired whether we held the fort—the question being put by *Farragut* and (Gen.) Foster.* The answer was, "No, the rebels hold it." But the assault was made and the fort taken in fifteen minutes, E. says, and then the General signalled *Yes.* He at once started Capt. Audenried and Merritt down the river in a boat to communicate with the fleet, and ordered another boat in which he himself and Gen. Howard were to follow them; and sent Ewing back to us and the army with the news.

What I missed by not going over! But it is some consolation that none of our staff were in the fight.

Before Ewing came back we heard our own men cheering loudly along our lines some half mile in front of us beyond the woods and swamp, and were almost sure the news of the capture of the Fort had been passed along the lines, but were afraid to believe it. No doubt the rebels have the news too, for they have been

* Bvt. Brig. (later Maj.) Gen. John Gray Foster, commanding the Department of the South.

firing their big guns in the most spiteful way all the evening and far into the night, for the first time.

The question with us now is whether the rebs in the city will evacuate and surrender it at once, or hold out and stand a siege. I expect the latter. But they might as well "git up and dust," for now that we have our base and communication with the sea, Savannah is doomed. It may be days, even weeks yet, before we enter the city—but this army *will take it.*

I close this long after midnight, to have it ready to go to the fleet in the morning if possible to send to my darlings at home. God grant it shall find them safe and well as it leaves me.

II

IN AND ABOUT SAVANNAH

LETTERS

THE following letter to Mrs. Hitchcock is the first of a series written during the seven weeks, from December 13, 1864, to January 30, 1865, while communications by mail were open between Sherman's army and the rest of the world. In the first and second letters the nature and object of Major Hitchcock's campaign diaries are set forth.

IN THE FIELD NEAR SAVANNAH, GA. December 13, 1864
(Tuesday Night 11 P.M.)

You will thank God with me that I can write you in perfect health and the best spirits, not only that three days ago we ended here our triumphant march through the heart of rebeldom, but also that today our gallant fellows—heroes they are—assaulted and stormed the rebel fort on the west bank of the Ogeechee River, on our extreme right, thus opening our communications with the sea. The problem was not solved till *that* was done—indeed, "a new base" on the sea-shore was vital, for without it our supplies would soon have failed, as we can no longer subsist such an army as this on the country, being no longer on the march. Fort McAllister was taken by *one division,*—there are three or four divisions to a corps, and this army consists of *not less* than four corps. I write from Gen. Sherman's camp at Headquarters, 5½ miles from Savannah; the General himself went down yesterday to our right, and remained there to see the assault, and doubtless before this a dispatch-boat has left the fleet with news that we are in communication with them. Our extreme right is eight or ten miles from here by the shortest route, and the Fort is four or five miles or more below that. The General and some of the staff witnessed the assault from the roof of a mill three miles off across a swamp;

we heard the cannonading this afternoon, and, knowing that the assault was to be made waited with anxiety
for the news, which came back tonight not long ago—
only the bare fact of our success, but that *certain.* I
write this in hopes of sending it tomorrow on board the
fleet to go North by first opportunity; I shall go down
to Howard's Headquarters (on our right) and if possible on board the fleet tomorrow—may or may not
have opportunity to add anything to this, but if not you
will know by receiving it that I was well when it left.

I send with it a sort of diary of the march, kept for
your amusement if you choose to look over it. You can
read such parts of it as you choose to such friends as
Mr. Yeatman, Mr. Shepley, Mr. Crow,—if interesting
to them—and of course Mother, Margie, and the boys
if they wish,—but you will not lend it or *put it into anybody's else hands but your own and Mother's.* It was
written under the disadvantages of a camp and shows
itself how hastily and by snatches—but it will give you
some idea of what interested me most day by day. It is
not a history of the campaign nor of the general movements of the different army corps—for those see the
Reports hereafter. I hope you will be able to decipher it
in many places—you'll have to make a winter's work
of it, I "reckon." The Roman numerals XV,—XVII,—
XIV,—and XX always refer to the numbers of the
Army Corps—14th is Gen. J. C. Davis', 15th (Logan's,
com'd^d by) Osterhaus',—17th, Blair's,—20th Williams'—In the beginning of the diary I used the character $ to designate *Sherman.**

You must take "Harper's Weekly" now. Their special artist, Theo. R. Davis, has been with us all the time
—with the army,—and from Kingston to Atlanta, and
from Milledgeville here, with our own party and mess.
His sketches are good and truthful. The pictures of

* In the diary as printed, the name of Sherman has been substituted
for the dollar mark.

General Sherman's staff in the "Review of Kilpatrick's Cavalry at Marietta, Ga." are intended in a rough way for the real persons—pray don't say mine is flattered. Davis is a pleasant fellow, quite young—twenty-three—and has real talent. . . .

Even if Savannah were surrendered tomorrow—which I don't think it will be by a good deal, though they might as well,—that would only end this campaign and set us about preparing for a new one. Thank God, for a while at least I can expect to hear from you now. Try to imagine how entirely cut off we have been from the whole world, save through the few meagre dispatches the rebel papers we could get hold of copied from our papers. If I had not resolved to banish entirely all doubt and fear, and to take it absolutely for certain that all my loved ones were well, I should have been miserable every day. I confess I am more agitated and anxious now than I have been since I left Kingston. And yet I know the same kind and merciful Father who has preserved me has watched over you all.

I will write you often—I cannot say how often—of course. Continue to write me regularly, addressing "Care of Major Gen. W. T. Sherman Headquarters Milit*y* Division of the Mississippi."—For the present this must suffice, and you can call my diary a long letter. Give my dear love to Mother . . . and "the boys" too. Tell them not to fret about being in the army—their place, both of them, is at home. Remember me affectionately to all friends who ask after me—tell them I was never better in health, and that this is the completest success Sherman has had yet. He is the man of the war as to military genius. . . .

[P.S.] Tell Gen. Ewing* his brother "Charley" is in the best possible health and spirits and sends him and his family his love.

---

* Gen. Hugh Boyle Ewing, one of Sherman's brothers-in-law.

IN THE FIELD NEAR SAVANNAH, GA. December 16 1864
Friday Noon

I wrote you Tuesday night stating our arrival here,
—that we had gone into camp on Saturday 5½ miles
from Savannah, and that our army was investing the
city—that on that afternoon (Tuesday) the capture
(by *one division* of the 15th Corps) of Fort McAllister,
so long the bugbear of the navy, had opened our communications with the fleet and solved the only remaining (but very important) question, of supplies and "a
new base"; and I enclosed in the same envelope with
that note two little books containing my daily journal,
in ink, of the whole campaign—hastily written from
day to day or rather night to night, but which I think
you may find interesting. I assure you . . . that but for
the hope that you would find it so, I am afraid I should
not have carried out the idea—but am very glad now
that I did.

Wednesday morning Col. Ewing, Capt. Baylor, T. R.
Davis ("Harper's Weekly") and myself, with some
orderlies rode round—about eighteen miles—to the
rice-mill on the bank of "Great Ogeechee" whence the
General, etc., saw the fight at the Fort the day before.
There by good luck, after declining a kind invitation
from Gen. Howard to go in his yawl—already full
enough—I got a slow passage in a flat-boat with two
other officers six miles down the Great Ogeechee's sinu-
ous course to the Fort; and there had the great good
luck of another invitation from Gen. Howard to go with
him out to the steam-tug whose yawl was sent to the
Fort for him—and gladly did so. The tug took us down
several miles to Admiral Dahlgren's flag-ship, where I
found General Sherman and staid all night,—had a
capital time, and concluded that navy officers are luxu-
rious rascals compared to us dwellers in tents—and
next morning the Admiral sailed up to the Fort, where
we all got ashore and the General took the Admiral all
round and over the Fort. I wish I had time to give you

an idea of the Fort, and of the *splendid thing* it was to make and take it by that assault. Our whole loss out of some 1500 men actually in the charge was ninety-one— 11 killed and eighty wounded, and of these a large number were hurt by the torpedoes, or shells buried just under the surface not over five feet apart in a line around the land side of the fort, arranged to explode when trod on,—not visible, of course,—but which our gallant fellows walked straight over like pebbles. Besides these lay the line of abattis,—tops of trees cut off with all the branches sharpened and pointing towards the assailants, impossible to climb or get over, and *apparently* impossible to get through—beyond these the ditch, at least fifteen feet deep perpendicular, and six or seven feet across at the bottom,—the sides so steep that it would be troublesome for a man to climb them anyhow—say thus ⌐⌐ with a row of sharp stakes five or six feet high set in the ground like a picket fence inclining outwards, at the bottom, through which our men had somehow to go and then climb up the steep bank. How on earth they ever did what they did is wonderful. The Fort was ours in twenty-five minutes after the first order was given—hence the small loss, in connection with the deadly fire by which our sharp-shooters in rear silenced their guns. The General says he never wants anything done better—well he may say so. Davis is now busy at his sketches of the Fort, etc., for Harper's Weekly, which will be reliable and which you must see. *You* must read "Harper" now.

After looking round the Fort, the Admiral and General S. and two or three of us staff had a charming row up to the rice-mill again in the Admiral's barge, and thence we rode back—the General and staff,—the Admiral returning to his ship,—to Gen. Howard's Headquarters where we staid last night, the General sending over for our camp to be moved down here on the right centre of our lines, 9 miles from Savannah and 4½ from "King's Bridge" over the Great Ogeechee, to which point *ships* can and will today come up with all supplies.

No special blow has been struck beside the taking of the Fort, but the time is busily employed in arranging our lines, making the investment closer, destroying more miles of the railroads leading out of Savannah, all three of which we have held since Saturday last,— and in completing reconnaissances, repairing and building roads through these infernal swamps and marshes, etc., etc. You will most probably not hear of any great fighting here. It is wholly needless, for if Savannah does not surrender it will starve in due time, and though no man nor any army can or will do more daring things than Sherman and his magnificent host, yet no man is more careful to avoid needless sacrifice of life. The men all know this, and that is one reason why when he tells them to fight they *do fight*—like heroes, or like devils, which you please,—of which this affair of Fort McAllister is a sample. The rebels inside were thunderstruck at the idea of such a charge. They say that they had confidently expected our line to be repulsed by the torpedoes alone.

But I have not time to write as I should like. . . . I put my letter to you (with the diary) in the hands of Capt. Williamson on the tug, who took it on board the Admiral's vessel with other army letters, so that sooner or later it ought to reach you. . . .

Aside from thoughts of home I could desire nothing better as to health, spirits or situation, unless it were— and that I do desire—more active duties. In coming across from our old camp on Wednesday we had a little prospect of being made an artillery target for a rebel battery which has, for 400 or 500 yards, a clear sweep and easy range across open swamps, of a causeway over which we had to ride, in full clear view of the battery about one half to three quarters of a mile distant, or else go round five or six miles farther. As it turned out, they did not think us worth firing at, though a day or two previously they had been firing at everybody who went over the causeway, and came near enough to several to make it interesting. I must tell you, however, that before reaching the causeway I objected strongly to taking that road instead of one which we knew to be safe,—on the ground that there was neither courage nor sense in running a totally unnecessary risk. I found however that Ewing was determined to go over it—he declaring that the rebs had quit firing at small parties or single riders crossing it, and that there was really no danger. Finding him in earnest about taking that road, of course I declined to let him take it alone and went with him—and as it turned out the rebs didn't fire. I was more concerned about my horse than anything else, for though a valuable one in most respects he plays the fool sometimes and I fully expected him to try to run off with me—perhaps into the swamp—if they had fired. However, he has never yet got the better of me, and I don't think will. The chance of their hitting us with a cannon ball was not one in one thousand; shells would have been worse.

A courier came here last night with important dispatches from Grant, to which I have been writing the General's reply, and some other letters for him, all morning. He sends back his reply this afternoon and I shall send this by same hands to Uncle Ethan for you. The dispatches from Grant relate to matters which will affect our future operations. I can say nothing of course, except to advise you to disregard any and all speculations whatever as to our future movements, and to take it for granted that it will all be right. It was the oddest feeling in the world to see New York papers again—one felt as if he had been buried alive and resurrected. I had a real fellow feeling for Rip Van Winkle. And it was still more odd to look over the files and read the absurdly would-be-wise speculations,—the lying stories of all sorts, which our own papers had about us (in a different spirit of course) as well as the rebel. One number of the N. Y. *Herald* had a big map of "Sherman's field of operations" with a very black line marked "Route of Slocum's column," which carefully avoided the actual line that column took, in a manner lovely to see. The biggest lie of all was that conference Sherman was to have at Augusta with diverse and sundry rebel Governors. There is not a rebel Governor in the South, in my opinion, who would *dare*—until Jeff Davis' military power is broken, to take any such step. Talk about "despotism"! I tell you that we have found a *white slaving* in the South of which I had no conception. Men and women both, who did not pretend to have been or to be "Union" have told us bitterly enough that they were *slaves*—I use *their* word; and we saw it without that. I wish some of our "Democrats" had one-tenth the reason for abusing the "Lincoln despotism" that these people have. Certainly there are many willing slaves—people, I mean, who have wrought themselves up to a blind hatred of the "Yankees," so utterly unreasoning, so frantic, so insane that all else is lost in that; but that this rebellion is and has all along been kept up, as to the mass of the Southern people, by the devilish audacity, unscrupulousness and skill of a few leaders, who have staked *all* and play accordingly, I more than believe—I know it.

We staid at Gen. Howard's Headquarters last night, our train coming over too late to make camp. His tents are pitched in the front yard of a fine residence, with what were handsome grounds. A quarter mile or more to one side of the main road, and in front of the house is—as in all the plantations hereabouts—a fine avenue of live oak trees. The place belongs to a Mr. Anderson, whose nephew, Major A.,* was commander of and captured in the Fort.

It was a most lovely moonlight night, the weather soft and balmy—(today is uncomfortably warm and a

* Maj. George W. Anderson, C.S.A.

thunder shower seems to be threatened) and we had a charming time. Gen. Sherman was in fine spirits—he is never low-spirited—and after supper we had a group of twenty-five or thirty officers around the camp-fire, kindled quite as much for light as heat, chatting, telling stories, singing songs—and there was some excellent singing to a guitar,—and having a good time generally, which nobody enjoyed more than the General, though he took chiefly a listening part, with intervals of the most entertaining reminiscences of former campaigns, etc. Besides this, the Headquarters band of the "Army of the Tennessee" gave us some very pretty music,— and so we managed to pass the evening very well for such suffering martyrs as I'm afraid a good many thousand tender loving hearts have been pitying us for.

Of course this is the bright side, but the simple truth is that *I* haven't seen any other—or rather haven't experienced it. I saw a little of it once or twice—as when we passed the torpedoes on Friday. But there is neither use nor sense in dwelling on disagreeable things, and a good heart strips even real trouble of its imaginary surroundings which a faint one always increases. So much for moralizing. . . .

Two months of the three which our friend the Colonel allowed me to "get sick of it" are nearly or quite gone, and it is the truth that I am very much less concerned about the reality—so far as my personal comfort, etc., is involved,—than I was before I knew anything about it. Probably no other campaign ever can be so free from all but the *poetry* of campaigning as this last has been—but I am not troubled about anything that can come in future ones. Every day almost shows how much imagination has to do with all the ills of life. I found it a very easy thing to ride over "the causeway"—it is very well known among us—the other day as soon as we left the woods and got fairly on it in view of the rebel guns, and expecting them any moment to send us their compliments—though until we reached there I

am free to confess that it was a disagreeable prospect,
—much more so because I felt that the risk, if there
should prove to be one, was uncalled for and unjustifi-
able. If I had had orders to carry, or for any other
reason my duty called me that way, I do not think it
would have given me any concern at all—for I understood and fully accepted all that with the commission.
If I were a veteran, I should probably have refused
absolutely to take that road, and have gone around—
as Gen. Sherman very properly did two days before, to
avoid that same battery; but one cannot begin in that
way, you know. As it turned out, the risk was imaginary, and Ewing was—by accident, for he knew what I
did not, that they had quit firing on small parties—
right. . . .

This long note has been written by snatches—partly
where our camp was first made this morning, and
whence it has since been removed,—finished at the
camping-place now selected, half a mile from Gen.
Howard's, on another plantation, in a still finer group
of live oaks, the General's tent being pitched in front
of a magnificent old fellow whose green leaves are
hoary and venerable with long Spanish moss. It is the
middle of December, and yet Audenried went by me
just now with a beautiful white camelia, plucked in a
garden, stuck in his hat, and my cloth coat is uncomfortably warm at a moderate walk. Everything immediately around us is as quiet as if we were a hunting
party in camp—though now and then a gun booms
from somewhere along the lines, louder or duller as
nearer or farther off—probably rebel shots, for they
have done a great deal of spiteful and useless firing
since we came. The afternoon of Tuesday, by the way,
before we heard on the left that the Fort was taken,—
their pickets were very saucy to ours—"Hello, Yanks,
—don't you want some hard bread? Come over here
and get something to eat," etc., etc. They knew very
well, and so did we, that though our fleet was outside,

that Fort was a disagreeable—they thought an invincible—obstacle to the supplies on board of it getting to us, and probably they supposed us more in want than we really were. At that time our boys had no particular reply to make. But about 8 or 9 P.M. a regular *wave* of cheering rolled along our whole line—say a dozen miles or so—from the extreme right where the news first reached them, all round to the Savannah River, as the word passed along from division to division. "Hello, Yanks"—shouted the rebel pickets—"what's all that yelling about?"—"Fort McAllister's taken—the *cracker line* is open—that's what's the matter—how are you, Johnny!" was the reply—and the rejoinder was the most spiteful firing from their batteries all night long—so much ammunition wasted.— Our present Headquarters are farther from the city than the others were, simply because their line of defense on this side is farther out and ours corresponds. We are nearest them on our extreme left, where one of our batteries is only three miles from the city, on the river bank, and so close to theirs that neither party can keep out pickets—not over 200 or 300 yards apart.

Heavy guns have already arrived at King's Bridge on the Ogeechee, where our supplies, etc., are landed from ships, and will be by tomorrow in position to throw 30-pound shells into the heart of the city. General Sherman will then make formal demand for its surrender, on the ground that he has the city in his power, its communications cut off, an army completely investing it large enough to prevent equally any succor or supplies, and his guns so placed that he can destroy it at his pleasure. It is for Gen. Hardee to say whether that alternative must come, and for it if it does he is responsible. If he refuses, and damage is done by our shells to the property and persons of non-combatants, he is the one to answer for it. He has the power to defend it for a time, because it can be entered only by narrow roads or causeways through swamps, which his guns command. We can force a passage in spite of his guns, but at the cost of many precious lives, which are worth too much to be thus thrown away and which will not be, for if we simply stay outside and bombard the city it must sooner or later surrender—to starvation if nothing else. I make no predictions except that we shall not attempt to storm their works—there is better use for this army than that. I do not even predict, in case Hardee should refuse to surrender—which he may do and take the chances rather than give up so important an opening into the interior for our gun-boats as the Savannah River affords, to say nothing of himself, his garrison, arms, stores, etc.,—even in that case I say I predict nothing, and you need pay no attention to what anybody predicts, no matter how plausible even from what I have told you. Time alone is all we need to take Savannah,—whether that or something else is the best way to use that time is a question which events will answer.

My *wood-pile,* on which I have been sitting writing this on my knee, is not a very secluded place, and divers interruptions have brought me to the end of my time before this must be closed to go.—Imagine the disgust of everybody at these Headquarters to learn that though there are *twenty tons* of mail in the river coming up for the Army, *all our Headquarters mail has been kept at Nashville* and we who have the misfortune to be with the General-in-chief have to wait—thanks to somebody's stupidity—probably a week or more before any letters come for us. I wish I had that somebody's head between my knees—Perhaps I wouldn't punch it! —You had best now send your letters for me enclosed to Uncle Ethan, and ask him to get Kelton to see that they are properly forwarded. . . .

[P.S.] I doubt if I shall keep a diary again, at any rate so long as we remain here; so you must not be disappointed if I don't send another. Modest, to assume it, I admit.

I have concluded to mail this to St. Louis. Don't think I have forgotten you if I don't write every day or even every few days. Our mails are not yet *regular*.

IN THE FIELD, SAVANNAH, GA. December 24, 1864
Christmas Eve 9 P.M.

These two days past I have been constantly busy writing letters and dispatches, private and official, some of whose contents I wish I could send you. As it is, you will wait,—patiently if you can, and hopefully you *will,* dear Mary,—until again, please God, you shall rejoice and admire at the genius and splendid energy of our "Chief." Yet there is something very sad, if one did not look beyond the present, to be in the midst of these sounds and sights of war, and immersed in plans of another campaign, on this evening, sacred to "Peace on Earth—Good-will to men!" Yet these warlike purposes and preparations for renewed efforts to crush and overwhelm the enemies of the country are indeed the only and indispensable steps to that Peace for which none pray more truly or earnestly than those who see and know how terrible a thing war is. If I did not know and feel this to be true, I would resign tomorrow; for you know that the hope of distinction in *this* profession would never have taken me from home and from you. You will know by tomorrow, thanks to the telegraph, that we are in Savannah, without a battle, Hardee having begun his hasty evacuation the very next day after his refusal to surrender, and our troops discovering it and marching in early on the morning of the 21st.

As I write, the superb "33ᵈ Massachusetts" band, which for an hour past has been serenading Gen. Sherman (in whose room I have been writing for him till just now and now for myself)—has struck up "Sweet Home." Do they want to torture us! A little while ago the sweet strains of another fine band not far off came bearing the plaintive melody, "When this cruel war is

over''; . . . now they have begun a lively march and I
can go on.

I wrote you a hasty note on the 20th from Hilton
Head,* where the General went to arrange with Admiral Dahlgren and Gen. Foster to throw a body of
troops round from our right flank on the Ogeechee
River to the east side of Savannah River, to cut off the
only remaining avenue open from Savannah—the
"Union Causeway," an old plank road running N.E.
from the city to Hardeeville. Could he have done this
in time or Hardee have waited two days longer, the
garrison would have been hemmed in completely,—the
city would have been bombarded, for our heavy guns
were in position, and both Savannah *and* its garrison
would have been ours. . . .

I believe I kept up the account of our adventures
pretty well to the 20th when I wrote you from Hilton
Head. I enclose the unfinished letter begun Xmas Eve,
intended to go on from that date. That night we went
on board Admiral Dahlgren's flagship again to return
via Wassaw and Ossabaw Sounds to Fort McAllister
and camp, but lost considerable time both in starting
and on the way by very rough weather. Next day, in
"Romney Marsh," one of the inland channels, our vessel grounded and while going on in the Admiral's barge
we met a tug with news of the evacuation and entry of
our troops that day; reaching Fort McA. by night and
waiting there till midnight for the tide, we met our
horses (signalled for from the Fort) at 2½ A.M. at
"the rice-mill," now historic to this army and rode
thence to our camp, some ten miles, before daylight—
got breakfast, and by 7 A.M. camp was broken up and
our party—Gen. S.—staff and escort,—off to Savannah, nine miles further, entering the city by 9 A.M. on
the 22ᵈ.

We went first to the "Pulaski House," the hotel
where *Capt. Sherman* used to stay when on duty here

---

* Not among the letters preserved.

many years ago. Very soon a number of the leading citizens called to pay their respects, among them a brother of Gen. Hardee,—Dr. Arnold, the Mayor,—etc., etc., and were all very kindly received. Besides, came Mr. Chas. Green, a wealthy banker, a British subject, who has the finest house in the city, and not only invited but urged the General very earnestly to take up his quarters there—which he finally consented to, on condition that we supply our own mess and set our own table. We "occupied and possessed" it at once and are now in it. It is a fine house, two-story double, larger than your Mother's, and very handsomely furnished *before the war*—looks a little worn now. In the wide hall are some very handsome pieces of statuary, banana trees, growing in tubs, etc., and several fine pictures in the various rooms, books of engravings, etc.

Just this moment Davis has been in my room and tells me he and Waud* are getting up the house for *Harper's Weekly*. Mr. Green is an elderly gentleman, extremely pleasant and courteous, and has been most polite and friendly to us all, and since we have become acquainted has taken several occasions to compliment us all on our good behavior in the most fascinating manner. On Christmas Day the churches—at least five or six principal ones—were open as usual and going with the General to St. John's (Episcopal) across the street, I was delighted to see it filled, not only by a large number of our officers and men, but also a considerable number of Savannah people, ladies and gentlemen. Next Sunday I go with Mr. Green to the Presbyterian church to hear Dr. Axson† preach,—he says a very able man. In reading the service last Sunday when the minister came to the prayer for the President of the United States, which I was amused to find in its place in the prayer books in our pew, he simply omitted that

* A. R. Waud, another artist for *Harper's Weekly*.

† The Rev. S. Edward Axson, whose daughter, Ellen Louise Axson, became the first Mrs. Woodrow Wilson.

prayer altogether and passed directly on from the preceding one to the Litany without pause. This minister, by the way, with his wife, were in Mr. Green's house when we came,—"my honored guest for some years past," said Mr. G., but vacated their room for the General, and went elsewhere, as we found when we came in. Mr. G. has no family, or none here, and so we have elegant quarters without the pleasure of confiscating them. Some of the general officers in town, however, have occupied and possessed the premises of absent rebel officers, while many officers are with private families. I am glad to say that the perfectly unexceptionable conduct of our army here is not only apparent in the streets, but most favorably remarked by the citizens. Since we came, a week today,* I have seen but two drunken soldiers, and both of these were on their way to the guard-house at the time. I meet ladies and children on the street whenever I go out, and tonight at dinner the General was speaking with great pleasure and feeling of the number of children he met in the Park, playing, etc., this afternoon. Still, the stores are not open, nor business resumed, for the simple reason that all communication with the interior having been cut off, and free river and sea communication with "the white settlements" being not yet established—haven't had time—there is no business as yet to be done outside of the army. But things are beginning to get into shape; "Adams' Express" opened three or four days ago in the same place they had formerly, and it was pleasant to see the old flag hung across the end of the room and a crowd of our men sending money—not C.S.A. rags—home to their families. The C.S.A. money is sold here to the curious at 5¢ on the dollar for greenbacks—I send you some which you may give Tom if you like. But in truth I can hardly tell you very much

---

* This places the day on which this letter (began Dec. 24) was continued—Dec. 28.

about the town, for I have been almost constantly busy within doors till yesterday ever since we came.

The weather was "very cold" when we came in, for two or three days—the mercury down 8° or 10° below *freezing,* I should think; since then my little room over the hall in front of second story without a fireplace, has been always comfortable, and I am writing now with the glass bow-window blinds open, to hear the band outside playing "Rally round the flag."

Christmas evening, Sunday though it was, we had a (military) "family dinner-party," Capt. Nichols—our mess caterer—having secured three or four lovely turkeys, and sundry other good things—Col. Barnum* contributing some very good wine presented to him by some wine-merchants here at whose stores he placed a guard immediately on our troops first entering the city —and Mr. Green's handsome china and silver being "kindly loaned for the occasion." Including Gens. Slocum and Corse, and Mr. Green, we had some twenty at table, Gen. Sherman presiding, and a very pleasant dinner it was. Gen. Sherman's health being drunk first, he made a little speech, patriotic, modest, and pointed. Mr. Green made as happy a little after-dinner speech as I ever heard—Gen. S. proposing his health. I withdrew quietly soon after the toasts began fearing a little, I confess, that they might become too lively, but in that I was mistaken. It was as quiet and pleasant a Christmas dinner as one could wish—away from home. But you may give Maria† my compliments and tell her I don't expect to see any dinners like hers anywhere else. I went upstairs, and my thoughts were far enough from here, happy in the hope that your Christmas had been made a happy one by the news that Savannah was ours without the loss of a life. I ought and intended to have finished my letter to you that evening, but the

---

* Col., soon to become Brig. Gen., Henry A. Barnum.

† An old colored cook in the family of Mrs. Hitchcock's father, George Collier. Originally a slave, she was freed before the war.

truth is that when I woke up my candle was burnt out and the hour past midnight.

But the greatest in-door feature of our residence in Savannah has been the General's new-found colored friends who have come by hundreds, I was going to say, to see "Mr. Sherman." The morning we entered the city he rode down at once to the river-bank and went up to a signal station on the roof of a warehouse; and by the time we got down to the street again a crowd of them had gathered who pressed round him to welcome him and shake hands and tell him how long they had watched and prayed for his coming. After we came to this house they soon began to find out that he would see them, and for several days there was a constant stream of them, old and young, men, women and children, black, yellow and cream-colored, uncouth and well-bred, bashful and talkative—but always respectful and well-behaved—all day long, anxious to pay their respects and to see the man they had heard so much of, and whom—as more than one of them told him,—God had sent to answer their prayers. Frequently they came in a dozen or twenty at a time, to his room up-stairs where he usually sits, and where, as my writing is done there, I have been in the way of seeing it all. He has always had them shown in at once, stopping a dispatch or letter or a conversation to greet them in his off-hand—though not undignified way— "Well, boys,—come to see Mr. Sherman, have you? Well, I'm Mr. Sherman—glad to see you"—and shaking hands with them all in a manner highly disgusting, I dare say, to a "refined Southern gentleman." Almost all of them who have talked at all have spoken of our success and their deliverance with an apparently religious feeling.—"Been prayin' for you all long time, Sir, prayin' day and night for you, and now, bless God, you is come"—etc. One old preacher likened himself to Simeon of old, kindly reminding the General of all

CHRISTMAS-DAY IN SAVANNAH—GENERAL SHERMAN'S CHRISTMAS DINNER AT MR. GREEN'S.—[SKETCHED BY THEODORE R. DAVIS.]

FROM HARPER'S WEEKLY, JANUARY 28, 1865

the particulars as given in the Gospel. Indeed there have been some quite touching scenes, and I have wished Dr. Post* could have witnessed them. The General gives them all good advice—briefly and to the point, telling them they are free now, have no master nor mistress to *support,* and must be industrious and well-behaved, etc.

Meanwhile, the white citizens are "subjugated," and, what is more, they—or their leading men, lately "loyal" to Jeff. Davis,—say openly that the C.S.A. is "played out." The meeting held and resolutions adopted today—such as they are—were absolutely voluntary, without suggestion from us; and the signers to the call and others who took part embrace leading and influential citizens, heretofore active rebels, now convinced.

(Dec. 29th, 11 a.m.)

Gen. Foster is up here today and *the* General has just gone to a review of Blair's Corps; but as I can send this to Hilton Head today by an officer if finished at once I stay in to do so. The weather is bright and lovely—a fine bracing fall day we should call it. There is nothing very new to add. Indications daily increase of the tremendous moral effect our campaign has had and will have in Georgia in "knocking out the underpinning" of the C.S.A. Two men, one an ex-Captain "C.S.A.," both sent as delegates from a large meeting of citizens of two counties west of this—beyond our lines—brought the General last evening a set of resolutions adopted by the meeting, denouncing the whole kit of conspirators and declaring in *what I consider*— (that's good evidence, you'll admit)—clear and patriotic Union language their adhesion to the Government. These men walked forty miles and more to get here, dodging the rebel scouts, etc. The General re-

* A St. Louis clergyman.

ceived them most kindly, wrote them an excellent and encouraging letter to take back and show their friends, and sent them off rejoicing. The resolutions adopted here yesterday I *don't* consider "Union"; that is they are not the expression of willing loyalty, but are perhaps even more significant for that reason, coming whence they do, and as I have said *wholly voluntary* and not even suggested or hinted at by us. Col. Rockwell, who reported them, was a Rebel Colonel, and I am assured by those who know that the movement includes the leading men here. They are completely beaten,— they "feel it in their bones," and they have the sense to acknowledge and act upon it. There is much yet to be done, no doubt,—whether the story of Jeff. Davis' death be true or not, though less if he is; but while I do not think the war likely to end within a year from this as some do, I do think we now see clearly "the beginning of the end." And our General is the man who under God will bring it.

I cannot say when we leave here—the sooner the better for me, for except that I cannot get or even hope for your dear letters, I greatly prefer camp to city life so long as I am in the Army. You know now that I had a right to ask you to "trust my assurances" when we left Kingston. I have no less, and no less reasonable, confidence in the future, and if I could only feel that you were not anxious and sad I should be as happy as it is possible for me to be away from you. I cannot express the satisfaction it is to feel that I decided to enter active service. The content it brings would alone have made hardships light if I had encountered any yet. The only drawback is my almost envy of the men around me who *have* endured hardship and faced danger for three or four years already and who deserve far better than I the pleasant surroundings of my position. . . .

Your devoted H.

. . . .

From Mr. Yeatman's letter to the General, dated 26th, sending him a heartfull of congratulations,—which, let me tell you I can plainly see my "Chief" values to an extent that I am not sure you would approve, though he rarely *says* anything about them—I see that you all had the news of our being safely here on that day. Tell Cousin James from *me*, that his letter came to the General, as he will doubtless be duly advised,—and that I am strongly of opinion that "Pandora's box" will be taken *good* care of, in due time. But I repeat to you, that so far as our movements are concerned, the less attention you pay to newspaper speculations and assertions as to what *will* be, the less you will probably be disappointed. They predict so many things that 'tis quite possible that here and there some one or part of one of their infinitely numerous and various *guesses* may afterwards prove to have hit somewhere near the truth; but *which*, you cannot tell till "afterwards" comes. The most amusingly impudent thing I have seen was the "special Washington dispatch" telling what Gen. Sherman had written to the Secretary of War about his plan for the next campaign; which was a pure and complete fabrication. "Mais il faut vivre"—you know. . . .

When we do move—or soon after—I suspect there will be more puzzling over Sherman's plans than ever; and the rebels will brag as much louder, and fiercer, and bloodier, than during the last march, as their threats, etc., then exceeded those of the Atlanta campaign. By this time you must surely know the worth of all such wretched trash. Let alone Sherman's genius, it is simply and physically impossible for them to defeat his army; and we move again with an increased *moral* strength, the inevitable result of past success, which you can hardly estimate. But for the present we must remain here and await supplies, which have been coming in but slowly, compared with what they ought. . . .

(5 P.M.)—I wrote the foregoing at noon, while the General was gone out to a review. Before and since then my time was taken up with his mail, which he turns over to me and with some other matters requiring attention; and I now seize another interval to add what I may to this before the mail closes here to go down to Hilton Head. By the way, I was delighted a day or two since when with an odd mail by a supply steamer there came a short but most cordial and highly eulogistic note of congratulation from Uncle E[than]to the General, which evidently gave him very great pleasure. He has often spoken to me of Uncle E., and always in the very highest terms—higher, I think, than of any other man whose name I have ever heard him mention. At first he told me to answer—or said something about wishing me to answer it; but I had no idea of doing that, even by taking it down at his dictation. I took up some other letters, and handed that to him again and when he read it over again he said—as I expected and *wished,* for it contained an allusion to me, simply thanking him "for allowing my nephew a place near you"—he said he must answer that letter himself. From appearances he wrote quite a reply—but I did not see it. You will have to modify your ideas about great men not caring for praise, if you agree with me that Sherman is a great man—at least that he is a man of genius; for though no man is more independent of others' opinions, or more splendidly fearless and confident, though not arrogantly so, in his own, he nevertheless notices and *feels* deeply both the merited praise and the undeserved censure which he has received during this war. I should think less of him if he did not. But he does not tell everybody about it, nor has he told me so. I see it.

I enclose you a relic which you must take good care of; many people would pay high to get it. The note inclosed in it shows how it came to the General; he told me to acknowledge it, say, etc., etc., and "that I'll keep it"—and then added with a laugh—"about a week.— Do you want it, Major? You can have it if you like." So I answered the note very politely—for the General, of course,—and, having made him put *his* autograph on it, with the date, I send the paper to you, to keep for me. This venerable paper, ninety years old, containing as "news of the day" *both* (British and American) accounts of the battle of Bunker Hill—the commencement of the struggle to secure our national existence,—has to me a special interest at this crisis of the struggle to preserve it against internal foes.

We had a party two nights ago, quite a gay one, and very pleasant, if that word can be applied to an evening party of a hundred men, with *five ladies* for them all to pay homage to. Mr. Green's two large and very handsome parlors, together about 50 x 22 feet, lighted up and the light reflected from four or five splendid mirrors, with a crowd of officers, generals by the dozen and colonels and majors plenty as blackberries—Mr. Green himself, and Mr. Sorel, an old citizen of high standing, whose daughters the General and other young officers used to visit here years ago, being the only civilians. The ladies were Mrs. Elliott, a widowed, and Miss Sorel, a younger, daughter of Mr. S.— the latter quite pretty and both really "Southern *ladies*"; also Mrs. Mackland, wife of Col. M., the U.S. military P.O. agent here, and an elder and a younger lady, also residents here. The two former ladies are connections of Mr. Green also. I was introduced by Mr. Green to them, at his particular desire, but was interrupted before I had more than begun to chat with them. Mr. Sorel has four sons now in the Confederate army, and these ladies do not disguise their "sympathy" but, like all the people I have seen or heard of in Savannah, they show none of the vile rebel vindictive spirit you find elsewhere. Old Mr. Sorel said to me very earnestly that the contest was utterly hopeless and ought to be given up; and by the way, *this morning* Mr. G. B. Lamar, a prominent citizen (Mr. Yeatman knows who he is) with several others, waited on the General, by special appointment made at Mr. Lamar's request,—for what he did not say. I was very sorry I was busy elsewhere. The General told me afterwards that they came to talk about "reconstruction"—that they profess to want to "get back into the Union" but "wanted to know," said he, "what terms and conditions they could have." "I told them," said the General, "I had no terms or conditions to make—that *we* didn't consider that the *State of Georgia* ever had been out of the Union, and that as for them, we didn't care what they did—that was their business, but the United States was going to put down this rebellion anyhow." I don't give his words, but about the substance. You may think this a careless and even harsh way of talking, but it is founded, and I think very shrewdly, upon the very character of the men he was addressing. The first step to "reconstruction" is to show these "high-bred Southern gentlemen" accustomed to rule as by birth-right, first that they are utterly powerless, and then that nobody cares to solicit their obedience,—that they have *got* to obey, whether or no. Not to obey *us*—not at all, but the Government and the laws which we also obey; and that if they don't they will be crushed like flies on a wheel. This is Gen. Sherman's "policy," and it is the kindest and the *only* one; and he will crush them if need be. Hence this march and its devastation—and now the leading ex-rebels of Savannah are bitterly cursing J. D. & Co., and voluntarily abandoning their hopeless cause. And in seven or eight counties west of this we now have information that Union meetings have been and are being held, that the C.S.A. is openly denounced, and at last accounts the hitherto submissive citizens were attacking and driving out the rebel troops and scouts among them. In this way, not so rapidly as some people probably expect, with the usual foolish haste to think each success final,—but *surely,* the rebellion will be broken up. How soon God only knows. The best news I have heard in a long time is the new call for "300,000 men." The worst,—and it is enough to make a man sick,—that the N.Y. city and county authorities now offer $1000 *bounty* per man. They ought not to offer one cent; they *ought* to provide for the families of poor men who are drafted. The only real danger I see is the financial one; and this, every half-hearted expedient, every miserable "bounty," increases. As to the military features, I believe Sherman and his army will end this war; I wish I could say I believe they will end it this year.

The General's Official Report of his operations from the fall of Atlanta to the 1st January /65 is ready and will be sent to Washington probably by this mail. I dare say it will be published befort long;* when it is, pray read it, and if you don't feel equal to the whole of it, read it on the same principle that our bright boy wanted Papa to tell his story—*"begin at the end."* Don't fail.

What do the Butler people in St. Louis say of the miserable affair at Wilmington?† I could not think, of course, of saying anything disparaging of my superior officer, and he a Major General in the regular Army. But if it were not for that, I might express opinions of my own which you would smile on approvingly. . . . Of course Gen. Butler's Report will make it all right; but the single fact that though the terrific fire of Porter's ships—150 guns, the smallest of them 9-inch,— had completely silenced the guns of Fort Fisher and driven its garrison into the bomb-proofs, although volunteers from our skirmish line outside of the Fort

* It was soon printed in *General Sherman's own Account of the Great March, etc.* (New York, 1865.)

† Referring to the failure of Gen. B. F. Butler to coöperate with Adm. Porter in the first assault on Fort Fisher—a failure which led to Butler's removal from his command.

actually walked into it (only four or five of them) brought away a flag, shot an orderly off his horse, took dispatches from his person and rode his horse out of the sally port,—all without any opposition,—*yet no charge was even ordered,* this single fact, which is a fact, not resting (for us) on newspaper authority, either—followed by the pusillanimous and disgraceful withdrawal of Butler's troops, is beyond all comment and beggars all explanation. It is sheer folly to talk about the strength of the Fort or its batteries; *these were absolutely neutralized,* and the garrison huddled or hidden in the bomb-proofs were worse off than if drawn up in an open field, for there they could form and manœuvre. It was a wretched and cowardly failure, without apology or excuse, and Butler is the man responsible for it. Capt. Gadsden tells us that when his ship left New York it was the theme of universal contempt and derision, on the street, in the cars, everywhere; and that Butler's reputation was *gone.* I rejoice to hear it; nor have I heard any lamentation over it here.

I am afraid this rambling letter will not repay perusal, written at divers intervals with frequent interruptions and closed late at night to be sure of the mail which closes very early in the morning. . . .

I inclose an autograph of Admiral Dahlgren's which you can add to your collection if you like. He was at our "party" two nights ago, and a number of his officers, and was very much pleased at the opportunity to meet our officers. He is a most polished, kindly, and agreeable man, and there are some very pleasant and manly fellows among the gold sleeve-bands. . . .

III
NORTHWARD THROUGH THE
CAROLINAS

LETTERS

In the Field, January 22d (4½ P.M.) 1865
On Board Steamer "W. W. Coit"—Savannah River

But for bad weather we should have left Savannah
at least two days ago, by land. As it is, a steady and
heavy rain compelled delay, and today the General and
his staff embarked on this steamer, *en route* for Beaufort, S. C., and thence—? Probably I shall not have another opportunity for the present of writing to you, as
we shall be at Beaufort and beyond there by tomorrow
morning, and will then be out of the reach of mails for
the time. Impatient as I was on all other accounts to be
moving again, I confess I rejoiced a little in secret over
the storm which I was sure would delay us long enough
for the "Arago" mails,—as it did; and in them came
(enclosed by Uncle E.) your letter of 7th inst. Just here
let me say that your letters will come more direct and
equally certain if simply mailed at St. Louis addressed
to me at "Maj. Gen. Sherman's Headquarters *In the
Field*"; with *"via New York"* in the corner of the envelope. The army mails are all carefully distributed
and come (that is, all mails for this army) to Col.
Mackland at Savannah direct; and having them re-
mailed at Washington or anywhere else does no good.

Imagine my pleasant surprise this morning when,
being told that some ladies were in the parlor and
asked for "Maj. H" I went down and found the ladies
to be our friend Mrs. Brown,—of Morristown memory
—and a very pretty young friend of hers, a Miss Hoad-
ley, of New York,—accompanied by Mr. Brown and
Capt. Gadsden (Commanding "Arago"), just up from
Hilton Head, where the "Arago" arrived last night.
Capt. G. told me the first time I saw him at Savannah
that he thought "Louey" and his wife would come

down with him, but somehow I had not expected them. It was like old times to see them again. They had come up on this boat—Gen. Foster's boat—this morning from Hilton Head; and were going back again on her; and we had this morning received notice from the General to pack up and be ready to leave on the "Coit" when she came. And so I write on board the Coit, having suddenly bid adieu to Savannah; and I improve the opportunity to send this to New York by Mr. Brown,—my last letter for the present. I am really delighted at the good luck which not only enables me to see them again, but also enables them to see more of Gen. Sherman than they could in any other way.—We have just left the dinner table where Mrs. B. sat opposite the General, and I at her right; and I have left them all in the cabin. . . .

As to where we are going, or what we are going to do, that will all appear in due time. Nobody knows the details except Gen. Sherman himself; *very* few know even the general outlines, though my position is such that I am one of those; and you may be assured that neither the rebels nor the newspaper men know anything about it—and value what you see in the papers accordingly. This campaign cannot but be even more important in its bearings on the war than the last; it will very likely not be as much of a mere "pic-nic," because we may not go into so desirable or rich a country, —nor will it, in all probability, be as *apparently* remarkable because the novelty is worn off, like Columbus' discovery of America or his standing an egg on end.

But we have the same genius to guide us,—an even more "demoralized" enemy to meet, and the same good and loving Father to watch over us. And I assure you I am heartily glad to be moving again. I did not enter the service to "loaf" anywhere. . . .

IN THE FIELD, NEAR POCOTALIGO, January 29, 1865
Sunday Morning

Major Dayton, who has charge of the couriers etc., tells me that letters can be sent off this morning if ready soon; and I have long ago discovered that Dalgetty's rule for a soldier's eating holds equally well as to his writing letters—he had best do all he can of it every time he has a chance.

It is understood that we leave here tomorrow (Monday) morning, "for parts unknown," but you know by this time that a soldier's punctuality consists in his being ready to move at the appointed hour. Whether he does move depends on "orders" at the time. Still, if some other people have done their part by that time we shall be off. I have already written you once from this place,* and have nothing in particular to say now. Indeed I must write in constant expectation of a summons to seal up and send off, which may come at any moment and may not come for half an hour.

I shall enclose in this one of the pocket maps we had photographed for the Georgia campaign,—which I carried in my pocket all the time, and consulted daily—I was going to say hourly—from the day (19th Novr) that we "got on it." It will aid you in tracing our march from that by reference to my diary, if you choose to take the trouble and can decipher the microscopic scrawl of which I don't wonder you complain. But of course space in that, as in all other incumbrances, was everything. I have still four more of those little books not yet used; for I have not kept up the Diary at all as such since I sent those two to you. I may begin another today for this campaign but cannot promise it, for I am not sure I shall be able to keep it up. I have already told you we take no wall-tents but only "flies" which are not as large nor as convenient, especially in the being able to have a light at night—

* Letter not preserved.

for both ends of a "fly" are open except you close them with bushes or hang a blanket or poncho over them. However, if I do keep a diary it will be for your benefit, and I would do a good many things to please you that I should think too much trouble otherwise.

This map* I enclose to be kept for me as a memento of the campaign, which will be of interest to me hereafter. The General many times used and referred to it on the march, it being a reduced photographic copy of the large one prepared for himself and which he carried in those well-worn old saddle bags of his. Since I began this letter Col. Poe (Chief Engineer) has come into our room and distributed our copies of the new maps just prepared for this campaign, and I shall now begin to feel like knowing where we are. In due time I hope to send you these also, and that they will be equally valued mementoes of a more important, probably more tedious march.

The weather continues cold and clear—really very cold for this latitude, whence we infer that there is bitter weather farther North.

I received last evening in a straggling mail a note from Mr. McPherson of the 14th inst., seven days later than my last from you. . . . I have replied to him—and had half a mind to remind him of his advice to me when he heard I was going into the Army—"It's none of my business, but I think after *staying out so long* I'd stay out the rest of it." He didn't know that that was one of the sore points with me. However, I have not alluded to it, but only expressed my satisfaction at being in the service.

By the way, it is now "3 months" and 3 days since I left home; and Col. G. is not yet a true prophet. As I told you then, I was as "sick of it" the day I started as I ever could be. By the way tell Mr. How† with my compliments that I was rejoiced to hear of his hanging

---

* Unfortunately not preserved.

† John How, a St. Louis neighbor of the Hitchcocks.

out that flag with "Honor to whom," etc.; it was a
merited rebuke to "Frank's"* unprincipled enemies.
Yet I dare say I don't agree with "John" about the
"Emancipation Ordinance." It was time, long before
this, to clear away the rubbish and cut loose from the
dead remains of what never lived save by tolerance. I
am glad to remember that in the State Convention,
. . . at its last session, I advocated emancipation to
take effect January 1st, 1864—though desiring humane
provisions and protection both against the whites and
themselves for the freed blacks which, if we could
mould and model the world to suit ourselves, would
have been very fine. But it is useless to haggle at details
and insist on impracticabilities, however desirable in
themselves, "in such times as these." When a thunder-
storm clears the air some trees are apt to be blown
down and some houses struck by lightning; but after all
we must have thunderstorms. I think the analogy a
good one, and while the wanton perpetrators of outrage
are wholly guilty, yet the outrages, etc., of war I recog-
nize as being after all as much a part of the inscrutable
and all-wise providence of God, and as necessary and
ultimately as beneficial, as the terror which His wisdom has made part of the visible phenomena of Nature.

I am writing, you see, at a gallop, awaiting the summons at any moment, and with Ewing, Poe, and T. R.
Davis standing and sitting near, chatting over maps,
looking at D.'s sketches, and discussing things generally.

We—and by "we" you understand of course that I
mean the General and his Staff—are occupying the
house formerly owned by a Dr. Ficklin; a Southern
country house, on brick pillars and arches some 6½ or
7 feet high all round, with four principal rooms and an
odd little room projecting at each rear corner; and with
no second story, though there might have been a good
garret made under the roof. Ewing, Davis, Dr. Moore

* Gen. F. P. Blair's.

(chief Medical officer) and I have our pallets on the floor of the right hand front room. The General, Dayton, and McCoy are in the rear room behind us,—and Gen. Barry and his staff and the rest of ours occupy the other rooms, save that our Staff Quartermaster and Eddy, the telegraph operator, are outside in "flies."

The first night *we* reached here our wagon train hadn't come up, and we had to make the best of it with one blanket apiece on the floor. Since the train came up with the rest of the blankets we have done well enough, Spanish moss five or six inches thick under the lower blanket making the floor a good deal softer, and an extempore table having been rigged up yesterday out of an old hospital bunk,—on which I am writing—with a valise, when needed, for a seat. It is amusing to find how small one's absolute necessities are when one is forced down to it. But it is simply a mistake to suppose that because men can "do without" their usual comforts, etc., and take it very cheerfully too, that they cease to value them when attainable. On the contrary, they value them the more; but when they are not to be had, why that's enough and no fretting. I can and do enjoy our plain fare—all except the heavy biscuits which Manuel makes now and then, and which I rate him soundly for, apparently to his amusement—as heartily as anybody, or as I do the choicest meats, etc.; indeed with the air and exercise, etc. comes a relish that nothing else gives. But neither I nor anybody else here —not even the General, in my opinion, for all his praises of "hard tack"—but thoroughly enjoys the delicacies we get now and then, when some young lady sends a barrel of fine apples, for instance, to the General and gets an autograph note of thanks in return, as a day or two since (per Capt. Gadsden)—to say nothing of the jellies, and *fruit cake* and canned fruits "and sich like" which from time to time have appeared on our mess table, to disappear with a rapidity at which your ideas of soldierly appetite I fear would be shocked.

After all Dugald Dalgetty (in the "Legend of Mont-
rose") had some of the truest characteristics of a genu-
ine soldier about him, and his practical wisdom finds
its counterpart in the experience of many a man in this
army. The fact is—strange and novel as the assertion
may seem—that human nature is a compound affair of
which both body and soul are elements; and it is a false
and one-sided theory of human life which omits either;
—though I do not say they are equally exalted.

This place evidently has been settled a long time, for
though all round it and almost within a stone's throw
of the house are dense woods and thick underbrush and
swamps "convenient" (especially for outlying pickets
and "guerrillas") yet just around the house are many
noble live oaks and cedars, not less than seventy or
eighty years old, planted in regular rows. It is bad for
the live oaks and cedars that so many soldiers are
camped round here in cold weather. Not far from the
house are strong and well built earth works—heavy
pine logs filled in and fronted with earth, with embrasures for guns, and a ditch on both sides, thrown up by
our men as soon as they came here, probably a mile
long or more. A single division could hold these works
against a very large force; but the rebels have made no
demonstrations since they "got up and dusted" on the
15th. Only their pickets and mounted scouts are thrown
on this side the Salkehatchie every day or two, that being one of the little rivers which form the Combahee
and which runs some four or five miles east of us. Our
picket line is from half a mile to a mile outside of these
Headquarters; but every thing is so quiet around us
that you would not know what is going on. We have all
we want thus far, and their game is to watch us when
we move and penetrate those puzzling plans of Sherman. *"Nous verrons."* . . .

IN THE FIELD NEAR POCOTALIGO, January 30th 1865
Monday P.M.

We leave here tomorrow morning (Tuesday) for certain. The troops recently camped around here are all moving, the long line of wagons showing their white tops through the distant trees as they wound along the road this morning. The last packages of office papers, orders, etc., and superfluous articles, cut down this time even more than at Kingston, are being made up by the clerks near me in the office-tent as I write, and I expect to send this by the orderly who carries them to the landing to go down the Pocataligo River and back to Savannah—perhaps in a few moments, perhaps longer.

I am rejoiced to say that the weather continues to be and promise all we could wish. The nights are cool, and quite cold towards morning, even sleeping as we have done here in a house. When we get into our "flies" it will be necessary to sleep *under* instead of *on* three out of four blankets; otherwise it will be pleasanter in them. Today is a most lovely specimen of a fine day in a Southern winter—the air, since the sun got fairly up into the heavens, only bracing, the sunshine bright and warm, and the sky a beautiful and cloudless blue, save where in one or two directions clouds *not* of the heavens dull or darken it a little near the horizon. I think I shall never see a distant column of smoke rising, hereafter, but it will remind me of Sherman in Georgia and South Carolina.

We are all well and in good spirits, of course. When or where we shall come out nobody seems to have any idea, only that Sherman knows what he is about, as usual. . . .

My turn as caterer for the mess begins tomorrow morning, but I shall not invite you to dine with us yet a while. Capt. Nichols (now Bvt. Major) has been "running the mess" ever since I joined, and might indeed have thrown it on me at Savannah; but as I was pretty busy then and he had nothing else to do whatever—being an Aid-de-camp,—he held it till now to accommodate me. As he laid in some supplies before we left Savannah—sending to New York for them— and moreover I could not lay in any now if I tried (that is any "store goods") my chief duties as caterer *en route,* besides giving Manuel (the cook) any necessary directions, will be to try and prevent what we have being stolen, and to see that our darkies and some of our mounted escort keep up a judicious and "liberal" system of foraging as we go along. Whether pigs, chickens, turkeys and the like will be found in equal abundance this time, or whether I shall succeed as Nichols did at Ogeechee Church in disinterring anywhere a barrel of sugar, or a lot of preserves, or any other good things, remains to be seen. We start with part of a barrel of flour and part of a barrel of soft crackers, and four boxes of "hard tack," among other things, and I have already given directions to use the two former with sufficient stinginess to make them last as long as possible and the "hard tack" often enough to meet the General's approval, I am sure. . . .

As I told you in my last, the idea that because a soldier usually cannot get good things he doesn't enjoy them *when he can,* is a grave and dangerous error, and one which cannot be too earnestly avoided by those gentle and adored divinities who preside over the putting up of "boxes" and the like. Mother may send as many *crullers* as she pleases—or might if they did not take up so much room as to make the freight too heavy; and if you know of any superfluous mincemeat, which wasn't used up last Christmas and won't keep till next, or are embarrassed to dispose of any of the tomatoes Maria put up last summer for *us,* or of any other small stores including jellies, on hand when you left the house, I will undertake to find a most proper and patriotic use for them if you will simply send them to Wm. W. Parkin, (Olyphant & Co) 114 Pearl St., New York and tell him to have them put on board the

"Arago" in the personal charge of Capt. Gadsden, addressed to me at "Maj. Gen. Sherman's Headquarters *in the Field,*" and marked "Mess Stores." . . .

Sherman's march northward through the Carolinas, with communications suspended, was now about to begin. Major Hitchcock accordingly resumed his diary, but persevered in writing it for only about a week. The small volume containing it was the third he used.

CAMPAIGN DIARY

These diaries not being intended as complete histories either of army movements or events generally, but simply partial memoranda to be made when convenient, of such personal experiences *on the march* as I may think of note, this one is taken up in anticipation of *our* "sallying forth" (a pet phrase of W.T.'s—*vide* his letters) tomorrow.

Fort McAllister was taken Dec. 13/64—most of that night H. H. spent in completing the former diaries to that date, and the next day they were taken on board the fleet by him and in due time reached home. After that current events were noted in letters home. This evening the last of these for the present—and for how long?—was written and sent.

It is pretty thoroughly understood—fully by those who know—that this is certain to be a very different campaign from the last; and probably—so *W.T. tells H. H.*—"a dangerous and difficult movement." Why so, will appear hereafter. Lucky I, to have been so pleasantly introduced to the service before; luckier I, if I shall safely go through this, and if so, the harder it was, the pleasanter to remember. It would hardly be satisfactory to have campaigned only in sunshine, even though one's self was not to blame for it. But—*nous verrons.*

About the 3d January, Howard *begun* to move part of his wing round on the right; the 17th Corps came to Beaufort, S. C. and camped near there, and on the 13th and 14th marched to this place—or rather to the fort at the town of Pocotaligo, some two miles S. of the railroad. On the way they found several rebel works covering "causeways" on which the road ran through the swamps and rice-fields; first at "Garden's Corner," then another further on, and finally at Pocotaligo, some two miles S. of the railroad. By the night of the 14th all these were taken up to the last above, by flanking them, with not much of a fight, and losses not over thirty in all. One of Leggett's staff was killed and one of G. A. Smith's was wounded. By night our men had reached the causeway leading to the Pocotaligo fort, which is a strong work, pierced for twenty-four guns, and in which the rebs had eleven or twelve field pieces. It was too late that evening (Sat. 14th) to attack, and besides, it was intended to make a detour and take it on both flanks as well as in front; so nothing more was done than to push our skirmishers well up toward the work, who when seen and fired on with grape and canister, lay flat in the grass. Col. Fairchild* of 16th Wisconsin, commanding 1st brigade in this advance, tells me as a fact that our men got up so close as to hear the rebels shout and talk to each other in the works; and that an officer inside (rebel) was plainly heard to tell his men—"Look out, boys, you haven't got the d— nigger troops to fight now—this is Sherman's army." Next morning the work was evacuated and the rebs gone—unfortunately their guns also. Col. F. says they could plainly hear the cars running on the railroad that night till nearly 2 A.M., and easily guessed what was going on; but the country was so swampy and bad, that, ignorant of it as they were, our forces could only wait for daylight. Blair at once occupied Pocotaligo and cut the railroad, and the rebels fell back to the Salkehatchie River. Howard sent word of this success to Gen. S. at Savannah on the 16th, and characteristically rejoiced that he had secured Pocotaligo with the loss of so few "precious lives" and also without fighting a battle on the Sabbath (15th), which he said he had feared he would be obliged to do. Both the humane and the religious feeling were like Howard.

* Later Bvt. Brig. Gen. Cassius Fairchild.

On the 22d January Gen. S. and staff left Savannah, exactly one month from the day we entered it. I am ashamed to say that I never went down to "Bonaventure," the cemetery four or five miles from the city, celebrated for its magnificent avenues of live-oaks, whose dense foliage and overhanging branches, grey with pendulous "Spanish moss," give it by all accounts a peculiarly sombre and imposing scenery. The truth is that I went seldom anywhere; being much of the time actually busy writing for the General, and always liable at any time to be called on by him—so that I disliked to be out of the way when I *might* be needed, for though he never finds fault, he does notice very closely the manner in which officers do their duty. Besides I wrote a good many letters of my own—and so day by day slipped by; and though I made two or three appointments to go there—Bonaventure—with other officers, something always prevented. It is a bad plan ever to let slip *any* opportunity of doing what one wishes to do. "Some other time" is generally *never*. . . .

We reached Beaufort by 8 or 9 P.M., still raining, dark and ugly night. Had disagreeable time enough—went ashore with Col. E., tramped about through the mud and rain, couldn't get any room at hotel, etc. Ewing roused Harbor Master and insisted on having the boat unloaded forthwith, etc., etc. . . . We all staid on the boat that night. Next day we turned out Dr. Treanor* (Chief Medical officer of the Department) and his assistants, from a house in which they were comfortably located, and took possession of the same for "our staff." Thus, as the wise and excellent Dr. Franklin long ago remarked, the big fishes eat the little fishes and the little fishes eat the minnows; and so we of the staff whom Mr. Secretary Stanton, Gen. Meigs, Gen. Townsend, etc., etc., turned out of *our* rooms (at Mrs. Green's) in Savannah, restored the equilibrium

* Bvt. Lt. Col. John Trenor, Jr.?

by turning out the Doctors at Hilton Head. Dr. T. "didn't see it" when Dayton and I went there with Gen. Saxton* and told him to leave—but a few pointed though paternal words from Gen. S. cleared his vision rapidly and he was soon as courteous as need be. He was in a U.S. house, and a U.S. officer—and ought to have taken it quietly at once. These gentlemen get spoiled by their good quarters.

The General came up to Beaufort on the 23rd, Monday, and staid one day—quartering at Gen. Saxton's. The latter owns the house he lives in—a fine large double house on Bay Street, fronting the sea, with a handsome yard, evergreens, etc., in front. He bought it at one of the U.S. tax sales, and I was told gave $1000 for it. These tax sales—for U.S. direct taxes—are simply a means of confiscation in fee simple, and, as that thing ought and is to be done, are a very good way to do it. On the 23rd I took breakfast at Gen. Saxton's with Gen. Howard. . . . Gen. S. talked to me about St. Louis where he was stationed in and before 1861, expressed great admiration for *Margie,*† and also spoke of other young ladies and houses where he visited. . . . Saxton is not popular with our officers generally, many of whom—justly or unjustly—think or say they think he took up the "nigger business" in order to get advancement. He has not seen any active service in the field, and I have heard it repeatedly stated has never been under fire; but don't know how this is. *Per contra,* Gen. Howard is said to think very highly of him as a sincere and conscientious man; Gen. Sherman evidently does not hold that opinion. Either is likely to be prejudiced, one for and the other against him—Howard's kind disposition and truly Christian charity, and Sherman's quick way of judging men, with his dislike to theorists and "abolitionists," etc., and his special

* Brig. Gen. Rufus Saxton, then "Inspector of Settlements and Plantations."
† See note, p. 15.

appreciation of men of action, perhaps disqualifying either. I have not seen enough of Saxton to form a just opinion. He was very polite to me, of course, being *on the staff*, etc. He does not make any great impression on one, at first sight.

General left next day (24th) for Pocotaligo, taking only Ewing and his orderly, and the ambulance, and going with Howard, who took Strong,* his Inspector General; both their Headquarters trains to follow on Thursday, 26th. So the rest of us staid two days longer at Beaufort.

I have not time now to say even the little I might about Beaufort; for though we were there three days— what with writing letters, some long ones as to E.A.H., and home—selecting photographic views to send Mary, looking for sundry small articles needed for the next march, etc., I saw less and learned less of its peculiar features than I ought. It is not a pretty place, nor even has a fine sea-view like Hilton Head, though considerably larger. It is the place where the "experiment" of educating the negro, etc., was begun and is going on; Saxton being the Moses and "Father French,"† who is irreverently called "Holy Joe" by officers who don't believe him to be more sincere or disinterested than he ought to be, the Aaron of the enterprise. I had seen Mr. F. at Savannah, and heard him hold forth to Gen. Sherman in a tone so like cant, if it was not that, that I could have foretold the impression it would surely produce. I saw him again here; and my first impression of him is bad. He has a face far more sanctimonious than sanctified, and I confess to some amusement at the General's sharp comments upon his having impressed upon all the negro couples who wished to live together, the necessity of their being duly married—he performing

* Lieut. Col. (later Brig. Gen.) William E. Strong.
† The Rev. Mansfield French, a Methodist pioneer in work for the Negro during the War.

the ceremony *for one dollar apiece!* No doubt it was a lawful fee, etc., etc.,—but it looks bad.

On Wednesday evening, 25th, through Capt. Cole, signal officer with us, I was invited to and took tea with Judge Worden and wife, at the "Rhett House," so-called, where Edmund Rhett* formerly lived and where (so they say in Beaufort, but 'tis doubtful) the South Carolina ordinance of Secession was got up and drafted. How the old South Carolina nabobs who formerly made this place their summer home, must gnash their teeth over its present use and occupancy! It is odd that this house, if its local celebrity is deserved, should now be occupied by one of the 3 "U.S. Direct Tax Commissioners" whose business it is to carry out the law which is stripping those conspirators of their property. Judge W. is a Wisconsin man, but once lived for several years in South Carolina—a "nice old gentleman," very quiet, kindly, plain old man, but intelligent and of excellent standing (C. says) at home, and entirely devoted to his duties. He showed me his record book of sales already made, to both black and white men— among others to "Prince Rivers," the colored sergeant mentioned in Col. Higginson's article ("Leaves from an Officer's Journal") in the Atlantic for Jan. 4/65. Rivers has bought quite a number of lots. I mentioned the "Atlantic" article, which I thought very injudicious in its praise of him, as likely to make him conceited—and was told by Mrs. W. that he was a good deal spoiled and very conscious, etc. Still she is not exactly the oracle I would consult—a plain, rather elderly, rather hard-featured woman—dare say a good woman in her way, though,—but a contrast to the "Southern ladies" who used to rule here. Yet she is a type of a better because more useful and more truly respectable class.

We left Beaufort Thursday morning, 26th, train and

---

* A son of Robert Barnwell Rhett, editor of the *Charleston Mercury*, and member of the Confederate Congress.

all. Forgot to say that I was agreeably surprised on
Tuesday by Mr. and Mrs. Brown and Miss H. coming
up there, with Capt. Gadsden, from Hilton Head. They
only spent the afternoon, and I did not know they had
come till night; but as Nichols did the agreeable, drove
the ladies out to Smith's plantation, etc., it was all
right.

Jan. 26th. Went from Beaufort to Pocotaligo, a long
day's ride, about twenty-one miles, though called
twenty-four. Sky clear, but air very cold and wind
bitter and piercing, so that after 2 P.M. the ice by the
roadside, over an inch thick, was not at all thawed.
Everybody felt and complained of the cold, though
after an hour or so I felt it very little, toes and fingers
having got pretty comfortable. Wore only the cape;
with overcoat would have been all right. Road lay
through woods and swamps and very uninviting country, little settled; frequently bad, though much better
than if not frozen stiff; much corduroying, and usually closely bordered either by the dense woods full of
almost impenetrable underbrush, or marshes, swamps
and wet rice-fields, on both sides. If this was a sample
of South Carolina roads, Georgia will be a joke to it.
At Port Royal ferry crossed on Foster's pontoon
bridge; two or three miles further came to Garden's
Corner where rebs made first stand against Howard.
Here as everywhere they had earthworks and guns
commanding the narrow "causeway" through the
swamp, but were "flanked out." At a number of points
beyond this we found earthworks of similar purpose.
Passed directly through the fort or large earthwork at
the settlement or town of Pocotaligo, which is two
miles or so E. of *Pocotaligo Station* on the Charleston
& Savannah R.R.; had no time to examine but saw it
was a strong work, fully commanding the long causeway in front. Went on to and beyond the R.R. at Pocotaligo Station, before reaching which we met Gen.

Sherman, Ewing and others in the road—General being out reconnoitring in person.

We crossed railroad at the Station and went to Dr. Ficklin's house say half a mile north of it, already selected by General for Headquarters. It is a mere country house, on brick pillars, one story, four main rooms with hall dividing either pair, and two more stuck on, one at either rear corner. Around it and in yard are numerous, and some very fine, old live oak trees, also cedars and a few well grown magnolias, planted in rows, evidently at least fifty years old—General says seventy or eighty—the live oaks forming a fine avenue on one side and in rear of house. The place was abandoned when our troops went up there first, and no furniture, etc., remained save an old sofa or two. Some of the 15th Corps were camped between the house and the road—the house fronting south. Saw Gen. Force* there commanding brigade—formerly Cincinnati lawyer, wounded July 22d, then thought fatally, by ball (minie) passing in below one eye and out below the other; but wonderfully recovered without permanent injury even to sight, and with an enviable scar. Fine looking man, and General says fine officer.

Our Headquarters train could not make the whole march, and so that night we did as best we could, lucky in having house to sleep in. Eddy, Davis and H. H. took one front room, and the rest the other rooms, Dayton and McCoy in rear room. The General and Ewing staid at Blair's Headquarters and were comfortable. Fortunately I had bought two more pair of good Government blankets at Beaufort, and strapped one pair on the cantle of my new saddle the night before we left, instructing Aleck to keep it permanently there for accidental needs; and had also put a liberal lunch in my saddle bags before starting. Thanks to this, I had something to eat—not otherwise easily attainable, as I knew none of the officers encamped there and

* Brig. Gen. (later Bvt. Maj. Gen.) Manning F. Force.

would not have gone to their messes—and had a blanket to wrap up in that night before the fire. But save me from sleeping on a bare floor in one pair of blankets on a cold night with the wind pouring in at every rattling window. The ground cannot be and is not nearly so hard. On the road I did not feel the ride at all, and when it ended felt fresh enough to ride ten miles further. But once dismounted, cold and hungry, I felt stiff, sore and used up, and the floor did not rest me much. They accused me of talking in my sleep all night. Very likely, for I dreamed all sorts of uncomfortable things.

Next day however (Friday, 27th) Lieut. Howard, our Headquarters Quartermaster, came up with train, and we were all right. A few armfuls of Spanish moss from the trees with my blankets—three pair in all— made a capital bed, and with Manuel at work and the mess wagon to draw from, cold lunches were soon forgot.

We are waiting here now to hear from XX and XIV, who were to move up and cross at Sister's Ferry. General is surprised not to have heard from them by this time, but hourly expects a courier and we probably leave here tomorrow.

Nothing specially worth noting since we came here. Nothing for us to do save some little "making of orders" for Dayton. Except indeed that the day before we left Savannah the General handed me for review the only Court Martial proceedings that have come up to him since I joined, and which—as the sentence is *cashiering* and *imprisonment in a penitentiary,* require his approval as the Commanding General in the field. I have carefully examined them and reported approving them. One of the charges is mutiny, and defence (in part) that no "plan" or *conspiracy* was proven. Mentioning this to General he said rather hastily that one man cannot commit a mutiny. On renewed examination and consideration I was satisfied one man *can,* and so reported—and he approved my (verbal) report and directed the necessary order made at once.

This point is as yet our most advanced post—is not over three miles from the Salkehatchie, the rebels' line, and our pickets are only a mile or two beyond this. The picket guard mounting takes place just before our house every afternoon, and I intended to walk out with them and see the pickets relieved and posted, but have not. Blair's Headquarters are two or three miles off, S. and W. of us, nearer Poco's landing, and Howard's not far from his.

Yesterday Hatch (who is of the Department of the South, and immediately under Foster) sent a brigade part of white, part black troops (two reg'ts of the latter, I believe) who passed us and camped out near the Salkehatchie. Walked out to their camps. The white troops are "vets" and march and look best; but the blacks are a fine looking body of men, and one of the regiments fought at Olustee. A captain in it, an intelligent man, though not of much culture, who was at Olustee fully confirms the good account then given of the negroes' good behavior there; claiming, I do not doubt truly, from other evidence also, that their steadiness under very adverse circumstances, saved the defeat from being a total and serious rout. I asked him about the qualities of the negroes, but he did not answer *by comparison* with the whites as I wished, but gave good accounts of them in general terms. I saw them building their huts (with shelter tent roofs) and they seemed as apt, as careful and as industrious, as whites could be. They told me, on inquiry, that their Col. (Willis—35th U.S.C.T.) had set them at it; but the white officers were not superintending them.

Today Hatch's force broke camp and marched back to this point where they will remain for the present, within the line of earth-works—good strong ones too— thrown up by the 17th Corps in rear of this house and for say half a mile down to the main road, as soon as

they came up. These works were very quickly made—
ditched on both sides, heavy pine logs and earth forming parapet say four feet high and three or four feet
thick, pierced for guns commanding road to N. with
good embrasures, and with "head logs" all along;
whose use, by the way, Hatch knew nothing of when he
came here and saw them. A division can hold these
works against an army.

POCOTALIGO, SOUTH CAROLINA
Tuesday, Jan. 31/65.

Still waiting here for advices from Savannah River
which General is disappointed not to have received, but
supposes the heavy rains a week ago—just as we left
Savannah—which were very general, have delayed the
movements there. He expected a courier last night, and
if one had come we should have left here early this A.M.
None came, and departure was postponed first till
noon, then till tomorrow, when we leave *anyhow*. The
weather continues clear and is for two or three days
past very pleasant—much warmer than when we came
up, when it was very cold. We ought to have received
today, or by tonight anyhow, the mails which came on
the "Fulton" to Hilton Head Saturday night last—
but hear nothing of them. My last letter from M. was
dated 7th inst., and unless we do yet hear tonight, I
may not get another for five or six weeks. But a note
from W. W. McPherson of 14th inst., enclosing a letter
from Mrs. Blackwood to go by flag to Charleston, says
all were well then.

It is a great bore to be idle thus, expecting all the
time to have something to do, but having nothing. Next
to an Indian's life a soldier's has the strongest and
most sudden contrasts of labor and idleness—danger
and safety—activity and rest. Today everybody, except
those on duty in their turn, is unemployed, listless,
wondering what will come next; tomorrow all are busy,
on the move, hard at work, perhaps. It is these inter-

vals of absolute leisure—so far as my duty is concerned
—with the irregular and unequal pressure of duty
when it does come, that is the worst feature of camp
life. It is impossible to escape a certain restlessness,
and almost as difficult to many, it is evident, to resist
the temptation to while away the idle hours with cards
and drink. Nor do I blame a soldier,—I mean a common
soldier—for yielding to these temptations as much as
I would the same man in the steadier employments of
civil life. He cannot turn from the hard, dangerous, and
exciting duties of the field to the quiet occupations
which *at home* would naturally fill up his leisure half
so readily as there. His little "dog-tent" gives little
opportunity for reading or writing—hardly more than
room to crawl into for sleep—even if there were
"transportation" for books or papers. He is obliged
to live "out doors" when the weather permits, and
among his comrades; and of course he finds it easier to
pass the time in some amusement which does amuse
without effort. Still a man who has sense enough and
character enough to see the dangers may avoid them;
I only refer to the peculiar influences and temptations.

The General walked down to Gen. Hazen's Headquarters this morning, at the R.R. station (Pocotaligo)
about a fourth to half a mile from ours, and asked me
to go along with him. Sat an hour or so with Hazen who
is a pleasant man in manner—apparently thirty-five to
forty years—thirty-five probably, a West Pointer, and
a good soldier. He occupies a double log cabin at the
R.R. station.

As we returned I mentioned to Gen. S. an incident at
Beaufort characteristic of Gen. Howard, which I happened to see when strolling with him and Dr. Duncan
near the dock; a civilian Quartermaster's clerk ordering us in an insolent tone off of a platform scales—
Howard mildly remonstrated as to his tone and manner, the fellow continued noisy and insolent after
learning who H. was—H. broke out on him for a mo-

ment, ordered him in a sudden loud and peremptory
tone to shut up (he ought to have knocked him down)
and then suddenly turned round and walked rapidly
away, evidently fearing to trust his own temper. Duncan saw Gen. Saxton a few moments after, reported the
facts, and Saxton very properly dismissed the fellow
instantly. He then came to Howard and made a very
humble apology; and upon that Howard not only for-
gave him but prevailed on Saxton to reinstate him in
his place. Gen. S. agreed with me that the whole thing
was characteristic, and went on to praise Howard, as I
have heard him do before. "Howard is a good man and
sincere Christian," said he, "he is an instance that a
man may be a good Christian and *yet a good soldier*"
(*sic*). By the way I heard Gen. S. at Beaufort, in a conversation at Saxton's house, tell Howard that if anything happened to himself (S) on the campaign, he (H)
was to take command of the Army, although (which
Howard alluded to at the time) Slocum is Howard's
senior in commission.

Today I took charge of the mess, *vice* Nichols, who
retires after "running" it some three months. I have
no fancy for it, and might have thrown it upon Eddy,
the telegraph operator, but felt that he was not the
man for it and that I had no right to shirk it. Somebody
must "run" it, and as at one time or another all the
officers—Eddy is not an officer—have had charge of it
except myself and Lt. Howard, our new Quartermaster, and Howard really has his hands full with his regular daily duties, taking care of the train, etc., I felt that
I ought to take it and did so. On taking account of
stores on hand I sent over at once to Capt. Corayn,
A.C.S. 2d Div. (Hazen's) 15th A.C. and bought flour,
hams, coffee and white sugar, in all about $80. Corayn
presented us with a quarter of very good fresh beef. I
also write tonight to W. W. Parkin to buy sundries in
New York as directed and have them packed and sent
to Van Vliet, C.Q.M. in N.Y., ready to be sent to us

by the first opportunity after we strike salt water
again. When will that be? Hope I may not have as bad
luck as Capt. Steele of Blair's staff, at Beaufort. He
was sent to New York from Savannah and returned
with "stores," etc., etc., bought in New York amount-
ing to over $800 worth; had them unloaded on dock and
a guard placed over them for the night. Next morning
the whole lot were gone save a barrel or two of very
little value! Rather a hard joke on Blair and staff!
Nothing recovered, of course; one learns to expect to
have things stolen in the army, and to keep at least one
eye open accordingly.

Tomorrow we start for certain. I have Nichols again
for my room-mate or rather tent-mate. . . .

"HICKORY HILL P.O." SOUTH CAROLINA
Wednesday, February 1/65.

Today *our* march commenced—the General and staff
—from Pocotaligo and "The White Settlements." The
campaign really began two weeks ago, when the 17th
Corps took Pocotaligo; but till we left that place we
were not beyond easy communication. From today we
can expect no more mails and are fairly on the move
again.

Marched today eighteen miles in all, from the R.R.
station at Pocotaligo to "Hickory Hill P.O." Weather
fine and clear and not too cold. Roads comparatively
good, country not much settled; woods border the road
almost every foot of the way. Found sundry creeks,
which are swamps as usual, and all of which had been
more or less obstructed by felled timber. In several instances large pine trees had been felled across the road
at these places, and at all of them plenty of brush, small
trees, branches, etc., had been piled up. But our pioneers went into and through them with such vigor that
our party was not delayed at all the whole day. We had
started from the rear (Hazen's) division, and passed
through the whole column, overtaking Logan with the

advance (Woods') division at this place by 3 P.M., about
an hour after they had reached there. Jno. E. Smith's*
(3d) division came into the column from the left during
the day and camped a mile or so down the road, just
across the last swamp (not on map)—Hazen about
three miles S. of us. The enemy, said to be Wheeler's
cavalry, were not far ahead all day, retreating. They
had expected us on this road, for the trees cut down in
all the swamps *but the last* before reaching Hickory
Hill had evidently been cut two or three days—the
quantity of turpentine or pine sap exuded from the cut
ends of the pine trees showed it. But it was also evident
they had expected to delay us, for all the creeks and
swamps up to and including "Alligator Swamp" had
been thus obstructed, the trees in the swamp nearest to
Hickory Hill had been *chopped* at, and many of them
cut half through, *but more of them had been cut down.*
Our advance was so rapid that we got through and beyond all their finished obstructions, and came upon
them while trying to obstruct this last swamp and
drove them out before a single tree fell. They did not
stop to fight, but ran. Near this swamp, S. of it, we saw
where they had bivouacked along the road the night
before—corn shucks, remnants of fodder, sheds of
fence-rails and extinguished camp-fires, for at least a
quarter of a mile along the road in the woods: signs of
probably a brigade of cavalry, our officers thought. We
reached Hickory Hill by 3½ P.M. Like so many other
Southern "Post Offices," it was no town but simply
the homestead of a planter. We found quite a large and
unusually comfortable frame house, with numerous
out-buildings, on something of an elevation, but of
course *no* hickory trees that I saw, though plenty of
large pines. The house faces south, and a branch road
directly from in front of it crosses the Coosawhatchie
River, which is in plain sight at the foot of the hill on
that side. Across the river and on this road part of the

* Bvt. Maj. Gen. John E. Smith.

rebs had retreated, but were still visible and as we rode
up Logan had just got two guns in position and threw
three or four shells into them from in front of the
house, which soon drove them from the bridge over the
river and then from a rail barricade further down the
road beyond it which they had thrown up say 800 yards
from us; and also crossing some troops, a regiment or
two, they left. The artillery was used by us partly to
show that we had it, partly also to notify Corse, who
was to have been marching up that road from Robertville to join his Corps at this place, and it was hoped
was with his (XV[4]) division in this hearing.

But later in the day came an officer from A. S. Williams commanding XX,* reporting that he (Williams)
with two divisions (Jackson and Ward) less two brigades, was still at Robertville, and that Geary (XX[1])
and all of XIV, and Corse, *were still at Sister's Ferry;*
a second freshet in the Savannah River having flooded
the road on this side for two or three miles opposite
and above S. Ferry to Palichocola Bluff, and that Slocum thought it would be three or four days before they
could cross, K[ilpatrick]'s cavalry division being also
on W. side of the Savannah River.—Bad news this, and
vexatious delay. The officer who brought the note had
ridden forty miles today, from Robertville S.E. to
Coosawhatchie, thence to Pocotaligo, thence following
and overtaking us here. But the General made orders
to push on all the same, sending back word to Slocum
and K. to hurry up as fast as possible. Meanwhile we
with the 3d Division of 15th Corps had been pushing
up this road, Howard and Blair with XVII had taken
the road up and along the west bank of Salkehatchie,
to our right, they aiming at Rivers' Bridge and we at
Beaufort's Bridge, both over the Salkehatchie River.

This place was owned by a Mrs. McBride, a rich
widow, reported by the darkies as a very hard and
cruel mistress. She was gone long before we came. All

* Bvt. Maj. Gen. A. S. Williams.

the whites seem to have fled before us, except that in a few instances "poor whites" have been left in the dwellings of their rich neighbors in hopes to save the houses. Dr. Moore rode ahead and stopped at one of these; says the man in charge, whose family also there, described himself as of the "poor white" class, and spoke in no friendly terms of the rich people; asserted that he had known more than one instance in the neighborhood of the rich planters taking "poor whites" on accusation of trading with their negroes—which is a heinous offence, for it encourages the negroes to steal, etc., etc.—tarring and feathering them and riding them on a rail across the Savannah River. But like *all* the planters' houses I have seen in the interior of Georgia and South Carolina so far, this "rich widow" does not seem to have had half the *comfort* out of her money that many a Northern farmer on 80 or 160 acres has. Rough rail fences, except just around the house—unthrifty looking yard, cabins and out buildings, and general air of slovenliness, dirt and waste. But we find already more forage than we expected, and are agreeably disappointed in the available chickens, etc., for the mess.

CAMP IN THE FIELD
AT X ROADS NEAR MOUTH OF "DUCK CREEK,"
ON N. SIDE OF "COOSAWHATCHIE SWAMP," SOUTH CAROLINA
Thursday, February 2/65.

Marched today thirteen miles,—general direction N.W., nearly parallel to and along left bank of Coosawhatchie River (called Coosawhatchie Swamp this far up)—from "Hickory Hill P.O." to these X Roads, from which "Duck Branch P.O." is distant about two or three miles, across the Coosawhatchie. Weather still fine and clear, but not so bright sunshine as hitherto: signs of rain ahead.

Roads today quite good, that is, for this country, and considering our expectations of the roads in South

Carolina. The same general features continue. Almost constantly thick woods on both sides the road; here and there a clearing here and there a pretty good house with occasional pretensions to style, embosomed in dreary looking forests, and with wild growth in native forest, tangled with underbrush, in sight and within a few minutes' walk all round it. The growth perhaps chiefly pine, but also oak and other trees. Every creek that crosses the road makes a swampy place, almost invariably needing to be "corduroyed." The enemy are still ahead and retreating, but make no serious attempt to stand.

I forgot to note that yesterday P.M. when driven by Logan's advance from Hickory Hill they fired (musketry) from across the river on the left, and killed one or two of ours. Also that the officer from XX at Robertville reported Wheeler's Headquarters at Lawtonville the day before. Of course this movement of the XV "flinked him out" of *that*.

Apparently yesterday's total failure to delay us by felling trees has convinced the rebs that it doesn't pay, for today, though we crossed several creeks and small swamps, we found none of them obstructed at all. Hazen's division, which was camped in rear last night, three miles S. of Hickory Hill, became the 2d division in order today, and marched sixteen miles to this place, we camping near it, and a few rods from Gen. Logan, in a large open field. J. E. Smith (3d Div.) went north 2½ miles beyond us; Woods (XV[1]) in rear. More or less slight skirmishing ahead all day, our *foraging parties* driving the rebel cavalry rear.

During the forenoon we halted a few moments before a large and good looking double frame house, facing the road but set back from it some 100 to 150 yards. In front of the house was something like an open grove, though no very old nor fine trees. But within 200 yards of the house on either side was the same dense tangled forest, with dead logs and underbrush, in apparently its primitive wilderness condition, and though the house—which I had not time to go into, being called off as below—had evidently been built for the dwelling of some "heavy fellow" (as the old Georgia darkey called them) yet its surroundings were not inviting. I have seen none that were. True this is in the swampy and least cultivable part of the State; but a Yankee farmer would make the same place *look* far more comfortable. We learned that the house first mentioned was that of a Brig. Gen. Ellis, or some such name, and was formerly the residence, 'twas said, of W. H. [*sic*] Colcock,* of South Georgia political notoriety. The owner or owners have gone; understood that it was occupied for them by some "poor whites." While dismounted Capt. Bechtold came out of the woods near by and told me there were two or three hives of honey there. Started for them at once with sundry of our darkies as foragers, and went though the brush and trees and over logs to the place, but found the honey just about all gone, thanks to earlier individual enterprise; meeting sundry high privates and darkies just coming thence with large pieces of dripping honey comb in their fingers.

Halted about noon and for lunch at a log house by the road further on, on a farm of 400 acres owned by a "poor white"—a land owner but not (I understood) owning any or but very few slaves. *He* was gone, of course, conscripted, his wife said, and forced to go with the company raised in that neighborhood. She was a middle-aged woman, slatternly and almost stolid, but not ill-humored, and talked civilly enough when addressed. Her three or four children were noticeably plump and *ruddy-faced* for Southern children—a boy of twelve or thirteen the oldest, and an infant in her arms. There was no "snap" about the woman, and no thrift or evidence of even what had been comfortable

* William F. Colcock, member of Congress, 1849-1853, was Collector of the Port of Charleston under the Confederacy.

living on the place. Her dress was dirty and slovenly, complexion the usual sallow, and expression good-natured but listless. Yet she told us that her boy had been doing ploughing for two years, and evidently they had all been sufficiently well fed. In the front part of the yard, next the road, was a good sized double log cabin with open hall or space between the ends, which at first I thought they lived in, as it was shingled and weather-boarded, with room at each end, and porch along the front. But they were living in another large shingle cabin still further back of this, she telling us that the other was too decayed to use—though in truth only the roof was much decayed and two or three days' hearty work would have set it to rights. The General made friends with the children, as usual, sharing his lunch with them, and greatly delighted a red-cheeked little girl of four or five years with a scarcely more rosy cheeked apple. The woman answered his questions and mine about the road ahead very readily, and as it turned out correctly. There was some corn and fodder in the place, which our men took, of course; she saw it, but seemed perfectly indifferent to it, as though a thing she expected of course. But she spoke with some feeling of ''Wheeler's men,'' who she said had passed up the road ahead of us the day before, and had taken from her whatever they wanted, and been rude to her too—''I didn't expect that of our own people,'' she said.

We reached this camping place by 4 P.M. or earlier, and found that just across the swamp which borders it, *i.e.,* in this field and the road along it, and just before reaching the X roads at its farther end, the rebs had tried to oppose us. But Hazen had deployed skirmishers and easily drove them to and beyond the X Roads just before we rode up, though they had pretty substantial fence-rail barricades across the road and on either side. As we rode into the field—a very large open one, slightly rising for some distance and the ground all cleared and formerly cultivated for some 100 or 200 acres around—my horse almost stepped on the body of a dead rebel soldier, lying at full length on the ground, face upwards, his bloody head showing where the fatal ball struck in or rather just over the forehead. He was young—not over twenty-two or twenty-three—dressed in the coarse gray private's suit; but his regular features and well shaped hands and feet indicated him to be of the better class. Poor fellow! What sorrowing mother will mourn for him, what sister watch for his return in vain? Our men buried him where he fell, that evening. We had none killed there, and but two wounded. Riding into the field, the General ordered camp made, and thanks to Lt. Howard, who is an excellent and energetic Quartermaster, our train was up in a little while, and tents—I mean, flies—pitched, fires lit and supper cooking before dark. Hazen, as ordered, pushed his troops on after the retreating rebs, and for an hour or more we heard the shots of the skirmishers ahead of us. The direct road up which we came today, runs N.W. and is crossed not far from this point by "Duck Creek" emptying into the Salkehatchie. On this creek was a mill. The rebs fled from the X roads to and beyond the creek, and by cutting the dam flooded the road, causing some delay. At our camp we plainly heard the musketry skirmishing going on there for some time, and two or three guns (ours) which threw shell. But by dark Hazen had *turned* this mill-dam, his men crossing above, and drove the rebs two or three miles further and across another creek emptying into the Salkehatchie higher up. At the mill-dam we had an officer, Capt. ——, shot dead; no other killed, I understand, and very few wounded.

A good story is current in camp:—that some of our men who came up to the mill first, got to it and drove off the rebs posted there; that the latter had been grinding corn, and left quite a considerable quantity unground. Our boys were unable to finish grinding it, there being no one in their party who could run a mill. After some consideration they decided what to do, and when presently the rebs came back and attacked them they retreated and gave up the mill, but not going very far. The rebs again went on grinding the corn still there and when our boys thought they had had time enough to have finished it, they attacked and re-took the mill suddenly, this time capturing *meal* with it instead of corn. I don't vouch for this, but it is told, and is not only "ben trovato" but thoroughly in character.

Maj. Gray* of Gen. Foster's staff, arrived this evening at our camp, direct from Hilton Head—about fifty-two miles—with dispatches, having ridden all day. He took supper with us, waited an hour or so for replies to be written, and started back tonight. This ride back is not entirely safe from possible guerrillas, and he will have had a long and hard trip. He is a quiet and very gentlemanly man, pleasant mannered. Though the weather thus far has been good, it threatens rain this eve'g; sorry to see it. If rain comes it will fully test our "flies." I had ours pitched last night at Hickory Hill, preferring it to the house where most of the staff staid —we (N. and I), Col. Garber's party, and Dr. Howard and Eddy, taking the front yard. But the weather was fine and of course we were comfortable. It is amusing how little one *can* be comfortable with when one *must*. We found *abundance* of fodder en route today. Wheeler has burned some, but not one-fifth even of what is on the main road. Chickens also plenty on the plantations around.

* John Chipman Gray, of Boston, ten years younger than Henry Hitchcock, and later to hold a place in the legal profession in his community corresponding closely with that of Hitchcock in St. Louis. His own account of his hazardous visit to Sherman's headquarters may be found in one of his letters to his friend, John C. Ropes, preserved in the memorial volume *John Chipman Gray* (Boston, privately printed, 1917), pp. 16-18. It is not recorded there that he carried back from the front the letter to Mrs. Hitchcock which follows this entry in the diary.

[To Mrs. Hitchcock]

IN THE FIELD NEAR "DUCK CREEK," February 2d 1865
Thursday (7 P.M.)

I embrace an opportunity wholly unexpected, to send you a line—I think I may say very certainly the last from *this end* of our march. Major Gray of Gen. Foster's Staff has just overtaken us, in camp, with dispatches from Hilton Head and goes back tonight—and I shall send this by him. I wrote you last from our Headquarters near Pocotaligo, on Tuesday night. We left there next morning (yesterday) early—up at 4 A.M., breakfast at 5, and wagons and all on the road by 6.30'—and in these two days' march have made thirty-one miles. Do you know where "Duck Creek" is? —Well, trace a line nearly due N.W. of Pocotaligo, constantly approaching the Coosawhatchie River, to a X Roads just below the mouth of Duck Creek, and you will know where we are; just a little south of the latitude of Milledgeville, and a little north of the latitude of Louisville, (in Georgia), and east of the meridian of Barnwell, S. C. We have had so far a sufficiently "agreeable march"; the weather fine, roads not bad, on the whole, as the distance shows,—trains all up, and everybody in good spirits. The enemy's cavalry are in front of us, of course, and have made some show of— hardly resistance, but objection, let us say. Their "sign" was apparent yesterday whenever the road was crossed by creeks or lay through swamps, namely felled trees, etc., some of them large ones; but the "obstructions" did so little obstructing that we marched eighteen miles and went into camp with our wagon-train up by 4 P.M., which is a full day's march. The last swamp we passed just before reaching Hickory Hill P.O. showed not only their good intentions but our discourteous speed, for though many trees on either side the road were marked with the axe and some nearly cut through, they had not had time to fell any. Perhaps yesterday's experience taught them the folly of this sort of thing, for today, though we have crossed sundry creeks and swamps and have been preceded by the same rebel force,—not a very large one, and one which could not hope to make any serious stand against this column, even, or a fifth of it,—we found no trees felled at all. Our foraging parties ahead of us have skirmished a little with them now and then at the rail barricades they would throw up along the road, but we have had no occasion to deploy men at all, nor even to send forward skirmishers until these X roads were reached, which was our appointed camping ground for tonight; and those easily pushed the rebels the other side of Duck Creek.

Our camp is in a large open field, on a very gentle slope, near a bordering pine grove, with water convenient. We are fairly and literally "in the field" again, and I am heartily glad of it. But it does vex me a little—yes, a good deal, to think of that letter from you, perhaps more than one, which I *know* reached Savannah by the "Fulton." If I didn't know that Mackland must have had some good reason for not being able to send it and all our mail up to us at Pocotaligo before we left, I should be in a terribly bad humor with him. Of course we are in our "flies," and though neither so roomy nor so comfortable as tents, still we can manage well enough. The pine trees furnish mattresses,—we don't need much furniture, and you see that I can write on Margie's portfolio on my knee —I mean *my* portfolio that dear thoughtful Margie gave me,—with a camp candlestick to serve for gasfixture as legibly or illegibly as ever. So we have good weather, we shall be comfortable enough, and even if it rains one can double up in india-rubber.

I am happy to say, since my duties as caterer give me special interest in these matters now, that we find more "supplies" in this country than I feared we might. Chickens, sweet potatoes, fresh pork and honey and fresh lard, all rewarded the zealous inquiries of our headquarters foragers today; and the dinner table to-night reminded one of Georgia and its abundance. Yet we are not fairly into the region where supplies are to be looked for.

Major Gray leaves in a few minutes and I have only time to send my dear love to Mother and Margie and all the household—kind words to friends. . . .

[Diary resumed]

CAMP IN FIELD NEAR MOUTH OF
"DUCK CREEK" SOUTH CAROLINA
Friday, February 3/65

Did not break camp today; 17th Corps is moving up on our right to "Rivers' Bridge," and part of 15th moves forward toward Beaufort's Bridge—both over the Salkehatchie River. The threatened rain came last night, and today it has rained pretty much all day, giving our "flies" as fair a test as I desire for a beginning. Nothing special to do, nothing exciting in immediate prospect. Sky leaden, heavy, dismal; wind steady from the N.E. or E., promising more rain yet; air raw, cold, disgusting. One cannot ride, for there is no place tempting enough to pay for riding there in the rain. Even to walk about means to drag this mud. Learned *not* to bank earth along the sides of the "fly," especially in rainy weather. The earth from the ditch around the fly may be banked up *to the edge* of the canvas; but if it is piled higher it catches the rain as it runs down the sides of the fly, *prevents* it dripping off at the edge and ensures the canvas becoming wet through and muddy besides at the bottom. General sent —— over to Howard today—he rode off after break-fast with an amusingly mysterious and important air; and when he came back at night talked more and more loudly about his (he says) thirty miles' ride, though he didn't figure up that much, and about the rebel cavalry, etc., whom he expected to meet (but didn't), in the course of ten minutes, than Gray did last night in

two hours about his really hazardous ride of 100 miles.
Bah!

Gen. Logan has his Headquarters in the same field
with ours, say 300 yards off, and he and Gen. Hazen
were at our camp last evening. Logan also remains
camped here today. During the day he sent over to
Gen. S. a *"white slave."* This was a man, 38 years old
(so he said and looked), with a skin as white as mine,
and not a tinge or trace of swarthy or mulatto tint,
though he was sunburned—exactly as fair complex-
ioned white men are; with well-shaped, unmistakable
clear blue eyes, nose thin, well formed and *aquiline,*
hair very dark brown, nearly black, worn rather long
than otherwise, and lying in waves, so to speak: *i.e.,*
not curly, *nor in the slightest degree* "frizzled," yet
not straight like mine. I stood close beside him for
nearly half an hour while Gen. S. talked to him, and
once stepped round immediately behind him,—not two
feet from him—and closely examined his hair and skin.
Not a feature or thing about the man indicates negro
blood in any degree, and an ordinary observer would
instantly pronounce him a white laboring man. But his
story, which is positively corroborated (as to his being
a slave and so treated) by a negro man who has joined
Logan's Headquarters here (the two coming in sepa-
rately) is, that he always has been a slave and held as
such; first at Charleston, till eighteen years old, then
sold at auction with six other children of his mother,
and brought to this part of the country where he has
lived for twenty years. He answered readily, and intelligently enough—*i.e.,* just about with the average intelligence of an ignorant laboring man, neither particularly stupid nor very bright, the questions put to him.
He seemed to have taken his slave condition as a thing
of course; said he had never tried to escape, nor to get
his freedom through the Courts—"wouldn't have
known how to do that"—and had apparently, indeed
he said so, never inquired. Said his father was a white

man named De la Roche, in Charleston and had in all eleven children by his mother, of whom he produced a small daguerreotype. I saw this: her face and features were *not at all like his,* not any trace of resemblance that I saw. It was the picture of a woman over forty years old, rather stout (a three-quarters length, sitting) with (I thought) an Indian cast of features and wearing divers rings and ornaments; her face heavy and commonplace. By his story she had borne several names and a large number of children, some to others than De la Roche, whose name this man says he bears. He further said that his mother and De la Roche were never married; that she and her children belonged to a Judge Smith (I think)—that after *his* death they were sold at auction *for $91 apiece,* a "speculator" (whose name he gave, which General recognized as an auctioneer, etc., in Charleston) buying the lot of them at that price, all sound, and himself being afterwards sold up here; some of the children thus sold being then very young. He also said something not very clear—apparently having himself no distinct understanding of it— about a suit respecting (apparently) the title to himself and the other children; that his suit was "four years in court," and that "they tried to bring in the Indian law." He seemed to have just about such an idea of it, whatever the fact was, as a man of ordinary mind, without education, and without ambition, would be likely to pick up. His stolid way of acknowledging that he had never made any effort for freedom, and that his mother was not married, as to both of which he answered the General's questions with the same almost stupid unconcern that he did all other questions, was remarkable. He said he had always been a slave, always worked and associated with the negroes, etc. Yet he used good—i.e., correct—language as a general thing, with little or no negro brogue. It was a queer case altogether. His story was doubted at first, and he was suspected as a spy; but the negro above mentioned, also from this neighborhood, asserted that the other *was* really owned and known as a slave, and the white man's answers were apparently entirely consistent. Gen. S. seemed finally disposed to think that he was not really the son of the woman whose picture he carried, though supposing himself so, and positively asserted that he was, but the child of white parents whom it was convenient to dispose of thus in infancy. He went back to Logan's Headquarters and I have heard no more of him. Gen. Logan was much interested in the case and declared that this alone would have "made an abolitionist of him." Loafed about camp all day, read old newspapers, sent out foragers, who returned with good supply of *pea-nuts,* but reported chickens and potatoes all gone. There were plenty yesterday, but the 15th Corps is around! Everybody is delighted with the unexpected amount of supplies we find, and great abundance of fodder stacked; Hazen counted thirty-five stacks in one field. *The people* are not destroying anything; what is burned is done by Wheeler, and that not much.

CAMP IN FIELD
½ MILE S.W. OF "BEAUFORT'S BRIDGE"
(BANK OF BIG SALKEHATCHIE RIVER, SOUTH CAROLINA)
Saturday, February 4th, '65.

Broke camp about 7 A.M. this morning, marched thirteen miles to Beaufort's Bridge, arriving by 11 A.M. Weather still cloudy and raw, wind easterly; roads bad. Nothing special to note on the march. The point designated "Anglesey's P.O." on the map, is not known hereabouts. "Jackson's Branch" is a small stream, swampy like all of them; on it, at the road crossing is a mill known as "Barker's Mills," with a small bridge across it just below the dam.

We find no further attempt at obstructions by felling trees, etc., since the first day out, as above noted. The streams in this country might be pretty much all drawn by one picture—just as the General told T. R. Davis and W. Waud (Harper's Weekly artists) that they had better send *one picture* to N.Y. "for all South Carolina"—viz: "one big pine tree, one log cabin, and one nigger," as types. These lovely streams all have the same swampy approaches, the same thick woods, of trees large and small, dense brush and dead and decaying logs, on both sides; the same infernal mud to wade through, the same (usually) *brown colored* water, otherwise clear, fresh and *drinkable,* the same sluggish current—sometimes no perceptible current—and most of them the same intervals of dry ground here and there, between which the short bridges are built. As *we* pass on them in rear of the troops, we find them "corduroyed" with fence-rails or small saplings for the passage of the wagon trains; and pleasant walking is it for a horse to pick his way over these even after they are somewhat covered with mud or sand. Luckily my horse is a careful stepper at all bad places, rarely stumbles and never has slipped seriously or fallen down. But he went down today on what—in this weather—is by courtesy considered good ground. The road just lay through the woods with not very much small timber or brush on either side; and as usual when we can, we were riding along on one side of the road, both to keep out of the mud in the road, and not to delay the wagon trains. Without the slightest warning, as he planted one fore foot on apparently good ground, though damp-looking, as it all is today, it sunk clear down to above the knee, the other fore foot went down in like manner but nearly to the shoulder, and in another moment down sunk his hind feet also, till he was nearly belly deep in the soft mushy earth, and struggling to get out. Fearing he might roll or fall over I jumped off very quickly, and just saved my right leg from being caught under him; but in two minutes more he had jumped and kicked his way out on the really firm ground beyond, I retaining the bridle still; and so remounting, we went on again.

These invisible pit-falls are dangerous. They are caused by the complete decaying—or more frequently the *burning out*—of a stump; the gradual decay or slow fire filling up the cavity with soft mold or ashes, the surface remaining apparently level, perhaps covered with dead leaves or pine straw, but ready to sink the whole depth of the roots under the weight of a horse or even a man.

We knew this morning by message from Gen. Howard that he had carried the crossing at "Rivers' Bridge," some eight miles below "Beaufort's Bridge," and as expected before we reached this place word came back that the rebs had abandoned the latter, and Woods, whose (1st) Div. of XV was today in advance, had thrown a brigade across without opposition. These rebs, though they cannot tell how or when "W.T." intends to "flink 'em" are always alive to the *fact* and its consequences the moment it is done, and act—and evacuate—accordingly. The passage of the Salkehatchie at Rivers' Bridge by the XVII of course turned their position at *this* place; and it would have been *vice versa* had the XV crossed here (or at any other point) first. They evidently expected to hold the line of the Salkehatchie much longer and more successfully than they did. We have been told all the way up here that the C.S. and South Carolina authorities had advised and indeed ordered the people below this to come north of this river, and that almost everybody had come to and beyond *Beaufort's Bridge,* which they seemed to think the Yanks could not pass. No wonder they thought so— only they did not know the Yanks.

We found Gen. Logan and Woods at a large frame church (called "Big Salkehatchie Church") just this side of the "river"—or rather of the big swamp through which the road approaches the river proper. A few minutes later, Gen. Howard rode up with some of his staff, having come up from Rivers' Bridge to meet Gen. S. Evidently from his account of it the crossing there was a very handsome thing, and an ugly job for any other army. The usual crossing was through a long swamp—I am told over three quarters of a mile—over a narrow "causeway," water, mud and dense trees and swamp thickets on both sides, and the causeway itself having sixteen bridges over the water which every now and then had to be crossed instead of dammed. This road or causeway at a point 700 or 800 yards from the other side (northern) took a sharp turn, and then went nearly straight to the further bank. To carry these by a direct assault across the causeway was simply impossible—any column would have been swept away as fast as it appeared. But Mower with his division went higher up and G. A. Smith's Division went lower down, and the former waded through the swamp, the water up to waist and armpits, cartridge boxes slung round their necks or held above their heads—and so the astonished rebs were *flanked again.*

Gen. Fuller* tells H. H. (since this date) a story of the crossing, viz: While the men were in the water, cold enough too, and rain falling, and immersed to and above waist, and the bottom so bad with mud and roots, etc., that Fuller had to dismount and wade, his horse falling with him, a big Paddy roared out to the Brigade Surgeon, wading near—"Ah Dochter, Dochter, I'm sick—I cannot go any furder." "Very well," was the cool reply, "sit down and wait for an ambulance!"

Howard says Rivers' Bridge was the ugliest place he has ever seen; our loss was ten or eleven killed, seventy wounded; but *our men crossed.* In approaching it, Capt. Taylor† of Howard's staff was seriously wounded in throat, and Col. Kirby, Blair's staff, shot through calf of leg.

While at the church curious case of vagabond brought

* Brig. Gen. John W. Fuller, commanding a brigade of the 1st Division of the 17th Army Corps.

† William N. Taylor: this incident is described in the *Autobiography* of Gen. Howard (II, 105-106).

in—says he is one of band of two hundred who follow
army to steal and plunder; dirty, degraded looking
wretch, talks bad French, says is of Wisconsin regiment, but cannot tell names of officers, etc. Turned over
to Provost Marshal.

Our camp ¼ mile back from church, across a large
field, in edge of pine grove, crowning gentle knoll, with
pond at foot in rear. Location of tents fixed after some
squabbling by J. C. A–d with Dayton. A. got angry
and talked very sharp to D. who "glowered" and
looked vengeance but kept cool. Gen. S. heard A. fretting—"this must stop—any grumbling, one of you
must leave." My fly (and N.'s) is just next Col. Garber's—good neighbor. I might have made a fuss too,
but thought it too small a business. Dayton gave —— a
hard rap about never having been announced on the
staff; —— gave me a long account of his joining; says
General told Dayton to announce him, and D. never did.
Don't believe it.

Woods' division went to work at once to repair this
(B[eaufort]'s) bridge which rebs had abandoned after
burning and tearing up twenty-seven small bridges
across the swamp and river. Needing planks, etc., General ordered the frame church torn down and lumber
used to build the bridges, which was done. Before night
troops were crossing on bridges rebuilt. Woods says
this place could not have been carried by assault—
natural obstacles too great; but Howard below turned
it. Pleasant camp; tried to burn "altar" pine stumps
in front, but no great success.

CAMP ON N. SIDE OF "BEAUFORT'S BRIDGE"
SOUTH CAROLINA
Sunday, February 5/65

Crossed Big Salkehatchie this morning and went into
camp *at*—not *in*—dwelling a mile or two this (N.) side.
Don't wonder Woods thought the place so strong.
From "Big Salkehatchie Church" you descend the hill

at once on a road lined with dense woods, thickets, underbrush, and some cane, to the swamp bordering the river. It is nearly or quite *a mile* across the river and swamp, the river proper being on the further or northern side. The road is narrow, hardly wide enough for two wagons to pass; the ground always soft and muddy, the impenetrable trees and bushes on both sides standing in water and mud, all along, the road itself being a dirt causeway thrown up. Every little while, there was a "bridge," or rather a sort of wooden culvert, twenty-seven in all, to allow passage to the sluggish current. The rebs had burnt or torn up all these, and they had been repaired by our men, sometimes by using the half-burned "stringers" or beams of the former bridges, sometimes replacing them by new ones roughly made from trees cut down or the timbers brought from the church; and on these "stringers" were laid, "corduroy" fashion, the planks, etc., of the church, small trees, rails, etc., etc.; rough enough and in many places very difficult for horses to pick their way over, but still affording a passage. The road was more or less winding through the swamp, and the water grew deeper as we approached the other bank, and in some places flowed over the hasty bridges or "corduroys." Finally we came to the river itself, which was simply the largest of the numerous streams we had to cross. The water here was apparently pretty deep and something of a current; but one could pass, though not pleasantly, over the loose planking laid over the stringers, almost on a level with the water. This "river" itself was some — feet wide. On the other (now *this*) side were clay bluffs and firm ground rising at once some fifteen or twenty feet, and along this shore, along which were open fields, evidently long cultivated, were large trees along the road—and on the lower side of it were earthworks thrown up for about 100 yards long, high enough to fully protect infantry and pierced for two guns. From this parapet and em-

brasures the *debouchure* of the road through the
swamp and across the river was completely commanded, and fifty men with two guns could have *swept
away* any column whatever which tried to cross it, no
matter how daring or reckless. No assault here—so the
best soldiers with us say—but must have failed and
with terrible loss to us. And the nature of the swamp
itself just at this point, its great width, depth of mud
and water, and the extremely dense and tangled growth
of brush, small trees and cane on both sides the "causeway," gave no chance to flank the works here. As it
was, the position at Rivers' Bridge, also naturally a
very strong one, being flanked and the river crossed
there, *this* one was turned and the Johnnies abandoned
this one in haste, before we came up, giving up their
works without a shot.

We rode on from the bridge a mile or so to a comfortable looking frame house, built on brick columns
some four or five feet high, as so often seen in the
South. It had been abandoned by the family who lived
there when the rebs left, and our foragers had torn to
pieces pretty much everything inside. There was quite
a little settlement just around here, it seems—not quite
a village. Two negro women still remained at the house,
in the "quarters." Gens. S. and B. took rooms in the
house, on one side the hall, and Dr. Moore and I took
the two opposite rooms for our messes—otherwise we
made camp as usual, in the yard in front.

The weather today was delicious, clear sunshine,
with occasional fleecy clouds, a gentle air stirring, tem-
perature so warm that I took a bath, all over, in my
tent fly without any discomfort, having luckily borrowed of Col. Garber an extra fly to hang across the
front meanwhile. Got one of the women to wash the
underclothes taken off, and paid her 75¢ for six pieces
including towels. The arranging of tents, etc., and bath,
filled up the time till dinner; afterwards Merritt, Marshall, Davis, Nichols and others, had a jumping match,

etc., in the yard, which I did not stay long to see, and spent the evening in my tent with thoughts of home and better things. Just two months ago we had that pleasant pine woods camp and pine stump "altar fire," and sweet music just above Ogeechee Church.*

CAMP AT DR. FISHBOURNE'S HOUSE
—N.E. OF DUNCANVILLE AND 5 MILES

Monday, February 6/65.

Marched twelve miles today from camp at Beaufort's Bridge to this place. Roads much better, country higher and rolling, with good many large fields and other evidences of cultivation etc.; weather cloudy and colder, quite raw but not rainy. Stopped to lunch at house of Dr. Rice—quite large and very good house, yard well planted, good out buildings, etc. Like all the houses the kitchen is separate building in the yard. Dr. R. was a practising physician, well off—interior shows habits of reading and comfort. As we rode up to the gate Mrs. Rice came out of the house and met us, a young woman, say twenty-five to twenty-eight, really very pretty, and a lady. She had an infant in her arms. She asked General for "protection" before he dismounted—evidently anxious and alarmed but quiet and ladylike. He replied by curtly asking her why she brought that little baby out of doors on a cold, raw day like this—and she replying that she had been carrying it about all the morning, he told her she ought to know better and to take it into the house. He then dismounted and went in with her, as did we. Staid there over an hour—General sat with Mrs. R, several of our officers also there from time to time. I went into that room after a while. General was talking kindly to her and she evidently much reassured. She said Dr. R. had gone off "with the army," but had insisted on her staying at home with the children, assuring her that Gen. S. and his officers would protect her and them, and that by staying she

* See *ante*, p. 141.

would save the house from being burnt; in which Dr. R. showed he had sense. I had no talk with her and did not sit there long.

Manuel, our cook, came and reported to me that in the store room there had been found sundry things that would "suit us mighty well." Went there and found a quantity of good candles, also some first rate wax candles—soap (washing) and sundry other things, also some very nice china, etc. Evidently Dr. Rice has had friendly relations with blockade runners. As we need soap, which is as much a part of the regular army ration as hard bread, I authorized M. to take a part of one box of soap, and some of the commoner quality of candles—all the candles by the way were of foreign (German) manufacture and in the original packages and wrappers—but required him to leave more than he took of these and to touch nothing else. Saw sundry books in the bookcase I should like to have had in camp.

Approaching Little Salkehatchie River, which is about nine miles (not sure of this distance, but near it) from Beaufort's Bridge, we stopped at a deserted house, a common log and boarded farm house, where Gen. Logan was awaiting result of troops sent forward to that stream. The road crossed this also through a swamp, not a very long one; rebs were on t'other side, with trees felled, etc., in the swamp and rail and other barricades beyond—and in a field beyond a force of say 1000 rebel cavalry were drawn up in line of battle, but they had no artillery. Logan was vexed at the opposition—met General as we rode up with, "Those fellows are trying to stop us at the creek down there, and d— sassy they are acting about it." He sent some guns forward and shelled the rebs out of and beyond the swamp, and then threw skirmishers across the swamp—and before very long word came back that the Johnnies were gone, and we all rode forward. By the time we reached the swamp, the pioneers had removed all the obstructions and we went through. All these swamps are much

alike—water not often deep—woods and thickets dense
on both sides, sometimes almost absolutely impassable
even for a single footman, sometimes not so; road generally a "causeway" or "made road," not always corduroyed for common use, but which we are obliged to
corduroy for our many animals, wagons, etc.

Passed the town of Duncanville, I understand, and
so the map says—but I saw no town. I do remember a
large frame meeting-house ("Springtown, M.H.") a
little way this side the Little Salkehatchie. Reached Dr.
Fishbourne's house—must have been really a handsome place. House two and a half stories, porches in
front, rooms small, house and place both old, I guess.
Large garden in front of house, with very large circle
laid off in it, about 100 feet diameter, with well grown
osage orange hedge around it, and beds laid off in old-
fashioned style inside of it. Found Gen. J. E. Smith
(XV³) already in the house. Gen. S. and he divided it.
I preferred to have our fly pitched outside, as did Col.
Garber his, and Lieut. Howard. Rained heavily almost
all night. Our tents were in the yard under a large oak
whose branches extended over forty feet across. Am
inclined to think the dripping from branches in a
steady rain worse than to be out in the open ground.
But though the fly was pretty well wet through—nevertheless I slept soundly and dry all night.

CAMP AT "BAMBERG" OR
LOWRY'S STATION—SOUTH CAROLINA RAILROAD
Tuesday, February 7, 1865.

Started this morning for the South Carolina R. R.,
to cut which at *sundry points* is the first great object
of this march. So far we have had the best success;
we have passed almost without serious opposition the
swamps which the rebels—not unreasonably—boasted
were impregnable, and instead of aiming at Branchville where we should have found them fully prepared

for us, have aimed at and *struck* the railroad above
that, thus cutting off Augusta from the east.

As usual the General has threatened several points
simultaneously and so divided the rebel forces and will
finally gain them *all*. We have been with the XV from
Pocotaligo and are still; and while we have come up on
this route, Howard with XVII (Blair) has come up on
our right, generally a little ahead of us from Rivers'
Bridge across Little Salkehatchie at or near Millers-
ville (I believe) and thus up to Midway Station on the
railroad. Last night Gen. Williams reported himself
with two divisions of XX (Jackson's 1st and Ward's
3d) in camp on this side Little Salkehatchie at Springtown M.H. Thence he turned off to the left and strikes
the railroad at "Graham's Turnout," seven miles W.
of "Lowry's." These two divisions are all that are yet
across the Savannah and up to us, of the left wing—the
rest have been sadly delayed by freshet and high water,
as also the entire cavalry force, and Corse's XV[4]; and
these two are now up because they crossed at Savannah
and came up to Robertville from Hardeeville.

We left Dr. Fishbourne's this A.M. in the rain—
steady and detestable drizzle, though not heavy or vio-
lent; and expecting certainly some sort of a fight before we got to the railroad itself, now only five miles
off. I never saw the men in better spirits, the prospect
of a fight seemed fairly to rouse them. Riding along the
column, at first by the wagon trains in rear, and then
overtaking and passing the rear and then the main
body of the trops, who were moving forward light, with
all but the ambulance and ammunitions wagons in the
rear, I was struck with the spirit and gayety with which
they stepped along through the mud and rain as if un-
conscious of both. Some of them still carrying tokens
of yesterday's foraging, in the shape of pieces of bacon,
sides, etc., on their bayonets, and as there was no sound
yet of any in front, they marched along in their usual
easy but steady style—which, by the way, is slightly in

contrast with the picture book ideas of an army going forward to battle. But there was no battle.

While yet a mile or two from the railroad word came back to the General that the rebs had left and our advance was in the town without opposition. Aside from the rain and consequent mud the roads today were not very bad; country as already described—not often swampy, well wooded, a good many large fields and some good houses, the majority of them abandoned. Some distance out of Bamberg we passed one large and quite fine looking (frame) house near the road—don't know whose. Bamberg, now more commonly called "Lowry's Station" is a point on the South Carolina R.R. about nine miles W. of where that railroad crossed the Edisto River, and fourteen miles W. of Branchville, and seventy-six miles W. of Charleston. It is a railroad village, small, not over 500 souls, a few pretty good houses and two or three stores. There were two or three "Government" (frame) storehouses here, containing when we came at least 200 to 300 bales cotton, also some corn; besides which quantities of cotton smoking or in ashes lay on either side the track of the R.R. where the rebs had hauled, thrown it off, and set it afire. The fools —why should *they* lose time in destroying it? What use could we make of it but to burn it? How could we use or remove it if we would?

This is the last considerable entry in Major Hitchcock's diary. For four days more, including February 11, he pencilled a few notes which seem never to have been expanded. One of them, on the eleventh, when the day's march ended at Poplar Springs Bridge, consists of the words, "Audenried brought word house burned. General mad." It was on the seventeenth that Sherman and his army entered Columbia.

There is less occasion for surprise that Hitchcock made no attempt to continue his diary beyond February 11 than that he applied himself so long and so resolutely to it as he did. For the month beginning on that day the demands upon the members of Sherman's staff must have left little time for journal-writing. But when the month was over, and communications by mail were reopened, Hitchcock made ample amends for the cessation of his diary by means of the carefully detailed letters, reviewing in the first his experiences since writing the letter committed to John C. Gray on February 2— and among them his report of the burning of Columbia will be recognized as of special historical importance— and proceeding in a dozen more to relate his observations of such momentous scenes in the closing of the war as those that centered about Sherman in his dealings with the surrender of Johnston and his participation in the Grand Review at Washington on May 24. The letter which Major Hitchcock wrote to his wife two days later ends his record with all the appropriateness of a timely curtain descending upon a well-constructed play. The entire series covers the remainder of the northward march and the events with which the concluding division of the book, "The Final Days," is concerned.

LETTERS

[To Mrs. Hitchcock]

IN THE FIELD, FAYETTEVILLE, N. CAROLINA

Sunday, March 12th 1865*

I am perfectly well—spirits never better; the army is all here in first rate condition, and the campaign has been thus far—for though nearly over, the "objective point" is not yet reached—a splendid success, far exceeding both in interest and in the importance of its results already accomplished, the march through Georgia.

So much for the general statement, and now you will read without anxiety such details as I have time to give. Before you get this the telegraph will have given you the main facts, and with this or a day or two later the New York papers will add the details. I must refer you to these. I have not kept a diary—am sorry for it now, but it was on some accounts more difficult than before, and I wrote you not to expect one. I wrote you last on the evening of February 3d,† I think, by Major Gray, who followed us and took back dispatches. That night rain set in, lasting all next day; and we have had rains, sometimes very long and heavy ones, for more than half the time since. This has *not* been "a holiday march." The roads have been far worse than anything we saw in Georgia, and this has involved immense labor and much delay, to say nothing of the inevitable exposure of our columns, *inviting* flank attacks which the rebels have *not* made. Many miles of "corduroy" roads had to be made, and then re-made, day after day; eight or nine rivers have been crossed, varying from 150 to over 800 feet in width; swamps had to be *and*

* On the next day, March 13, Henry Hitchcock was brevetted lieutenant colonel volunteers "for meritorious service in the recent campaigns of Atlanta, Savannah, and the Carolinas."

† In reality, February 2.

were passed which the rebels had boasted—and no
wonder—were impassable, even without the strong
earthworks and artillery thrown up to stop us. Hardly
any *natural* obstacle but has been met and overcome,
and yesterday morning, *on the day appointed,* the heads
of columns of both wings of the army, approaching
by different roads and from different directions, and
which have not seen each other before for three weeks,
entered Fayetteville almost simultaneously in triumph
on the heels of a flying enemy. On Friday morning, at
Laurel Hill, forty miles S.W. of this place, a scout was
sent through (across) to Wilmington with dispatches
telling where we were and where we would be on Saturday. He went through safely that night, and this morning a tug which left Wilmington yesterday (Saturday)
at 2 P.M. was moored at the wharf here. It brought no
letters nor even newspapers—stupidly enough—and
we are still waiting for the gun-boats which were to follow it with both. But the Captain says that the good
people in "the white settlements" have been "almost
crazy" about us—that we are or were all reported captured or destroyed and Sherman himself a prisoner.
I can hardly believe that even rebel newspapers have
lied so impudently as this.

The march has been a long and—for the men and
most of the officers—a hard one; but the truth is that
there has not been either as much or as serious fighting
as there was in Georgia; that Sherman's strategy has
from the first day just as completely deceived and be-
wildered the rebels this time as before,—that the
"chivalry" has become a by-word of contempt for
boasting, whining and poltroonery and that there has
not been a single engagement from Savannah and
Beaufort to Fayetteville where either as much pluck
has been shown by the rebels—their regular troops and
Hood's veterans included—as was shown by the Georgia militia at the Griswoldville fight on November 22,
1864,—nor in which as much loss was sustained either

by them or by us as on that day. But the results of this campaign are tenfold more apparent and more really disastrous than that of the last. This army as truly *took Charleston* as it did Atlanta, and by a precisely similar movement, only a little farther off.

We only know as yet that it was evacuated and that Foster's troops took possession, after having landed at Bull's Bay and shelling it also from Morris and James Island. This was in strict obedience to Sherman's orders, *made at Savannah,* as part of and designed to co-operate with our movement in the interior by which the railroads were cut, which alone made it possible for the rebels to hold Charleston at all. But the truth is that the capture of Charleston had only a *moral* not a military value; and except in that view alone, it would have been, and would today be, *an advantage* to us for them to hold it, and in it to keep idle and useless the garrison which is now in the field promising to fight us—somewhere.

The really important things we have done are in the capture and destruction of Columbia and the railroads near it,—the destruction of immense quantities of machinery, ammunition, ordnance and military stores of all kinds; the complete isolation of Lee's army in Virginia from its hitherto unfailing sources of supply; the immense consumption of supplies destined for that army, already straitened for the means of support; the continued demonstration of the hollowness of the "Confederacy" and the overwhelming power of the Government,—and the steady and steadily growing conviction thus forced upon the most obstinate rebels that their "cause" is hopeless and that rebellion is only and utterly ruin. We have now marched a great army diagonally across and through the very heart of the first and most bitter and obstinate of all the rebel states, without a single check, defeat or disaster, (except the repulse of a detachment of 400 men *sent back* to break railroad at Florence, and who met 3000), sweeping everything before us, consuming their substance, burning their cotton, destroying their vital lines of communication, defeating their forces with our *foraging parties* and *skirmish lines* wherever they dared offer resistance—crossing rivers over 600 and 800 feet wide, passing "impassable" swamps, by our men wading *breast deep in the mud and water* (as they did at Rivers' Bridge over the Salkehatchie), constructing roads for ourselves over and through quicksand and mud where a single mule could not go in safety till it was "corduroyed";—we have captured the capital of the State whose men were all going to "die in the last ditch," without even a battle and with a loss of less than sixty men including those killed and wounded by their (rebels') shelling Hazen's Camp all the night before they ran away from Columbia; have forced them to abandon the sea-coast in order to concentrate their troops, and then have been unable to come up with their troops when concentrated, so fast have they retreated, burning every bridge as they went. And we have seen and heard more *whining,* more cowardly talk, more blaming of "the leaders who forced us into this war," more mean-spirited and abject submission to mere power and less manliness and devotion to even what might be erroneously believed to be principle, in that same State of South Carolina than in any other State in the South. This is my own observation and experience, and it is that of every other officer and man I have heard speak of the people of South Carolina,—indeed it has been the common talk of this army ever since we got fairly into the State. Of all mean humbugs "South Carolina's chivalry" is the meanest.

But my time is limited for the mail is making up. For myself, I have been in perfect health, except for one or two days and then was not seriously indisposed—as you will believe when I say that I was never once absent from the table at meal-times and only once did not do my regular share of knife and fork duty, and then as a matter of prudence. We rode through steady rain all day more than once,—rains which no rubber coverings could keep out and which left us pretty well soaked by evening; and sometimes the rain came through our "flies" and dripped on and into our blankets in a manner that was not favorable to repose. I woke up one night with my feet in a little puddle between the blankets, which I had thought were arranged so as to run the water off as it fell from above. Luckily we did not break camp next day—*February 25th*—and by the next night there had been intervals enough without rain to get the blankets all dry again; and since then I have taught "Thad"—my *house-servant,* formerly a colored citizen of Columbia, S. C., and who now divides the faithful Aleck's duties—how to make my bed bid defiance to leaky flies and the heaviest rains.

These things are good to laugh over even at the time; it is a serious matter, though, for the privates, poor fellows, to whom rainy days mean not only to be drenched in their little "dog-tents" but the heaviest extra work on the horrible roads. Yet they are as cheerful and gay as boys, full of unquenchable spirit, ready to march again at daylight, ready to fight—and a little rather than not.

As to danger, I am very sorry to say I have not been in any—to speak of—on this campaign. It so happened that when Blair's column crossed the swamps of Big Salkehatchie at Rivers' Bridge (February 5th) where there was for a time some sharp skirmishing, we, with Gen. S., were with the 15th Corps, on an inner line, eight or ten miles farther N.W.—and, though the point where we struck the river was a still worse swamp to carry if defended, when we reached it the rebs had left not even waiting to fire a gun. So all the way through, what little fighting there was, I was never sent anywhere, nor any of our staff, near enough to hear a shot whistle close enough to hurt.

Yesterday morning I rode into Fayetteville ahead of

the General, hoping to overtake Gen. Howard who was with the advance on the road we were on, in time to enter with him, and if possible ahead of him. But his camp on Friday night was only eleven miles from here, while ours was twenty-six miles,—and though I reached here by half past 12 o'clock I was an hour after Howard and too late to see the little skirmish of our advance with the few rebels who had stayed to prevent our men putting out the fire of the burning bridge over which the rest of them had fled.

Our march is not yet accomplished, though *this one* is nearly so. When we reach "the new base" I will write you again. . . .

I enclose a sketch by "our special artist" (Theo. R. Davis) of my own tent taken on that day,* which though not a very finished drawing you may be willing to receive as a birth-day present. The truth is I asked D. to make me a sketch of the whole camp—Gen. Sherman's Headquarter's on that day, which he very willingly promised, and made his rough notes for it on the spot, also making similar notes for this one of his own accord, intending to draw both for me. It happened that in making the drawing he took up this one first— and since then other things have prevented his completing the other, which was the one I wanted most. This to explain how I came to have *my* tent drawn. It is faithful enough, except that the sword is a mistake,— it should be a straight "staff sword" instead of a cavalry sabre.

One word about Columbia. It was not burned by orders, but expressly against orders and in spite of the utmost effort on our part to save it. Everything seemed to conspire for its destruction. The streets were full of loose cotton, brought out and set on fire *by the rebels* before they left,—I saw it when we rode into town. A gale of wind was blowing all that day and that night, and the branches of the trees were white with cotton

* The sketch is dated February 25, 1865.

THEODORE R. DAVIS'S SKETCH OF HENRY HITCHCOCK AND HIS TENT

tufts blown about everywhere. The citizens themselves —like idiots, madmen,—brought out large quantities of liquor as soon as our troops entered and distributed it freely among them, even to the guards which Gen. Howard had immediately placed all over the city as soon as we came in. This fact is unquestionable, and was one chief cause of what followed. Here in Fayetteville a lady has told Gen. Sherman that Gen. Joe Johnson told her, yesterday morning, that the burning of Columbia was caused by liquor which the people there gave our soldiers. Besides there were 200 or 300 of "our prisoners" who had escaped from rebel hands before, and when we reached Columbia burning to revenge themselves for the cruel treatment they had received; and our own men were fully aware of the claims of Columbia to eminence as the "cradle of secession." In that same town, in 1861, a woman, a school-teacher from New England, was *tarred and feathered* and sent North "for abolition sentiments."

The result of all this was that partly by accident, from the burning cotton, partly by design by our escaped prisoners, and by our drunken men, fire was started in several places,—and once started, with the furious wind blowing, it was simply impossible to put it out. *Nothing was left undone,*—I speak advisedly— to prevent and stop it; Gen. Howard, Sherman, and other Generals and their staffs, and many other officers and hundreds of men were up and at work nearly all night, trying to do it, but in vain. The guard was changed—*three times* as many men were on guard as were ever on guard at any one time in Savannah where perfect order was preserved; our own officers shot our men down like dogs wherever they were found riotous or drunk—in short no effort was spared to stop it; and but for the liquor it might perhaps have been stopped. This is the truth; and Wade Hampton's letter to Sherman—it will be in the New York Herald if not already published North—charging him with sundry crimes at Columbia is a tissue of lies. . . .

[P.S.] I enclose with this some leaves and flowers gathered *en route*—as to which see the pencil endorsements. Make a bouquet of some from Preston's house in Columbia and give them to Mr. Yeatman with my compliments. The house belonged to Wade Hampton—Preston is, I think, his son-in-law;—it was not burned.

In the Field, Fayetteville, North Carolina
Tuesday March 14th, 1865

I wrote you two days ago—something of a letter—announcing our safe arrival here, etc., and sent it off that day by a little tug which has been to Wilmington and returned safe—so I am rejoiced to know my letter went all right. . . . We have no mail yet, nor will have till we reach ——, which please Heaven will not be very long now. We have just stopped here to take breath and destroy a fine Arsenal which Uncle Sam built and the rebels stole but will never steal nor use again.

I continue in perfect health and my usual good spirits—only anxious when I think about you. You know by today—by telegraph—I dare say, that "Sherman is all right." I write this at a table in the ex-hotel of this town, now Gen. Slocum's Headquarters, with *the* General sitting at the same table writing and directing—as keen and *lightning-like* as ever. The army is now crossing Cape Fear River at this point. Our Headquarters train went over this morning, and camp is probably made for us by this time a mile or two the other side. We cross sometime today, and tomorrow will fairly begin the last stage of this march. The usual threats of what is just ahead of us amuse us daily, as ever since leaving Atlanta; you know how to value them by this time.

I saw Gen. Blair yesterday, in fine health and spirits. He and his 17th Corps—one of the grand divisions of this army—have done splendidly on this march; in

GENERAL SHERMAN'S ENTRY INTO COLUMBIA, SOUTH CAROLINA, February 17, 1865.

FROM HARPER'S WEEKLY, APRIL 1, 1865
A CONTEMPORARY CONFIRMATION OF MAJOR HITCHCOCK'S NARRATIVE,
ESPECIALLY WITH RESPECT TO THE BURNING COTTON

fact, it has been their luck to meet the most serious of what opposition there has been—at Rivers' Bridge, crossing Big Salkehatchie swamps—and nothing could have been finer than the way they did their work. Tell Mr. How this with my compliments.

I advise you, if you wish to see the ablest and best articles *by all odds* on army movements, etc., and the clearest and most correct accounts of what is going on to read the "Army and Navy Journal." It is edited by a man—I don't know who—who knows what he is about, and writes with clearness, shrewd sense, faithfulness, and moderation; tell Shepley this also. . . .

It is terribly *unsettling* to get near the "white settlements" again. So long as we were enveloped in the clouds of rebeldom and knew that we were beyond mails and newspapers and had nothing to look for beyond camp and the march and its incidents, one could take it quietly and—by postponing the thought of such things definitely for say three, four, six weeks ahead—be quite contented. But now we are just near enough to all our home treasures to be anxious about them—and to begin to think in spite of ourselves what may have happened! But I fall back on my old plan—the only sensible one,—and determine to believe that you are all well till I know the contrary. Tomorrow we dive in again for a while, and then—with Mr. Lee's and Mr. Joe Johnston's permission, or without it, we shall come up again soon, and I will write. . . .

H

In the Field, Tuesday March 21st 1865
In Camp Near Bentonville, North Carolina

I embrace the opportunity to send a line by Col. Garber,* Acting Chief Quartermaster, who leaves us this morning for Kinston to see about and send up supplies. I am as well as ever, and we are all in good spirits. I

* Michael C. Garber.

wrote you from Fayetteville on Sunday week, 12th
inst. We left there next day. Since then we have at last
found some rebels who were both willing and able to
fight. If their newspapers lie in anything like the usual
proportion you will have heard that Sherman is
"checked" for good, his army beaten in detail, and
ever so many more terrible things. We had a good
laugh yesterday over the New York Herald of the 9th
with the rebel stories of a fight near Cheraw, S. C. in
which we experienced great disasters, of which, however, we knew nothing before.

But since leaving Fayetteville there has been really
some fighting. On Friday last, 16th inst., our *left wing*
—with which the General then was,—which marched
without incumbrance for some sixteen or eighteen
miles nearly north from Fayetteville on the east bank
of Cape Fear River,—the right wing having turned off
directly East from F., and the main trains of the army
being massed between the two,—met a considerable
force of rebels under Hardee, intrenched. The roads
were horrible, from three days' rain, and it rained that
day; but we carried two out of three lines of works,
took a good many prisoners, (among them Brig. Gen.
Alfred Rhett* of South Carolina) and three pieces of
artillery, during that day, and *our* camp that night was
on part of the ground fought over in the morning. During the night the rebels evacuated their remaining and
strongest line of works and hurried off up towards
Smithfield, across the Neuse. On Saturday morning the
General crossed over to the right wing with which we
have since been and now are.

On Sunday we heard artillery firing from the direction of the left wing, but Gen. Slocum sent word at first
that it appeared to be only a small body of cavalry
ahead of him. But it increased and by night we learned

* Alfred Moore Rhett was the eldest son of Robert Barnwell Rhett,
whose third son, Edmund, has been mentioned (see *ante,* p. 228). On p.
288 A. M. Rhett will be found to appear under his true title of Colonel.

that Jo. Johnston had rapidly brought down all his
forces, variously estimated at from 30,000 to 40,000,
and was making a furious effort to whip that wing and
then beat Sherman in detail. Slocum held his own, however, and punished the rebels severely, with serious
loss to us,—probably 1500 in all,—and heavy loss to the
rebels, who made six separate and furious assaults on
our lines, but were repulsed every time by heavy artillery and musketry fire.

On learning the true state of things the General gave
the necessary orders to concentrate the whole army at
once, which was successfully done during night before
last and yesterday, the left of this wing being swung
round so as to connect by yesterday at 4 P.M. with the
right of Slocum's. Johnston's hopes of dividing and
beating us are a dead failure.

There was no heavy fighting done yesterday, though
a good deal of sharp skirmishing, our object being first
of all to make, as it was his business—if he could—to
prevent our making, the connection with Slocum complete, which has been done. Our camp (I mean these
Headquarters) is now at the right of our whole line, at
a point nearly due west of Goldsboro, and about twenty
miles distant from it. Our whole line forms a sort of
re-entrant angle ⟨ (E thus, with the rebels (E) in-
(left / right)
side of it, which is better for us than for them, by a
great deal. They are, however, strongly entrenched,
and those who were on the Atlanta campaign are much
reminded of the way things used to be then. I do not
suppose there will be any heavy assault made by us in
front, certainly not if the rebel position can be *flanked,*
which is being now looked after. The rebs and we also
are south of the Neuse River, of course, and our right
(where I write) is about ten miles N.W. of Cox's
Bridge across the Neuse. Meanwhile Gen. Terry, with

———* effective men, is at Faison's Depot, on the Wilmington and Goldsboro Railroad, with the railroad in working order up to that point (except one bridge) and is advancing steadily. Schofield, with ———† men was yesterday at Kinston, on the Newbern and Goldsboro Railroad, and will be in possession of Goldsboro tonight, having with him ample supplies for us. Thus we shall both be supplied anew—which is greatly needed in respect to clothing after our long march (i.e., the men need it—we officers are all right)—and very largely reinforced with veteran troops.

Quite likely no general engagement may take place for some time, for as Johnston has failed in his attempt to beat us in detail he cannot now risk an attack, and the occupation of Goldsboro and the railroad to both Newbern and Wilmington for a "new base" is—I may tell you now—the successful accomplishment of the object of this compaign. If J. Johnston had not made this attempt, this army would have gone at once into Goldsboro; as it is, we confront him and send back to Goldsboro, Kinston, and Newbern for supplies, etc., and manoeuvre a little before going there. Undoubtedly, if (yes, IF) J. J.'s attack on Slocum on Sunday had succeeded in "mashing up" that part of our forces, it would have been a severe blow to us—but it didn't succeed, and now he is on the defensive himself.

Most fortunately we have had beautiful weather ever since the 16th, and though the previous rains made the roads bad—very bad in some places,—and delayed the movements in support of Slocum so much as to make him feel anxious at one time, yet it all came out right. The fight on the 16th, when we were with Slocum, would have been called a battle early in the war,‡—that of Sunday, after we had left him (not expecting J. J.'s

---

* The figure, rubbed out in the pencilled letter, is evidently 10,000.

† The erasure of this figure was a success.

‡ Sherman in his *Memoirs* (II, 302) refers to it as "this action, called the battle of Averysboro'."

movement, I think) was a battle, and a serious one.*
The operations yesterday on both wings, were nothing
more than heavy skirmishing, but our line was steadily
advanced and our object—uniting with Slocum—was
gained.

Our camp—you understand this always means the
General's own Headquarters encampment—is a pleasant one, in a large open field, and a few rods from us is
Blair's Headquarters, while Gen. Howard's is also
very near. I am writing in my tent, on that dear little
portfolio, expecting every moment the summons from
Col. Garber to finish my letter and hand it to him. It is
about 8:30 A.M., and breakfast is over two hours ago.
The pickets on both sides, and the skirmishers, are
amusing themselves popping away as usual, but there
is no prospect of an assault—indeed I know that it is
intended to reconnoitre the ground today for other
purposes. If I were on any other staff I should probably
be out somewhere on duty, but the truth is that our
staff has less to do in that way than any other, and
what there is to do of that sort there are three or four
A.D.C.'s to do, so that you need not worry about me at
all. I wish I had more of it.

You can show this, or as much as relates to the army,
to Shepley, hasty as it is. Of course, I cannot go into
details, but you know perfectly well that what I do say
is a faithful and correct account, and that I shall neither exaggerate any success nor deny any reverses, if
we should meet any. As yet, we have met none, and the
only question is as to getting up the supplies we begin
to need.

(We have no mails as yet, though we have had two
or three scattering newspapers brought by messengers.
It cannot be long now before they come.) . . .

---

* The battle of Bentonville.

I send but a line to say that we—General and staff—
reached here today, all well, and "the South Carolina
Campaign" is accomplished, with what the General
himself in a General Order† written yesterday on the
battlefield, calls "a glorious success." Thank God for
it all.

I wrote you a few lines on Tuesday while Jo Johnston was still in our front at Bentonville and the contest going on. But it was even then practically decided
—for his failure to overwhelm the left wing by his sudden and desperate attack on Sunday was a defeat of
his plan, and our success in uniting the right and left
wings next day across his front made the result inevitable. On Tuesday, the connection between our two
wings was made complete; and beside that, Gen.
Mower, with part of Blair's corps, on our extreme
right, pressed forward his line of skirmishers through
the dense woods—so dense that you could not see a man
on horseback 200 yards off—and across the ravines and
swamps,—drove the rebs out of two lines of works and
—as *we now know*—penetrated to within fifty yards of
Jo. Johnston's own Headquarters. If we had known—
which was impossible at the time—the real extent of
this success, and our whole force on the right had been
hurried up to his support, it would have resulted in the
certain capture of a large part if not the whole of the
rebel army. As it was, quickly perceiving the terrible
danger menacing them, the rebels "double-quicked"
(so the prisoners tell us) everything they had, instantly, against Mower,—nearly surrounded him on
three sides with a much larger force than he was leading just then, and he was obliged to fall back from his

* For once not on the stationery stamped, "Headquarters, Military
Division of the Mississippi." See final sentence of letter.
† Special Field Order No. 35, dated "On the Field, Bentonville, N. C.,
March 22, 1865."

advanced position to the first line he had taken. This was late in the afternoon, and there was not time for a new attack—nor did anybody know then the real extent of the success.

That night, all night long, Johnston was in full retreat, leaving his dead and wounded, many of them. All night long too, though we did not—could not, from the nature of the ground—know that he was actually retreating, except that about 2 or 3 A.M. word came in that it was believed to be the fact,—one or two of our guns were playing on his only road of retreat. Morning found him gone across Mill Creek; our advance pursued him two miles beyond it, attacking and harassing his rear guard, until recalled. This was yesterday. During the forenoon the General and most of his staff rode out to where J.'s works were and his camp had been; by noon we were packed up, our troops recalled and on the road for Cox's Bridge (across the Neuse) and Goldsboro; last night we camped at Cox's Bridge, and today rode in to this place.

I can tell you now, what I could equally well have told you at Savannah or Pocotaligo, that *Goldsboro*—this place—was the precise point which General Sherman then named as the destined end of our march,—and by the precise route we have taken. The campaign is a complete, glorious, and wonderful success, and Johnston and Lee's desperate effort to check or crush this army a failure.

I write at Gen. Schofield's Headquarters. . . .

IV
THE FINAL DAYS

LETTERS

In the Field, Goldsboro, North Carolina, April 5th 1865

. . . The General's Report of his doings since January 1st—the date of the one he made at Savannah—to the 1st inst., was completed today, and this letter will go by the same courier who leaves with it for Washington tonight. I have been pretty busy since I wrote last, but am now nearly through, and—keep this a profound secret—orders were made today, "confidential to Army and Corps Commanders," preparatory to our speedy departure, and "blocking out" the next campaign. We are looking daily with deep interest for news from Grant, who "moved in force" last week. The rebel officers who met a flag of truce sent out from here today admit that Sheridan has cut the "Southside" railroad —the thing Grant has so long been trying to do, and whose importance Shepley will explain to you.

Supplies, clothing, arms, etc., have been furnished our troops here with the energy characteristic of "W.T." and those who act with and under him, and with the heavy re-inforcements added by our junction with Schofield (including Terry's (10th) Corps) and also the large number of troops cut off from our own Corps last fall but who have joined us here, we shall move hence with a much larger force than left Atlanta or Savannah, all in splendid condition, and *of course* in first-rate spirits. The *morale* of this army is superb; their confidence alike in Sherman and in themselves, is an immense element of success,—and it is the confidence of veterans, familiar with danger, skillful and wary in encountering it, *not* of rash ignorance.

By the way, one of the N. Y. *Herald* correspondents, describing the battle of the 19th March, near Bentonville,—the first day, when Johnston threw his whole force unexpectedly on our "Left Wing"—says that "a *rout* was imminent." This is false; a rout was not imminent nor in prospect at any time. I was not present that day, for early that same morning the General (and staff, of course,) had left Gen. Slocum's column, there being no indication of any serious opposition ahead of him nor any reason to expect an attack, and crossed over to Howard's. But both that same evening, and on and since the 22ᵈ, we had full accounts of all that passed from both staff and line officers who were in the hottest of it, and while they stated frankly—as is apt to be the case in such unrestrained talk among ourselves,—that the troops, two brigades, in advance, were driven back at first—having unexpectedly "run against" infantry and artillery in position and strong force where there was apparently only cavalry—our left pressed back considerably and the four Divisions (which were all that Slocum had immediately available that day) were severely taxed to hold their own against Johnston's largely superior force, yet there was at no time any symptom of a "rout," but on the contrary the men fought splendidly *and held their ground.* That night the remainder of the Left Wing came up, and the rear division of the 15th Corps from the Right Wing crossed over and joined Slocum; and the rest of the Right Wing swung round on Johnston's left, threatening his rear, —and he was put on the defensive.

After that, though there was more or less skirmishing all the time and heavy skirmishing on the 21st, there was no more such fighting as on the 19th. As I wrote you on the 21st, Johnston's effort—a well conceived, bold and well executed blow,—was a failure, and their last chance of destroying Sherman and his army was lost. Their stories about our having lost 3000 men and more were all simply falsehoods. I *know* that our total losses, killed, wounded and missing, on the 16th in Slocum's column—which alone was engaged at all that day—were 477; and our entire losses at Ben-

tonville were 1596.* At both places our men buried
more dead rebels than our own killed; and they retreated from both fields in the night, leaving their dead.

These affairs gave me a good idea of what a battle
really is. At neither Averysboro (16th) nor Bentonville
did any of our staff have any orders to carry; but we
were on the field, near enough to know how things were
going, as you may infer from the fact that Averysboro
the General himself directed—through Slocum, with
whom he was all day—all the movements on our side.
Once we all had to move a little to one side, to get out
of range of a rebel gun which sent some canister shot
down the road, splashing the mud not far off; and at
another time after the first rebel line had been taken
and we were following up the advance of our troops, a
bullet or two pattered among the branches overhead.
But as to "Tecumseh directing the battle *under a warm
fire*"—as one correspondent has it, truth compels me
to say he didn't. There is a good deal of "poetry," I
judge, in most of these thrilling accounts. The fact is,
I got very tired of lying around in the woods near the
General, while the fight—it was hardly a *battle,* nowa-
days,—of the 16th was going on,—hearing the firing
just ahead of us, sometimes very sharp and rapid for a
while, then dropping off into the monotonous pop-
pop-pop-pop—of the "skirmish line"—then suddenly
breaking out again, twice or three times, perhaps more,
into quite a spiteful rattle, with the heavier accompani-
ment of the artillery; while yet I had no orders to go
ahead and see it and no right to go without them. One
mustn't be "officious," you know—says uncle E[than]
—and beside, if one should go into danger without orders and pick up a bullet, it seems the verdict would be
"served him right"—and this most of all from the
General himself; so there is less satisfaction in trying
such experiments. I do not find that those who have

* It is interesting to note that ten years later Sherman, in his *Memoirs,*
gave this figure as 1604, differing by only eight from Hitchcock's contemporaneous report.

faced danger oftenest are any more disposed to go into it needlessly; on the contrary, it seems to be regarded as simple folly—which is about the truth.

On the 20th, however, near Bentonville, finding that if I stayed with the General in rear of the reserves I could see and know little or nothing, I went ahead twice—"to get information"—beyond the line of battle into the woods, where they were skirmishing;—learned what was going on, found out that thick woods are not favorable to landscape views, though very good to stop bullets, and went back better satisfied. The truth is, your lady friend who provoked your indignation and my amusement by the suggestion that I was in a safe position, came nearer the truth with reference to this staff than any other. The organization of the army is such that there has been necessarily very little for any of *us* to do on either of these campaigns so far as any danger was involved. Comfort yourself with that if you read any more lying rebel accounts of terrible slaughter of Sherman's men; at the same time remembering that whatever there may be to be done we are more than ready for.

I hoped to make this a long letter; but—of course— I am warned that the package of letters is waiting for me and I must close. The weather is lovely, the roads *dusty,* and the heavy rains over. I will write again before we leave. I am perfectly well, but miss and long for the daily exercise and interest of the march and anticipate more interest than ever on the next one. . . .

IN THE FIELD, GOLDSBORO, NORTH CAROLINA, April 7 1865

I have just received . . . your letter of 25th March, acknowledging mine from Fayetteville. . . .

I am delighted that the sketch of my *residence* was acceptable; that it looks, in the picture, a little more desirable than in the reality, I won't deny—for we were then enjoying just about the worst rains and the worst roads of the whole march. On that particular

day—your birthday—. . . there was but about one
hour, in the afternoon, when more or less rain was
not steadily falling upon ground already thoroughly
soaked, slushy and detestable. During that pleasing interval, which, however, was not an interval of sunshine,
—the faithful Aleck, under "the Major's" own energetic direction, decorated the premises by hanging up
all my blankets to dry at my camp-fire, some on a frame
most ingeniously constructed thus [small sketch], the
rest on the apex of the tent, in front. The brilliancy of
that gay new red blanket contrasted finely with the
"sombre hues" of the gray ones bought of the Quartermaster, as well as set off the *subdued white*—we won't
call it *dingy* yet—of the "Hudson's Bay" blanket with
its answering gaiety of stripes at either end. Before the
rain began to fall again the blankets were all dry, and,
protecting them this time both above and beneath by
folds of his gum blanket arranged with a skill taught
only by damp experience, the Major laughed the elements to scorn. He slept dry and soundly that night,
and does not desire sleep more sweet and refreshing
than he has many a night enjoyed in a tent-fly.

Indeed it is wonderful how quickly and how completely the pitching of a few tents and the busy movements of their inhabitants, the bright crackling of
camp-fires and the sound of human voices,—sometimes
merry, sometimes *mad,* depending much upon the
weather,—will metamorphose a muddy hill-top or a
lonely bit of pine-woods, into a scene full of interest
and animation. Though it has some time ago ceased to
be a novelty to me, I do not think it could ever lose its
charm.

As to "discomforts,"—I need only step into the
camp of the brigade nearest us and see what the men
endure with unfailing hearty cheerfulness, to be thoroughly ashamed if I had even felt like complaining.
The "corduroy roads" which our horses stumble over
through the mud, they *make* as well as march on; our

"flies" are carried in wagons, with our cooking uten-
sils and provisions, while they must often carry on
their backs the little "dog-tents" under which, put up
by their own labor, they crawl to sleep, wrapped in the
blanket which also they have carried all day, after dis-
posing of the supper which has loaded their haversacks
along many a weary mile, or been cooked in the little
skillets and pots which also have been part of their
burden, besides the musket and accoutrements and
the "forty rounds" at the back. Patiently, steadily,
cheerily, tramping along, going they know not where,
nor care much either, so it be not in retreat, ready to
make roads, throw up "works," tear up railroads, lay
pontoon or hew out and build wooden bridges, or best
of all, *"go for* the Johnnies," under hot sun or heavy
rain, over weary sand-hills, and through swamp, mire
and quicksand,—marching ten miles to storm Fort
McAllister,—breaking out into irrepressible cheering
when the rebel artillery opened on the skirmish line as
we approached the defences of Savannah,—how could
any man who has seen, but not shared, their labors and
exposures day after day think about *his* enduring
"hardship"? I tell you truly . . . I wish I *had* the
satisfaction of looking back on any real ones myself.
So far as I am concerned—though no more so than the
rest of our staff,—I feel like Mark Tapley, "it's no
credit to be jolly." As a matter of personal experience,
and always excepting your anxiety and fears, which
have been my only trouble, I know of nothing that I
would exchange for this episode in my life—and I consider myself both uncommonly and undeservedly lucky,
—so much so that if I had not reason to believe I have
been able to render some real assistance to the General
I should feel rather mean about it. . . . But for all that,
there will not be a happier man in all this world, I
think, than I, "when this cruel war is over" and I can
return, please God. . . . I would not have missed this
experience, partial as it is and much as I shall always

wish it had been longer and harder—nor do I think you would have had me; but it has also had features, unavoidable ones, which I would gladly forget. But they were unavoidable, yes, they were *necessary*.

I used to tell you, hard-hearted as you thought me, that the war must go on, there was no help for it. I know now what that means as I did not then; and yet I am but the more convinced of its truth. The only merciful theory of this war was the one which McClellan talked—nothing more—and Sherman has acted on— "short, sharp, and decisive." Viewed in the general— and individual exceptions go for nothing on such a scale as this—two things made the rebellion possible; the ignorance of the Southern masses—ignorance of their true interests, their true relations to the Government and to their Northern fellow-citizens, and of their own duty as *men*,—and the devilish incarnate selfishness of the so-called "chivalry," whose energy and audacity have been its motive power. The former I believed before I saw it—I have seen it now even more than I believed, seen and heard it from themselves. The latter I have seen too. Both are the legitimate fruits of Slavery and both inevitably tended to intestine strife, anarchy, ceaseless war and national ruin. Nothing but such tremendous lessons as Sherman's campaigns have taught them could have overcome or enlightened the former; and as to the latter nothing can secure the safety of the nation short of blotting out their influence and if necessary their existence, as a class.

You will think this hard doctrine, and will perhaps be grieved at my repeating it; but I am looking simply at things as they exist, and it is no more unfeeling in me to say this than for legislators to enact and Judges and Sheriffs to administer and execute the death-penalty upon any other murderers, and thereby to involve *their* innocent families in misery and shame. I have felt deeply the distress caused by our march and

have never lost an opportunity to prevent or relieve
personal suffering where I could; though I have often
also felt that even in the case of women,—Southern
ladies—what they received was but a just retribution
for the large share they personally had had in bringing
on and keeping up this war. As to the "Southern gentlemen" we had a specimen at our Headquarters not
long ago, whom I had in my mind when I wrote the
words "devilish incarnate selfishness." It was Col.
Alfred Rhett,* of a South Carolina Artillery Regiment,
. . . long in command of Fort Sumter, and who, when
they gave up Charleston, came thence with his men under Hardee. He was captured on the evening of March
15th, *inside of his own skirmish line,* by some of our
scouts, very much to his astonishment. He was brought
to our Headquarters and was treated with entire courtesy by Gen. Sherman, as also by Slocum and Jeff. C.
Davis, who were old acquaintances of his. He was at
our camp for an hour or two, sat in the General's tent
and chatted very freely, and took dinner at our table.
He was a complete specimen of his class; well-educated,
fluent, "a gentleman" in all *exterior* qualities, of an
easy assurance of manner and well-bred self-confidence
admirably calculated to make an impression. He was
quite as much at his ease as any of us, and expressed
his opinions about military matters and everything else
with a frankness quite refreshing. He denounced Jeff
Davis . . . (who beat his father Barnwell Rhett, for
the presidency of the C.S.A., though Col. R. did not
remind us of this)—as a "fool"; criticized severely the
C.S.A. blunder of allowing Sherman to march through
Georgia without a great battle—was politely positive,
Sherman himself to the contrary notwithstanding,—
the General arguing the matter with evident amusement—that "if things had been properly managed"

---

* This ampler allusion to Col. Rhett (see *ante*, p. 272) records the
highly unfavorable impression he made upon Hitchcock. He is seen in
Sherman's *Memoirs* (II, 300-303) more as an amusing figure.

(probably if Col. Rhett had managed them) our Georgia march would have been a disastrous failure, etc., etc.; though he admitted that it might have cost the rebels 30,000 or 40,000 men to whip us. "But," said Sherman, "you can't afford to lose 30,000 men—you haven't got the men left to spare"—. "Oh, yes" replied Rhett, with a polite persistency which I am sure would have convinced you, "we have plenty of men. I will undertake in one month to raise 100,000 men for our army—*with one cavalry regiment.*"—"And what will they be worth—how long can you keep such an army together—how much fighting will such men do?" said the General. "Oh, just as good as any others," said the imperturbable Rhett,—"Just let me have my regiment to do it with and I'll raise the men, and make 'em do good fighting too; yes, if I don't raise 100,000 men in one month's time they may chop my head off— I'll make that bargain. Conscripts are just as good as any other soldiers; *discipline's* the thing; all you have to do is to establish the principle. Why, I've shot twelve men myself in the last six weeks and not long ago I took a pack of dogs and went into the swamps and in three days I caught twenty-eight men with them."

I have given you almost the exact, literal words he used. This "chivalrous" Southern gentleman; this devil in human shape, who is but a type of his class, and whose polished manners and easy assurance made only more hideous to me the utterly heartless and selfish ambition and pride of class which gave tone to his whole discourse. Day after day we had been listening to the protestations of those whose own ignorance and cowardice have made them the victims, while also in some sense the accomplices, of these "leaders"; day after day we heard the same story in South Carolina just as regularly as in Georgia and in a more whining style. "The people didn't want this war—they were *drug* into it by the big men—if the soldiers had their say-so they'd come home mighty quick, but they's forced to go." Unluckily a conscript's bullet kills as quickly as any other. Do you wonder that I say this class must be *blotted out?*—The class of which Rhett, Jeff Davis, Toombs, and the like, are types?

It happened that the morning after Rhett's capture —which was the 16th March, the day of the battle near Averysboro,—while the fight was going on a rebel deserter was brought in to where Gens. Sherman, Slocum, Kilpatrick, and Williams were standing together, the former giving directions for the movement of troops, etc. He was quite a fine-looking young fellow, one of the most intelligent and self-possessed I have seen. He was asked and answered promptly sundry questions, and then some one told him Rhett was in our hands. "Lucky for him he was taken"—he replied—"he'd have been shot within a week anyhow." "Shot!—by whom, and why?"—"By his own men, if Wheeler's men didn't do it. They all hate him. He has had seven men shot since he left Fort Sumter, and one lieutenant in Wheeler's command has sworn to kill him for shooting one of their men, the first chance he gets." I heard this,—and it seems to me that all these things together pointedly illustrate this rebellion. I do not say, of course, that all "Southern gentleman" nor all rebel officers are like Rhett. I do say that he represents the class which has from the first lorded it over the South, and would put their foot upon all our necks if they could. As to those who have let these men inflame, deceive, bribe or drive them into the support of their schemes, and willingly or unwillingly have been made at once their tools and now their victims—while I see plainly the different position they occupy, yet are they not also justly responsible for what they could have prevented? Sad enough, terrible enough it is, that so many helpless, so many innocent, all over the land, must suffer; but I cannot hold any man guiltless, no matter how well-meaning or how admirable his character in other respects, who has allowed ignorance, or prejudice, or passion or cowardice of any kind to number him among the accomplices in this enormous crime. (10 P.M.) Thank God, we *know* now that the end draws nigh! We have official dispatches from Grant to and on the 4th tonight, telling of the occupation of Richmond and Petersburg, and doubtless as I write you have later news still by telegraph. There is something stunning in these successes. I do not feel like shouting over them, but rather like one who looks back with mingled gratitude and awe into the depths of an abyss from which he has escaped. For all I have written so bitterly above about Rhett and his like, I do not desire—that is, I should take no personal gratification in their punishment. The leaders of the rebellion are the greatest criminals, I think, in all modern history, and I know no greater in ancient times; nor could any punishment well exceed their just deserts, in view of the misery they have wantonly inflicted upon a whole people. But defeat itself to a man like Jeff Davis is a terrible punishment; and the only thing I care about is that the nation shall be safe, and the last spark which might blaze up again be utterly trampled out.

However, the war is not over yet. Grant's last dispatches report Lee's army reduced more than one half —"*It is said,* he has not over 20,000 men left," and Sheridan in hot pursuit. Johnston's army *was* about 40,000 men when he attacked us near Bentonville. If Lee and Johnston can unite whatever may remain to both, as of course they will try to do, these are yet to be defeated, killed, captured or dispersed. We shall leave here by Monday next—and you will be less at a loss this time to imagine in what direction, though exactly to what point depends more on Lee than on Sherman.

The fact is,—though this is nobody's guess but my own,—I do not see how it is possible for another great battle to be fought. We know that after Hood's defeat, which was not—on account of weather and roads—followed up with anything like the vigor Sheridan is now using, nor with anything like the force,—his army almost fell to pieces, though pursuit soon ceased, and his men went back without molestation to Augusta. Now, what has Lee's shattered and flying remnant to hang a hope on—and if Johnston could not defeat a part of "Sherman's army" proper, how will his men face it, largely increased and re-fitted, acting in concert with as many more, and they the captors of Richmond! But —*nous verrons.*

I have learned—not, happily, from misfortune,—the wisdom of Uncle E[than]'s rule, "nothing can be certainly predicted in war." By the way, you would have lost your respect for Gen. Sherman today if you had heard him reply to a question of mine—I think the only foolish one I ever asked him. A telegram from Newbern stated that the *New York papers* of the 5th (I think) set down the rebel losses at Peterburg and Richmond at 15,000 killed and wounded, *and* 25,000 prisoners. "General," said I, "do you think these figures can be correct,"—"Don't know—*I haven't facts enough yet to reason from!*"

But suppose that Lee's remnant and Johnston's force also should speedily fall or be broken to pieces, and the whole organization of the "C.S.A.," as such, be destroyed, east of the Mississippi, Texas still remains to be occupied, if not reconquered, and the "guerrilla question" then comes up. It *may* be a good many months yet before all serious armed opposition to the Government shall cease.

I confess to you, . . . whether it be a sign of unsteady patriotism or not, that while the first thought that came up on learning of the victories at Richmond, etc., was "Te Deum laudamus," the next, only not simultaneous with it, was—"How long now before I can leave for HOME?" But it is idle to ask that yet awhile; nobody can answer it. I cannot leave the army until it is clear that the military question is solved, and the *general* necessity for the services of the loyal men of the country is over. . . .

I have written this letter at intervals, as you can see, and finish it hastily to send back by private hands to Fort Monroe. It is lovely weather, and we no longer dread heavy rains—in fact, rain will be welcome, to lay the dust. I will write again before we leave. . . .

April 8/65

I have sundry rebel newspapers, etc., picked up on the march which I may send home to be laid aside as mementoes for my own eye.

IN THE FIELD, GOLDSBORO, April 10, 1865

Everything is packed up; the troops have been moving since daylight,—our Headquarters wagons are at the door nearly loaded, and in a short time (today) we shall be on the march again. The late victories have changed our programme somewhat; Grant telegraphed Sherman from Parksville on the 6th that "the rebel armies are now the only strategic points"; and while he is looking after Lee,—perhaps has found him by this time,—we start to hunt up "Jo Johnston." If he is able and willing to resist longer against such odds—much worse in every way for him than when he fled by night from Bentonville,—there will be a battle. I must say that I cannot see how Johnston *can* give battle unless we succeed in catching him and forcing it; and as to that, "a stern chase is a long chase" on land as well as at sea. Possibly this may be a long march into the interior, possibly a short campaign—nobody can tell. Thank God that it opens with auspices so different from even our last "difficult and dangerous movement"—as the General told me *at Savannah* he considered that march, but which was crowned with so complete success.

But I predict nothing, not even to myself. I continue entirely well, and always feel better on the march than

when we are at rest, for then I miss the exercise and
free air. . . .

I wrote you last on Monday, 10th inst., from Goldsboro, just before we mounted our horses and "sallied
forth" on the "North Carolina Campaign." As the
telegraph is today repaired and in operation from this
to Morehead City, you will have learned long before
you get this that we came on to Raleigh without any
trouble; and how much more than we know now or than
has happened yet, you may also learn by telegraph before you get this—*quien sabe?* Nothing will surprise
me now, I think.

We know that Johnston and his army have gone to
Greensboro, N. C., only eighty miles from here; that
Jeff Davis and his family, and his "cabinet" are there,
or were two days ago; that *Stoneman's cavalry* have
cut the railroad (towards Salisbury and Charlotte) a
few miles beyond Greensboro, burning two or three
bridges at various points, and leaving J.D. & Co no
escape by rail; and we move tomorrow in that direction. Meanwhile if Sheridan's horses are not used up,
or as soon as they are in condition to move—for up to
the time of Lee's surrender they must have had hard
work and would need rest,—he and Grant's infantry
will be thundering down from Danville,—and Stoneman and Thomas' infantry from the west. The terrible
net-work is rapidly drawing in around the leaders of
the rebellion.

We are told here, on what appears to be good and
direct authority, that John C. Breckinridge* is in
Grant's hands, a prisoner, and we *know* officially of the

* Vice-President of the United States under Buchanan; C.S.A. Secretary of War from January to April, 1865. In Sherman's *Memoirs* (II,
352) Breckinridge is seen, not in Grant's hands, but at the conference
between Sherman and Johnston on April 19.

surrender of Lee and his whole "Army of Northern Virginia" upon terms which I cannot but think express Lee's personal conviction that there ought to be no further effort or resistance made. He might—or at least it is probable that he might—have simply disbanded his army, with *"sauve qui peut."* But by accepting Grant's terms—which we have by telegraph in an official copy of the correspondence between them— he put his (Lee's) whole army under bonds, or on parole rather, which is stronger, to cease all further effort, go home and stay there in obedience to the laws, "until properly exchanged"—which will not be immediately. I take it that Lee did not intend to encourage "guerrillas," and his action was of course the best possible preventive. I do not doubt he so intended it. We are told here by respectable citizens that Hardee, before leaving here, having learned Lee's surrender, openly declared that if any more lives were lost in fighting for the C.S.A., it would be *murder;* this they say they heard him say. Hardee does not belong to the "last ditch" or chivalry set; and I do not doubt he did say it.

While the General's plans of course assume that Johnston will fight, we do not expect a battle. It would be mere madness—murder—for him to go into a general engagement with this army (more than double his numbers as it alone is) even were Lee's army intact. The only question is how far he will be disposed and able to run; and whether he will try to keep his men together at all. If he does keep them together, and does not get the heels of us, the game will be up within not many days. But as the General replied at Bentonville to some inquiry about what J. was likely to do—"Johnston and I are not on speaking terms"—and I make no predictions. Thirty days may wind up the business in the Atlantic States.

We reached here yesterday morning, the fourth day from Goldsboro; the enemy's cavalry being in our immediate front and falling back skirmishing all the way, though not heavily, during the first two days, as far as Smithfield. At Smithfield, on the morning of the 12th, about 4 A.M., two officers came into our camp—which was on the square round the Court House in the heart of the town, with dispatches from Grant for the General, dated 9th, telegraphed to City Point, and again from Morehead City to Goldsboro, whence they rode between 11 P.M. Tuesday and 4 A.M. Wednesday— twenty-six miles, over bad roads. The dispatches were copies of the correspondence between Grant and Lee proposing and accepting the terms of surrender. Within an hour later the columns of the "Left Wing"—or "Army of Georgia"—with which we were came booming along in splendid style to cross the river (Neuse) and go on to Raleigh. Imagine the waves—the billows of tumultuous cheering, which rolled along the lines as brigade after brigade came along by our Headquarters and were told the news. We did not start till the greater part of the Corps then passing had got by—about 9 A.M.—though our wagons were on the road at six— and meanwhile band after band, as the successive divisions came along took position in the Court House square, relieving each other, and made the little old town echo with music as beautiful as it was patriotic. We were all pretty gay that morning, you may believe, and haven't got over it yet. Even in Smithfield the public stocks "went up"—visibly; for some of "the boys" set fire to them. I refer to the wooden stocks, near the jail, a comfortable institution for the improvement of criminals which the "conservative" old North State has retained from colonial times. Nothing else was burned nor damage done there that I know or heard of.

Wednesday night our camp and Headquarters were at Gulley Station, a railroad village about thirteen miles from Raleigh. That evening five gentlemen came out to see the General—really envoys from Gov. Vance: Ex-Gov. Graham (formerly U. S. Senator, Secretary of the Navy, and "Scott & Graham" in 1852); Ex-Gov. Swain, who has for many years past been President of the North Carolina University at Chapel Hill; and three of the Governor's staff, Colonels and Majors in the State Service. They were most kindly received,—had a long talk with the General, got a good supper,—to judge by their trencher work and their own apologies for it—stayed all night in our tents (Gov. Swain occupying my bed while I bivouacked elsewhere) and went back to Raleigh at early daylight hoping still to find Gov. Vance there; but he had left. Of all this more when I see you, if you care then to hear. Imagine my pleasant surprise to find in Gov. Swain an old playmate of my Mother—"the Davie Swain" of Buncombe Co. of whom she often told me; and who when I asked him purposely—only whether he ever knew Col. Andrew Erwin, who lived fifty odd years ago in Buncombe, so promptly and warmly responded, and finding who I was spoke so warmly of my Mother and Father and of the whole family—with whom he had kept up an acquaintance whenever opportunity offered, that I quickly felt as if I had known him all my life. When they left next morning I went down with the General to see them off; and after a polite good-bye all round, the old gentleman—still a vigorous and interesting old man, with a remarkable memory of books, dates, and persons,—called me to him to shake hands with "good-bye, Major—*we* are not enemies, I hope?"

Somehow or other there are ever so many "own correspondents" along with us, and I refer you for particulars about Raleigh to the New York papers. . . .

We have had a very pleasant time in this very pretty town. The rebel army left just before we entered. Wheeler's cavalry, as usual, plundered the citizens, broke into stores, etc., etc., the night before. Our men have behaved as well as in Savannah,—guards are stationed everywhere and on all sides we hear mingled admiration and astonishment at the good conduct, the fine appearance and condition and the soldierly bearing of our army, and the unreserved acknowledgment that the rebel cause is hopelessly "gone up."

I heard a son of George E. Badger*—formerly U. S. Senator and one of the most distinguished lawyers at the U. S. Supreme Court bar,—who (the son) has served three years in the rebel army and but recently got out of it by some good luck,—say today that the *Southern people* would not be contented with anything short of the death of "the leaders of the conspiracy who took advantage of the irritated state of public feeling on Lincoln's election to plunge them into a civil war." I give his words; I was struck with their accurate statement of the truth of the case.

The General called at Mr. Badger's last night; and when I told him this morning that Mrs. B. and the family were intimate friends of Mrs. Bell in Washington, he asked me to go there and invite them—Mrs. B. and her daughters—to see one of our Corps pass in review at the State House. I did so and after escorting two young ladies—one the wife of a rebel officer now in Va.—to see it, returned to the house, and had an extremely pleasant visit.

I don't think of any more of my *hardships* to mention just now; except that when I left Mr. Badger's house, declining a very *cordial* invitation to stay to dinner but agreeing to call again, Mr. Badger, who is an invalid, shook hands very warmly and told me to give the General his thanks for sending me there. . . . [P.S.] As Gov. Vance left a fine house here,—his official residence—untenanted, the General is occupying it. This is the fourth State Capitol he has walked into. It's a way he has.

But don't be disappointed if Johnston does run,— for he has the start of us, and may not be headed off,— down to Augusta or elsewhere. We may have many

---

* George Edmond Badger, United States Senator from North Carolina, 1846-1855, a Southern opponent of secession.

miles to travel yet; but the heavy fighting is over, that
I do not doubt; it cannot be otherwise. The C.S.A. as
such *is done for* now.

IN THE FIELD, RALEIGH, NORTH CAROLINA
Saturday, April 15th 1865

Before you read this sheet, if you happen to take it
up first, read the other one herewith, dated yesterday,
14th. I wrote that last night, fully expecting then that
by this time tonight we should be on the march again,
and in camp some miles hence towards Greensboro. But
I left none too wide a margin with my *quien sabe*. During last night there came in a letter from Gen. Johnston, whose contents being already known here from
the General's own statement of them to sundry officers,
I violate no confidence in giving you; though unless
and until you see them published, do not mention it as
from me.

Gen. J. requested of Gen. S. a suspension of hostilities till he could learn from Grant whether the same
terms would be given to him (Johnston) as had been
given to Lee. Sherman replied that there was no need
of applying to Grant, he himself being fully authorized
to act,—that he would grant the same terms,—and that
hostilities should be suspended, on condition that both
sides remain *in statu quo* with troops, etc., until he received Johnston's answer. This reply went back at
once.

This morning after breakfast Maj. McCoy, the General's senior aid was sent up the railroad to Kilpatrick's Headquarters—our advanced posts,—to wait for
Johnston's answer to come back by flag, and to telegraph it thence at once; yesterday's orders to march
were countermanded, and we are still here, *in statu quo*.
"After so much," as the President says, it is needless
to say that we look for no more fighting hereabouts.
Thank God that the end of all this strife and bloodshed
does at last appear,—and that it will be the *end*, when

it does come, and not a mere armed truce. Terrible as the cost has been, the price had to be paid and it was worth paying.

So it seems likely, at this present writing, that we may be in Raleigh for some time yet. If like terms are made with Johnston to those made with Lee, complete muster-rolls of J.'s army will have to be made out and signed in duplicate, arms, ammunitions, stores, etc., etc., transferred; and to do all this will no doubt occupy at least a fortnight. After that, I suppose this army or the greater part of it will very likely march northwards —but 'tis no use to speculate. I have no idea how this new turn of affairs will affect me. It may keep me very busy or it may leave me little to do; when I know, I shall be able to judge somewhat as to my own future.

As yet, McCoy has not sent back any word from the front, and as we learn tonight that Kilpatrick has pushed his Headquarters some twenty-four miles up the railroad to Durham Station, it may be some time yet before Johnston's answer comes. It has been raining nearly all day—and so we have luckily escaped what would have been a disagreeable soaking; and I am already tired out with lounging around the house with nothing to do but help entertain the officers who come to Headquarters.

Tonight we have had a charming serenade from the famous "33ᵈ Mass." band, and besides, a patriotic glee very well sung by four or five officers. I have heard and enjoyed more really excellent brass band music within the last six months than ever before in ten times the period; it has been no small element in the pleasures of campaigning.

Sundry "prominent citizens" have been here tonight —besides former visits—to see the General and learn his views and what is necessary to set matters right. I dare say Gov. Vance himself may soon turn up here. Nothing could be more complete, more absolute, than the conviction of the people here that the "C.S.A." is utterly, hopelessly "gone up"; and they acquiesce in it with an evident relief and delight at the prospect of peace which is the best answer to the nonsense about our being "unable to hold the South after we conquer it." I send you a copy of today's "Progress"—a daily paper which has already resumed publication by the same parties who issued it under rebel rule. Its articles, —editorial—are not "inspired" nor overlooked by any censor; I do not doubt they are honestly the feelings of the writer, and I know them to express the sentiments avowed by many who were "good rebels" last year, and even till recently. It is a little amusing to read the complimentary notice of the "grand review" of yesterday. *One* of our Corps marched through the city, passing in review by the State House, and occupying some five or six hours, marching by "company front." There are six corps in the army now here,—under the General's immediate orders,—that is, six corps of infantry, including the artillery belonging to each, *besides* Kilpatrick's Cavalry Division. But the compliment was deserved; the men did look and march splendidly.

The railroad hence to Goldsboro is already in repair except the Neuse River bridge, and trains will be running through to Morehead City in a day or two, when our couriers will go and come. As yet we have neither sent nor received any letters. I shall keep this open till the first courier goes down and then send it with the latest news. But I fear my letters will contain little of interest which the newspapers will not also give more fully.

Sunday night April 16th/65—10 P.M.

Tomorrow at 8 A.M. Gen. Sherman and staff go out by rail to Durham's Station, our advanced post, and thence are to ride three miles further, between the lines, to meet Gen. Johnston and staff. The appointment was made this evening by telegraph to Kilpatrick's

Headquarters, where Johnston's staff officer had come with J.'s invitation to Gen. Sherman to meet him. I was with the General this afternoon, making two or three calls. After leaving Gov. Bragg's house he was met by a messenger with a dispatch from K. giving J.'s proposition. He went to the telegraph office, sent Kilpatrick a dispatch accepting it—agreeing to meet J. tomorrow—and as we left the office he said to me in his quick way—"the war is over—occupation's gone!" The terms of surrender will be fixed at the interview tomorrow; but they will be the same as Grant's to Lee.

Once before in my life the accomplishment of hopes long and anxiously dwelt on, ever present, and which entered into all my thoughts, left me without even the power to express or give utterance to the joy and thankfulness which filled my heart. Something similar is the effect upon me of this astounding close of the most terrible contest of modern times. At last, Peace, blessed, God-given Peace, is so near that we can hear her gracious voice and her gentle foot-fall over fields too long drenched with fraternal blood. True Peace,—bought not by the surrender but the manly vindication of principles above all price. God be praised! God help us all "loyal" and "rebel" alike, to take to heart the terrible lessons of the last five years, and alike to shun the errors, the follies and the crimes, which brought upon us all such discipline. . . . I leave this still open, as the first courier will not leave, probably, till after we return from the interview.

H.

HEAD-QUARTERS
ARMIES OF THE UNITED STATES,

WASHINGTON, D. C. April 21, 1865

The enclosed letters were written at Raleigh. On Monday, 17th and again on Tuesday, 18th, Gen. Sherman held conferences in person with the rebel Gen. Joe Johnston, at a point between the lines of the two armies, twenty-eight miles from Raleigh, on the R.R. I was present during part of the latter interview—no one else but the principals being otherwise present at all—to do some necessary writing, and immediately on our return to Raleigh that night was sent here with dispatches of great importance. I reached here this afternoon and delivered my dispatches—which are of such a nature that instead of sending a written reply,—don't read this aloud—General Grant himself goes back with me (or I with him, as you choose) to Raleigh, at once. I write this in Gen. Grant's office at 11 P.M., waiting for some final preparations on his part. Some of his staff also go with him. You may expect very soon to hear news of great importance, relating to the winding up of the war.

I have been here about seven hours; this afternoon Gen. Grant told me I might have to wait a day or two for the answer,—but tonight he goes himself at once. This is a fair sample of the uncertainty of military movements.

I have at least seen Uncle E[than], who is well, and also had a pleasant visit this evening at the Nichols'.* After I saw Gen. Grant this afternoon and was told as above, I telegraphed Shepley and Dwight Bell† both to telegraph me at once where and how you all were, as my latest dates from you are *25th March*—four weeks old! However, as Uncle E has heard of nothing wrong I take it for granted you are all right—and as I passed a mail for our Headquarters on my way from Raleigh I shall find letters there no doubt. I am perfectly well, and am not worse in spirits for having had the confidential duties in regard to these matters assigned to me. When I see you—which *may* be before July, *quien*

* Shortly after the war Gen. Hitchcock "married Miss Martha Rind Nicholls, a member of a family with which he had maintained very intimate social relations for a whole generation." (*Fifty Years of Camp and Field*, p. 483.) It may be assumed that Henry Hitchcock referred here to this family.

† Of Pittsburgh, a connection by marriage.

sabe?—I will tell you about the interviews with Johnston, etc. . . .

I must close at once—God bless you! . . .

In Chesapeake Bay

On Board Dispatch Boat "M. Martin"

Sat: April 22/65—12 M.

I left at Washington last night to be mailed to you an
envelope containing two letters written at Raleigh a
week ago, and which I brought thence with me, also a
note written last night, explaining my sudden visit to
Washington with dispatches, and my unexpectedly
sudden orders to return to Raleigh in company with
Gen. Grant himself. Unexpected, because in the afternoon, (yesterday) when I delivered the dispatches,
Gen. Grant said that a Cabinet meeting would probably
have to be held and it might be forty-eight hours before I could get off with the answers. But he afterwards
saw the President and Secretary of War, and, though I
am not informed as to their conclusions, I am at no
loss—knowing fully the contents of the dispatches I
brought—to understand what these were; nor am I at
all disappointed in the result. I told Uncle E[than] in
the afternoon—without telling him what the dispatches
contained—that I was satisfied when I left Raleigh that
President Johnson would not approve or carry out certain points submitted to him; and I think it will prove
so. Anyhow, he made up his mind without a Cabinet
meeting, and instead of spending that night and today
quietly at Washington and—which was what I was
most anxious for—learning by Shepley's and Dwight
Bell's replies to my telegrams to them both, where and
how you all are, I was summoned to Gen. Grant's office
at 10 P.M. and before 12 P.M. had accompanied him
down to the boat. We did not get off, however, till 3
A.M., it being found best to take this boat instead of
the one first ordered, and this one having to be got
ready after we came down.

It is very pleasant, certainly, to be a Lieutenant General and have as really elegant a "dispatch boat" as this to travel on at will; one of the swiftest and handsomest, if not indeed the handsomest steamer I ever was on, built expressly for the purpose, with every comfort, furnished in elegant taste, and everything in keeping.

Our party consists of Gen. Grant,—whom I never met before except a mere introduction to him at the Planter's House in 1861 or '2 just after the battle of Belmont—Gen. Meigs,* (Quartermaster General of the Army) and Major Hudson,† Major Leet,‡ and Capt. Dunn§ (son of our friend Col. Dunn∥), all of Gen. G.'s staff; the two latter of whom I have met before at our own Headquarters.

Gen. Grant is in almost every respect a very unlike man to Gen. Sherman, in demeanor as well as appearance. I have had some conversation with him, partly to deliver some verbal messages Gen. S. sent by me in addition to the written dispatches, partly also informing him of details of our march from Goldsboro to Raleigh not included in those. He is very quiet and taciturn, with none of Sherman's vivacity of appearance or manner and none of his off-hand, ready, entertaining conversation. That is, I see nothing of that, and though I do not doubt his mind is just now fully occupied with the gravest questions of the day, which would explain unusual thoughtfulness in any man, yet it is evidently also habitual. The current pictures of him give a very correct idea of his face, except that I find him a younger looking man than I expected, also better dressed, thanks to a new or nearly new uniform, and his expression is also something sterner than I imagined. He has asked

* Maj. Gen. Montgomery C. Meigs.
† Edward McKeever Hudson.
‡ George Keller Leet.
§ William McKee Dunn, Jr.
∥ William McKee Dunn, of Indiana.

me very few questions, but listened quietly, though closely, to what I had to say,—which I made as brief as possible,—and but once or twice made any comment, and then but a word or two. Finding that he had the erroneous idea—derived from the newspapers—that Sherman had Gov. Vance in his hands, I gave him the facts about Vance's "commissioners" coming out to our camp which I wrote you. "Then you haven't had Vance with you at all?" "No, Sir—he left Raleigh Wednesday night (12th) with Johnston." "I'm glad of it"—he replied. The reply was significant of a good deal, as things stand just now.

I write this at a disadvantage, visible enough from the shaky handwriting, thanks to the vibrations of the boat, which is going at full speed. We have had a very pleasant sail thus far, the day being lovely, and the water smooth, and expect to be at Fortress Monroe by or before 4 P.M., where I shall mail this. Another steamer will be ready there to take us to Morehead City or Newbern, and we shall doubtless be in Raleigh by or before daylight Monday morning. By the way, I was glad to find that though the propeller on which I came from Morehead City to Fort Monroe on Wednesday rolled very noticeably and we came by the "outside route," on the open ocean, I was not the least seasick.

You will easily infer that what takes Gen. Grant to Raleigh is of importance. The next week or two will undoubtedly develop *practically* President Johnson's views as to the proper mode of winding up the rebellion and dealing with its leaders.

I have said nothing about the horrible assassination of Mr. Lincoln, though here as everywhere it is the topic of all thought. Whether it was the result of a conspiracy or the act of a single fanatic, it was but the legitimate fruit of the rebellion itself, and intrinsically but its logical concrete expression. Perhaps it was necessary, as some think, that by some such act as this should be made visible to all the true guilt of those who assailed the life of the nation with a purpose no less deadly, by means no less cruel and cowardly, when rightly judged, than those of the assassin who shed the blood of that most kindly, patient, loving man. I can hardly convey to you the horror and deep indignation which the tidings brought to our army. Gen. Sherman learned it by telegram on Monday morning 17th, but did not disclose it till the afternoon, after his first interview with Johnston—except to Johnston himself, who expressed the deepest concern and regret, *on the account of the South itself*. He clearly saw what a terrible disaster it was to *them*. I was told when we returned to Raleigh that night, that the soldiers stood around in the camps, in little squads, silent or talking in subdued but bitter tones, and many of them weeping like children, after they heard it. I heard officers who, I know, always denounced and strove against violence and outrages in our marches through Georgia and South Carolina swear in bitter terms that if our army moved again they would never spare nor protect another house or family. The Commanding officer at Raleigh instantly doubled all his guards (protecting the citizens) that night. Still, I am glad to say no violence occurred, nor will any; our men are too well disciplined, and even those officers who feel most acknowledge that indiscriminate vengeance is not to be thought of. You will notice Sherman's order announcing the murder indirectly cautions against this; he himself feared mischief from it at first. . . .

IN THE FIELD, RALEIGH, NORTH CAROLINA, April 25th 1865
                                                                Tuesday 4 P.M.
. . . I wrote you on board the steamer going down the Potomac, on Saturday (22d) leaving the letter at F^t Monroe,—also sent back a line to Uncle E[than] from Morehead City to be sent you. We had what was to me a very pleasant passage back, all things considered, at any rate we made good time and had no acci-

dents. I was amused to find myself the only man of the party who was not in the least seasick on our ocean passage—the Lieut. General, the Quartermaster General (Meigs) two Majors and a Captain all confessing the nauseating power of the sea-god, and the younger ones audibly envying me the undisturbed and hearty enjoyment of every meal and the "inevitable segar" on deck after it, which the Lieutenant General himself was forced to lay aside.

Coming up at once from Morehead City (the same place known as Beaufort, N. C.) Sunday night,—where we had arrived but half an hour too late for the afternoon train up,—our little party (six officers and Gen. G.'s colored servant) occupied one open "platform" or common freight car; but as the evening was lovely, clear starlight, and the air delightful, and we came up (thirty-six miles) to Newbern in about an hour and a quarter, it was rather exhilarating. At Newbern they rigged up a passenger car,—not the sort you travel in, but still with top, sides and seats,—and put into it two beds on which the two Generals slept soundly all night, while we Staff Officers consoled ourselves with a good lunch put up on board ship, and such sleep as we could get—which you will easily believe was in my case most of the night. Travelling of all sorts suits me so well that I wonder how I have come to spend so many days and years of my life quietly at an office desk. We reached "these Headquarters" before the General was dressed—about 150 miles in less than twelve hours— and astonished him with the appearance of General Grant, by whose direction I had omitted, the night before, in telegraphing my own arrival at Morehead City, to mention that any one but Gen. Meigs had returned with me. I find that I have made the trip there and back quicker than anybody expected and was very glad to find it so. From the enclosed order, issued by Gen. Sherman the day after I left here—as every body here quickly learned—with dispatches for Washington, you

will not be surprised that everybody was awaiting with
deep interest and anxiety the answer from the powers
at Washington. I have had to laugh many times since
returning when one and another and another officer
would take me aside with—"Well, now,—*sub rosa,* you
know—just between us,—what is the result? What did
Grant come down here for? Now, just tell me what you
think, you know?" They knew very well that if I didn't
know, I couldn't, and if I did know, I wouldn't, tell
them anything about it. One question was—"Well, Major—do you bring back peace or war?" My answer was
—"I brought back Gen. Grant;"—and my curious
friend "saw it" at once.

Nevertheless, the impression seems to prevail here
universally that the conditional agreement made between Sherman and Johnston on the 18th was not approved; which is strengthened by the fact that army
supplies have been kept coming forward rapidly from
below, and that today is published in the city papers a
General Order from Schofield directing the "Army of
the Ohio" to be prepared to march at 6 A.M. tomorrow.
Everybody anticipates, and I think everybody regrets,
another march; for this time, if the Army does advance, it is necessarily in pursuit not of a single object,
as heretofore, or to reach a definite "objective point,"
but to pursue a flying enemy and meanwhile to live on
the country.

As I write, the General—I should say the Generals,
—are waiting for Johnston's reply to a communication
sent out to him yesterday; besides which a certain time
must elapse after notice given before—under the
agreement of 18th inst.—either their army or ours has
the right to move again. I cannot but hope even yet, as
I do most earnestly, that Johnston's reply *may* be such
as to obviate the necessity of our again "sallying
forth"; but I confess it is rather hope than expectation. As to Johnston's attempting to make a stand and
fight us, it is of course out of the question; even if he

could hold his whole army in hand and fight it with the
spirit of his best days, we have force enough to double
him up and ruin him. He can only retreat,—he could do
no more before Richmond was taken or Lee had surrendered,—and now, whither or to whom ultimately
can he go? His men understand this, of course, and
they are constantly deserting; and I have no sort of
doubt that whatever course he may take, his army will
in great part fall to pieces. But it is not enough to *dis-
perse* his army; what we want is to capture it, and thus
completely prevent any further chance of trouble from
it as an organization. In any event, no matter how
many desert, there are some—like Wade Hampton and
other representatives of "the chivalry"—who will not
surrender nor lay down their arms in good faith, and
who will be the "guerrillas," that is, the robbers, outlaws, and brigands, who will *for a while* more or less
infest society. In the end, all these will either go elsewhere, probably to Mexico, or will be hunted down and
killed like wolves, as they will deserve.

Gen. Kilpatrick told me last night,—and I heard the
same thing in effect before I left here the other day,—
that Wade Hampton declared he did not intend to surrender, anyhow; and that he expressed his intention of
going to Mexico to take service with Maximilian. Joy
go with him—why not Duke Hampton too? I saw him
at the first interview, on the 17th and stood by for some
little time while he and Kilpatrick were talking—out in
the yard, where all of us remained while Sherman and
Johnston had their private confab in the small frame
house where they met. Hampton's whole demeanor was
marked with the easy "well-bred" essentially vulgar
insolence which is characteristic of *that* type of "gentleman"; a man of polished manners, scarcely veiling
the arrogance and utter selfishness which marks his
class, and which I hate with a perfect hatred. There is
nothing of the true *man* in such "gentlemen"; their
external polish and tact, their knowledge of the world,

their easy self-possession—qualities which the most
finished rascals of foreign gambling-salons share with
them,—even the qualities which make them agreeable
to their *own* set or circle,—for a man may be as thoroughly selfish in his apparent generosity, etc., as in the
want of it,—count for just as much as the glitter of
paste diamonds and no more.

On the 18th to our great satisfaction,—Wade Hampton (so one of his officers who came phrased it) did not
"see fit" to present himself. I had, however, quite a
chat with a Maj. Johnston, one of Gen. Johnston's
staff, a quiet, gentlemanly, unassuming man, who had
evidently seen considerable service, though he had very
little to say about it, and who made—as to his personal
qualities—a very pleasant impression on both Col. Poe
and myself. I was really sorry the conversation was
broken off when I was called in to the *sanctum* where
the two Generals—and also *John C. Breckinridge,* the
rebel *"Secretary of War"*—were holding their quiet
chat. I was busy in there till the conference ended, immediately upon which all parties mounted and rode off
—they their way, we ours. As I went out of the gate
towards my horse I passed this rebel Major friend of
mine,—and at the same moment we both held out our
hands frankly and kindly with—"good-bye, Major—
hope we shall meet again!"—To which he added, a moment after, in a lower voice—*"In the right way."*

I am very far from entertaining a blind or indiscriminate hatred of "rebels" as individuals, even while
I most heartily endorse our good friend Dr. Post's
solemn denunciation of the *rebellion* as "the greatest
crime since the crucifixion of our Lord." So it is. To
this awful and enormous crime there have been many
who were unwilling, reluctant, enforced accessories. All
such I would forgive, though I would not lightly en-
trust them with the privileges which they have once
failed to defend. But for the leaders,—for the men
whose ambition created or whose influence sustained

this fearful war,—it is not magnanimity to forgive or
trust *them*. It would be criminal folly and weakness. I
have seen too much, even in my little experience, of the
miseries which these men are responsible for before
God and man, to appreciate the "magnanimity" which
would let them go scott-free because having for four
years waged a desperate and remorseless war, in the
unscrupulous use of every means in their power, they
have at last surrendered when not to do so was to die
themselves. Don't think me harsh, or disposed to be
vindictive, if—before I can assent to your implied eu-
logy on Lee's "greatness" in surrendering as he did—
I remind you that Lee *did not offer to surrender* but
only yielded to Grant's summons to do so made on the
ground—which none knew better than Lee was true—
that further resistance was hopeless; or if I further remind you that even after the correspondence began,
and when in fact he was so meshed in Grant's lines of
fire and steel that to fight longer would have been mere
murder of his men, still Lee attempted to deny that he
was in such a condition as to call for surrender,—a
denial on which his surrender itself was the best commentary. Gen. Johnston—the rebel—himself attended
to this part of Lee's correspondence the other day (so
Gen. Sherman told me) in conversation with Gen. S.
remarking in a quiet way that he didn't think, if he
found himself so situated as to be obliged to surrender,
that he would go to work in his preliminary correspondence to show that he wasn't oblged to, *and then
do it*. The truth is, if Lee had not surrendered when he
did, all that was left of his army was utterly and hopelessly at Grant's mercy, and would have been cut all to
pieces. It seems to me that the humane part of the business was Grant's offering to let them off on the generous terms *he proposed* to Lee,—and that by accepting
them Lee simply showed that common sense and common feeling which long ago made it an established rule
of civilized war, that resistance against hopeless odds

is a *military crime*. I cannot, I confess, see any greatness in Lee's not committing this crime; if he had done
it, that alone should have made him infamous. It would
have been sheer murder and he knew it.

I cannot forget whatever estimable personal qualities some of these men may have,—I can never lose
sight of the great damning fact, that they made war
upon a Government whose only fault, as they themselves declared, was its gentleness,—that they plunged
this whole land into war, and blood, and mourning—for
what? It is useless to talk about personal qualities in
judging of the attitude these men must occupy before
the impartial tribunal of History—except, indeed, as
among themselves. There is an immense distance, I
freely admit, between a "gentlemanly" villain like
Rhett, of whom I wrote you, who boasted of his success
in recruiting with blood hounds in the swamps, and a
man like Lee, if you please; but—suppose that Robert
E. Lee had even only refused to take any part in this
war, which he did pronounce—in a letter to his sister,
written just before he accepted his first rebel commission,—to be unnecessary. Does not an "unnecessary
war" necessarily imply an enormous crime somewhere?
Suppose that every man in the South who honestly opposed Secession before the demoniac audacity of the
original conspirators forced upon the nation, at Sumter, the terrible issue of arms, had even only refused,
steadfastly, courageously refused, like Petigru* of
South Carolina, and John Minor Botts† of Virginia, to
be either cajoled or bullied into joining them—how
much of this dreadful bloodshed and anguish had been
spared! Sometimes I doubt whether these same "Union
Men" of the South are not the most guilty parties—for
but for their weakness, at any rate their yielding, it
would have been impossible for Jeff Davis to present

* James L. Petigru, lawyer and historian of Charleston, a vigorous opponent of secession.
† Member of Congress, 1847-1849.

the apparently united front he did. You know that I try
to judge truly and fairly of all things, for I think a mistaken opinion is a misfortune, and error—no matter
how "honest"—*can* only breed mischief. Judging as
carefully and honestly as I know how, I am thoroughly
satisfied from what I saw and heard day after day in
Georgia and the Carolinas, that the apparent "una-
nimity of the South" was the result of a system of
terrorism of infernal and reckless falsehood, from the
highest officials down, and of combined ignorance and
cowardice on the part of the masses of the people, of
which you can hardly form an idea. Talk about negro
slavery!—if we haven't seen white slaves from Atlanta
to Goldsboro, I don't know what the word means. And
I think that for this state of things those men are
largely responsible who talked, begged, prayed, against
Secession—but *when they fought at all*, fought for it!
They see it now around this city, plainly enough. The
most honest thing I have seen lately is the manifesto
of C. R. Thomas, the Secretary of State of North Carolina, published here this morning and which you will
see copied into the Northern papers,—his letter to the
Raleigh "Progress"—or "Standard," I forget which.
He sees now how "conservative" men failed in *their*
duty.

But you are tired of this "political talk," I dare say;
only it is not "politics." More than ever, day by day, I
thank God that I have had the opportunity to have even
my small share of the actual experience of this tremendous conflict, and to try, at least, to do what I could to
help towards saving the life of the nation. It has been
little enough, and easy enough—much easier than I
either expected or deserved. How I envy the men who
bore "the heat and burden of the day!" Yet even this
is something to be thankful for.

Since I begun this last sheet Johnston's reply has
come. General Grant had intended to leave us tomorrow morning at 10 A.M. for Ft. Monroe; now he will

stay here all day tomorrow at any rate, and orders are given to have a car ready at 8 A.M. for Gen. Sherman to go out *again* to Durham's Station, on our front, whence he rode before to where the former interviews with Johnston were held. You may imagine what new speculations this gives rise to. I shall keep this letter open till Gen. Grant leaves us, and send it by one of his Staff to be mailed at Ft. Monroe. Everybody is in hopes tonight that Johnston will surrender tomorrow, after all. God grant it! I cannot bear to think of this army marching any further through the country in a hostile attitude; its simple passage and subsistence, aside from the commission of any violence or outrage, would be a terrible blow to the people of the state. Johnston knows this as well as we do, and at the interviews last week expressed great anxiety to avoid the inevitable further damage that would result. It rests with him—not with us. We *cannot* stop short of compelling absolute, unconditional submission, and as to the further consequences, the longer the delay the worse they will and *ought* to be for the rebels. Nothing can excuse nor palliate further resistance now,—nothing whatever.

IN THE FIELD, RALEIGH April 26th 1865
Wednesday 10½ P.M.

The expected interview took place today, and you will know already by telegraph ere you read this that Johnston surrendered. Indeed I had no doubt left about it yesterday evening, when—after writing the foregoing—I read his reply to Sherman's summons to surrender. I did not go out today; Gens. Howard, Schofield, and Blair each with one aid, went with Sherman, and only his own two "personal aides" went with him. They have all just got back tonight, and the general fact is all that is yet made public here—but you will have learned the details by telegraph. Of course this being now a fact the military *kaleidoscope* is again shifted. I shall send this in the morning by Major Leet, of Grant's staff,—Grant returning at once to Washington,—to be mailed there. I *understand* that Sherman now intends to turn over this army to Schofield who will march it—except such detachments as may be left or sent here and there, to Richmond; and that the General himself will now go down to Charleston and Savannah, and thence come back to Richmond and meet the army there. How soon he leaves here,—how many or which, if not all, his staff go with him, I have as yet no opportunity to learn; but assume till otherwise informed—of which you will be quickly notified—that I go with him. I confess I am sorry for it, but am ready for anything.

It will be a hundred times harder for me now to remain in the service than when we were deep in the mud and swamps of South Carolina or in front of an enemy near Averysboro and Bentonville. There was something like a definite object there; for the sort of occupation or want of occupation I look forward to now I confess I have no relish, especially the loafing part of it. However, the war is over now, thank God, in its breadth and strength. . . .

I wish you could look in at the scene here tonight at our Headquarters,—the Governor's mansion. Quite a crowd of officers have been sitting and standing all the evening on the portico in front; a fine brass band playing in the large yard in front of the house since 8 o'clock; and a little while ago, looking through the front window of the right hand parlor, from the portico, one could see Grant and Sherman sitting at the center table, both busy writing, or stopping now and then to talk earnestly with the other general officers in the room—Howard, Schofield, "Johnny Logan," and Meigs.

If you never did before, you will appreciate from my late letters the folly of promising or predicting—even if one had a right to—anything certain as to military movements, or as to those of any one in the service. I have told you all I know as to what I shall probably do; what changes may come, what my own orders may be, and how soon, or when I can expect to see you, I cannot say; we can only take things patiently, and thank God for the glorious, the overwhelming successes of the last few weeks. Alas, that so heavy a blow should have fallen upon the nation in the midst of its deep rejoicing! But—"He doeth all things well."

It is late and I must close this. If anything occurs before Gen. Grant leaves worth noting I will add it; if not you will understand that this leaves me well and all of us in the best spirits. . . .

IN CAMP, AT "GATES' WOODS" NEAR
WASHINGTON, D. C.—May 26/65

I wrote you on Monday, as soon as I arrived. Since then, what with the bustle and confusion, finding out where our camp was—which luckily for me was moved to this place just outside the city, about a mile N.E. of the Capitol, the very day I arrived,—attending the Reviews on Tuesday and Wednesday, hunting for our ubiquitous General all yesterday morning and attending to his letters, etc., all the afternoon,—I have let four days pass without writing you. At any rate I had nor have yet any letter *from* you, though I hope for one or two today. Direct hereafter to Uncle E[than]'s care; I shall always be in the city some time every day, and think likely I may arrange to stay with him at night, as the General stays in the city with his family and only comes out to camp a short time every day to attend to business here.

He told me night before last that his Headquarters would remain here he thought about a week, and would then go West, and be fixed either at Louisville or Cincinnati—probably the latter. He spoke as though he had no idea but I would go along, as of course I should if still on the staff. I have not said anything to him yet

about leaving him, and though I have not the slightest
idea, of course, of remaining in the service, yet it is and
will be harder than I even thought, to leave *him,*—
especially now, thanks to Mr. Stanton.* However, it is
possible he may be kept here longer than "a week";
and I shall not leave till the last moment.—This letter
I write in his tent, expecting all the time his arrival
from town, when I shall be busy looking over letters,
etc., with him and may be busy writing the rest of the
day. It may therefore be abruptly closed and must be
fragmentary.

You see that Maj. Gen. O. O. Howard has been put
in charge of the new "Freedmen's Bureau." The day
I came Uncle E. told me that Howard had at once applied to Stanton to have me assigned to duty with him,
but that Stanton declined to interfere with my position
near Gen. Sherman,—very properly. Uncle E. added (to
me)—"Gen. Howard is a very good friend of yours—
he spoke very warmly in your praise." Afterwards I
called on Fullerton at Howard's office in the city, and
saw Gen. H. himself, who also immediately told me that
he had applied for me, and had wanted to make me one
of his "Assistant Commissioners," and give me charge
of the affairs of the Bureau for the States of Missouri
and Kansas; but that the Secretary would not transfer
me to him. *Entre nous,* I am very much obliged to the
Secretary. Since then Brig. Gen. Sprague,† who commanded a brigade in (I think) the 20th Corps on Sherman's late marches, has been appointed to that place;
he is a man of fine reputation both as an officer and a
gentleman—about forty-five to fifty years of age, and
when we are at home again next winter we must be
polite to him. I remember him and his pleasant manners very well, and had much rather he (or 'any other

* Sherman's indignation with Stanton over his public comments on the
terms of Johnston's surrender had led to a quarrel holding a large place
in the annals of the time.

† Brig. Gen. J. W. Sprague commanded the Second Brigade of the
First Division of the Seventeenth Army Corps under Gen. Blair.

man') had the place than I. The truth is, Howard's new berth is a very difficult as well as a laborious one. The last Congress passed an Act creating the "Bureau," but very scantily and unsatisfactorily defining its scope or the duties of the "Commissioner"; and Howard has to create the whole thing, collect all information, devise a system, and report to the next Congress, who will *then* be in a position to legislate intelligently. I don't envy him. Fullerton is on duty with him in his office as A. A. G. and tells me he will have charge of the correspondence of the office. F. wanted me to advise him whether or not to accept the place; says he fully intends to leave the service and return to the "jealous mistress," and will settle only in either New York or St. Louis, and will *not* settle in New York. As he could do no business to speak of during the summer and there is no hurry, I advised him to stay with Howard for the present and till the affairs of the Bureau were got into some shape, and then he could better resign; and he will do so. He is in much better humor, by the way, about Sherman and his "treaty," and when I first met him said that though it had done the General injury at first, "it can be easily explained."

I have not seen very much of the General—*my* General—myself since I came. He is staying in town with his family, and of course for the first two or three days the Reviews put everything out of joint. I saw him only a few minutes on Monday afternoon, at our camp; but it was evident he was in high spirits. He met me as kindly as I could wish, and though I had but a few minutes chat with him, he began to tell me at once how President Johnson had received him with both hands outstretched, shook hands with him very warmly, and said—"General Sherman, I am *very* glad to see you,— *very* glad to see you,—*and I mean what I say.*"

He further told me that "Everything was working favorably here—about that *fiasco* with Johnston, you know, all going right"; and added that Stanton was al-

ready "backing down," and "had sent half a dozen
people to him to try and make it up," but that he (Gen.
S) had peremptorily refused to come to any terms with
the Secretary till the latter had publicly retracted his
attack on him. I dare say the New York papers of this
morning contain *by letter*—for it was not sent, probably not allowed to go, by telegraph,—an account of
Sherman's giving Stanton the cut direct *on the stand*
on Pennsylvania Avenue where the President, etc., etc.,
were sitting to see our Army pass. When the General,
riding in advance of his Army, with his Staff, etc., had
passed this stand, we all dismounted and marched up
into the stand where the General went up to the President, saluted and shook hands, and was welcomed by
the various dignitaries around the President. Stanton
was sitting next the President on his right, and among
others advanced and offered to shake hands with Sherman, but the latter *cut* him entirely. I was above and
behind them, on one of the upper tiers of benches, looking for a seat, and did not see it; but they were on the
front seat, facing the Avenue, and of course the observed of all, etc.,—and the incident was plainly seen
by many even across the Avenue with their opera
glasses. I heard of it a few minutes after. My first impression was of regret—which I have not got over altogether—and even of censure, almost; but there is
truth in Uncle E.'s comment that if Sherman had
shaken hands with the Secretary on Wednesday he
could not have refused to do it again on Thursday, and
so Stanton would have compelled him to renew their
intercourse *without* the public rectification of the injus-
tice done the General to which the latter is entitled.
Doubtless you will see in the New York papers an admirably well and ably written article in defence of
Sherman—whose author I do not know yet—published
in the *Chronicle* here yesterday; written with excellent
temper and coolness, yet very able and really very severe. This morning Sherman's letter to Col. Bowman

is republished here from the "N. Y. World," in the "National Intelligencer." I am sorry it was ever published; for though he had a perfect right to write it as a private letter to a friend, it is in my opinion a *mistake* to allow his public defence to be conducted in that way. As a simple question of political strategy, I think it a blunder, or in danger of proving such. Whether the General authorized its publication or not I do not know. I have not seen him today. He was to have come out to camp early this morning to attend to business, but it has been raining steadily all day and he has not yet (1 P.M.) come.

I leave you to the daily papers for details of the Grand Reviews; though no description can do them justice. The uppermost thought in my mind all day when our Army was passing was regret that I had not *forced* you, almost, to come and see it. Our glorious fellows did magnificently, and the officers of the Potomac Army themselves admit, and everybody else says the same, that "Sherman's Army" made the finer appearance of the two. Both armies were most fortunate in point of weather; our day, Wednesday, was *perfect,* cloudless and cool. . . .

Since I began this another large mail has come in for the General, though he has not come, and I fear that unless he does come out soon I shall not get into town today at all.

Uncle E[than] is very well, or was yesterday morning, and was highly delighted with our Army and its magnificent appearance. He called with me yesterday A.M. to see the General and Mrs. S., but they were both out. Gen. S. began to ask me about Uncle E. as soon as I met him, and whether Gen. H. thought that his convention with Johnston was such as to justify the abuse of him in the papers etc.; which I could truly tell him was not the case. In fact, though Uncle E. speaks quietly and rather guardedly even to me about it, and while he thinks—as I do—that the "terms" might have

been better put, he plainly shows himself very warmly
a "Sherman man." About the whole matter I find that
my own views square closely with his, except that he
was more disposed to approve that "cut direct" than I
was at first,—and I think gave good reasons for it.

This "imbroglio" affects me in two ways. So long as
Sherman is in a quarrel I hate to leave him at all, and
if occasion offered I should very likely "pitch in" anywhere on his side. At the same time my cooler judgment
is that as it is not at all impossible that this breach may
be—as it certainly will if they can—made use of by the
"opposition" to make a new political party and use
Sherman's fame to give it strength, it is not wise for
me to become even in my humble sphere identified with
any such thing; for with my views of public policy and
affairs and of the new political issues likely to arise
now or within the next few years it is *not* likely that I
could affiliate with that party. This makes me all the
more anxious to leave the service now that the war is
really over.

I cannot possibly say how soon I can be at Fishkill.
I may get my discharge here within a week; after that
I must and intend to make such preparations as to letters, etc., etc., as are necessary, for the trip to Europe,
before rejoining you,—and then I can stay with you
quietly till the time comes to go. . . .

So ends the record of Henry Hitchcock's military
life. What followed it, through the thirty-seven years
that remained to him, has been suggested in the opening pages of this volume.

INDEX

ALABAMA, 1, 2, 66, 85 n., 102, 129, 135; First Cavalry, 50, 100, 116, 118, 161, 162.

Alexander, Ga., 149.

Alexander, Dr. Richard Henry, 151 and n.

Allatoona, Ga., 44, 45, 49, 50, 52, 177.

Allen, Ethan, 2.

American, Bar Association, 5; Conference on International Arbitration, 5.

Anderson, Maj. George W., 192 and n.

Anderson, Gen. Robert, 41, 173.

Anglesey's P. O., S. C., 250.

Arago, 213, 222.

Armenia, Ga., 145.

Army and Navy Journal, 271.

Atlanta, Ga., 7, 8, 10, 11, 18, 21, 26, 34, 36, 39, 40, 50, 55, 56-59, 60, 63, 64, 72, 73, 80, 81, 91, 101, 103, 113, 135.

Audenried, Capt. Joseph C., 40-41, and n., 53, 63, 64, 75, 89, 123, 155, 173, 175, 177, 178, 180, 194, 254, 261.

Augusta, Ga., 65, 73, 74, 75, 98, 100, 104, 107, 112, 119, 124, 129, 135, 260.

Averysboro, Battle of, 274 and n., 283, 290.

Axson, Rev. S. Edward, 199 and n., 200.

BACHTEL, CAPT. SAMUEL, 138, 140, 151, 170.

Badger, George Edmond, 298 and n.

Ball's Ferry, Ga., 100.

Barker's Mills, S. C., 250.

Barnard, G. N., 150 and n.

Barnum, Gen. Henry A., 201.

Barnwell, S. C., 245.

Barry, Gen. William F., 20 and n., 23-24, 31, 40, 41, 43, 44, 218.

Baylor, Col. Thomas G., 41 and n., 60, 188.

Beaufort, N. C., *see* Morehead City.

Beaufort, S. C., 213, 223, 225, 226, 227, 228, 229, 234, 235, 238, 247, 250, 252, 254, 257, 258.

Beauregard, Gen. P. G. T., 29, 32, 33, 41, 45, 46.

Beckwith, Gen. Amos, 40 and n., 56, 65, 75, 79, 81, 155.

Bell, Dwight, 303.

Belle Peoria, 27, 38.

Belmont, Battle of, 305.

Benoist, L. A., 34.

Bentonville, N. C., Battle at, 275 and n., 276, 281, 282, 283, 284, 291, 293.

Birdsville, Ga., 120.

Blair, Gen. Francis P., 54, 55, 59 n., 106, 107, 109, 111, 113, 120, 135, 136, 137, 141, 142, 153, 154, 156, 157, 160, 161, 163, 164, 166, 167, 171, 174, 203, 217 and n., 224, 230, 232, 236, 238, 253, 260, 267, 270, 275, 276, 315, 318.

Botts, John Minor, 313.

Bowman, Col. S. M., 9.

Brady, Capt., 178.

Bragg, Gen. Braxton, 33, 131.

Bragg, Gov. Thomas, 302.

Branchville, S. C., 259, 261.

Branham's Store, Ga., 148.

Breckinridge, John C., 46, 294 and n., 311.

Brier Creek, Ga., 123, 124, 129, 149.

Bright, John, 4.

Brimfield, Mass., 2.

Bryce, James, 6.

Buck's P. O., Ga., 148.

Buckhead Creek, Ga., 125, 128, 129.

Buffalo Creek, Ga., 91, 92, 97.

Bull's Bay, S. C., 265.

Burke County, Ga., 121 and n.

Burnside, Gen. A. E., 81.

Hickenlooper, Gen. Andrew, 162 and n.

Hickory Hill P. O., S. C., 236, 237, 239, 244, 245.

Higginson, Thomas Wentworth, 228.

Hilton Head, S. C., 198, 203, 206, 214, 226, 227, 228, 233, 244.

Hitchcock, Anne (Erwin), mother of H. H., 1, 2, 186.

Hitchcock, Gen. Ethan Allen, uncle of H. H., 2, 6-8, 21 and n., 25 n., 191, 196, 206, 213, 283, 292, 303 and n., 304, 307, 318, 320, 321-322. *See also Fifty Years in Camp and Field.*

Hitchcock, Hon. Ethan Allen, brother of H. H., 2, 3, 22.

Hitchcock, George Collier, son of H. H., 3.

Hitchcock, Henry, character and personality, 1, 2, 5, 6; family, 1, 2; at college, 2, 3; as teacher, 3; as editor, 3; law practice, 3; marriage, 3; in Missouri state convention, 4; early service to Union, 4; travel, 4; return to law, 4, 5; death, 5; director, Washington University, 5; faculty member, St. Louis Law School, 5; president, American Bar Association, 5; L.L.D., Yale, 5; civic activities, 5-6; enlistment and reasons for, 6-8, 36-37, 216; on Sherman's staff, 11 ff.; first impressions of war area, 18-19; staff duties, 16, 19-20, 24; "restitution," 27; attitude toward war, 35-36, 99; conception of service, 46-47 n.; at burning of Marietta, 52-53; retaliation discussed, 56; destruction in Atlanta, 56-57; army discipline and the problem of stragglers, 61-62, 86, 87, 88, 94, 109, 124, 130-131, 134; "laws of war," 62; necessity for severity, 82-83, 87, 97, 125, 143, 287-288, discussion of, with S., 92-93; foraging and "acquired goods," 64, 66,

87; results of March, 89, 167; opinion of war, 99; of "Southern man," 102-103; of "Southern gentleman," 173, 288, 289, 290, 310; Christianity in the army, 139; torpedoes, 161-162; responsibility for war, 167-168; hardships, 193, 218-219, 231, 253, 267, 298; attitude toward danger, 193, 194, 283-284, 285; Christmas, 1864, 197, 199, 201; attends party, Savannah, 207; on bounties, 209; evils of war, 217, 287-288, 290; "running the mess," 220-221, 246-247, 250, 258; court martial proceedings, 231-232; camp life, 233-234; brevetted Lt. Col., 263 n.; march to Fayetteville, 264 ff.; S. C. chivalry, 266; explains burning of Columbia, 268-270; at battles of Averysboro and Bentonville, 272-277, 281-284; N. C. campaign, 294 ff.; Johnston's surrender, 299 ff.; to Washington for Grant, 302 ff.; Grant and S. contrasted, 305; assassination of Lincoln, 306-307; Lee's surrender, 312-314; Freedman's Bureau, 318 ff.

Hitchcock, Henry, Jr., 3.

Hitchcock, Judge Henry, father of H. H., 1, 2.

Hitchcock, Luke, 2.

Hitchcock, Margaret D. (Collier), 3, 15 and n., 41, 186, 226 and n., 246.

Hitchcock, Martha Rind (Nicholls), 303 n.

Hitchcock, Mary (Collier), wife of H. H., 3, 10, 11, 38, 185 ff., 197, 227, 244 n., 263.

Hitchcock, Judge Samuel, grandfather of H. H., 2.

Hood, Gen. J. B., 11, 16, 19, 21, 23, 28, 29, 32, 39, 41, 44, 45, 108, 109, 154, 157, 158, 264, 291.

Hooker, Gen. Joseph, 55.

How, John, 216 and n.

Howard, Col. Charles H., 94 and n., 98, 159.

287; reconstruction, 208; reports about North in, 61, 64, 66, 70, 71, 119, 122, 151, 154, 155, 158, 175, *and see* Newspapers; Union men in, 313.

Sparta, Ga., 107.

Special Field Orders, No. 35, 276 and n.; No. 120, 64, 66, 68, 76, 82, 158; No. 130, 166.

Spencer, Gen. George E., 50, 51, 100 and n., 116, 126.

Sprague, Gen. J. W., 318 and n.

Spring Hill, Ala., 1.

Springfield, Ga., 148, 150, 154.

Stanfordsville, Ga., 80 ff., 81.

Stanton, Edwin McM. (Sec. of War), 7, 34-35, 225, 318, 319-320.

Stephens, A. H., 74, 97, 102.

Stoneman, Gen. George, 84 and n.

Story of the Great March, The, from the Diary of a Staff Officer, by Bvt. Maj. George Ward Nichols, 9.

Strong, Gen. William E., 227 and n.

Sumter, Fort, S. C., 288, 313.

Swain, David, 297.

Swainsboro, Ga., 107.

Tarver, Judge T., 114, 115.

Tarver's Mill, Ga., 113-115.

Taylor, Capt. William N., 253 and n.

Tennessee, 2, 32, 33, 39, 46, 95; Army of, 107, 166, 172, 193; River, 16, 21, 23, 27, 32, 45, 109.

Tennille Station, Ga., 97-98, 99 ff., 106, 107, 119.

Terry, Gen. A. H., 273-274, 281.

Thomas, C. R., 314.

Thomas, Gen. G. H., 11, 46, 101 and n., 118, 158, 294.

Thomas Station, Ga., 149.

Tilton, Ga., 56.

Tompkins, Maj. Logan, 108 and n.

Toombs, Robert, 290.

Trenor, Bvt. Lt. Col. John, 225 and n.

Tullahoma, Tenn., 21.

Tupper, Lt., 161, 162, 163-164.

Ulcofauhatchee River, Ga., 67, 68, 69, 73, 81.

Union, the, 4, 6, 11; men in South, 79, 82, 125; prisoners, treatment of, *see* Confederacy.

U. S., Armies of, 302 ff.; Colored Troops, 35th, 232; Circuit Courts of Appeal, 5; Congress, 5; Department of South, 232; Department of State, 7; Direct Tax Commission, 226, 228; Freedman's Bureau, 318; Sanitary Commission, 17, 34-35; Supreme Court, 298.

Vance, Z. B., 296, 297, 300, 305.

Vaun's, Ga., 80 ff., 108.

Vermont, 1, 2.

Verplanck, Lt. Abram G., 63, 178.

Vicksburg, Miss., 30.

Virginia, Army of Northern, 295.

Walcutt, Gen. Charles C., 98 and n.

War Trace, Tenn., 21.

Ward, Gen. William T., 90 and n., 238, 260.

Ware, Lt. William E., 108 and n.

Washington County, Ga., 88 ff., 106 ff.

Washington, D. C., 5, 7, 10, 21, 302 ff., 304, 316 ff.; University, 5, 6.

Waud, A. R., 199, 251.

Wayne, Gen. Henry C., 98 and n., 100.

Waynesboro (Wainesboro), Ga., 107, 121, 123, 124, 149, 177.

Western Sanitary Commission, 34-35.

Wheeler, Gen. Joseph, 85 and n., 95, 96, 98, 100, 103, 104, 105, 107, 109, 112, 115, 120, 123, 124, 129, 149, 157, 177, 237, 242, 244, 250, 290, 297.

Williams, Gen. A. S., 59 n., 90 and n., 103, 238, 260.